DIS

Practice

DISCRIMINATION
Law and Practice

Third Edition

Chris Ronalds

THE FEDERATION PRESS
2008

Published in Sydney by

The Federation Press
71 John St, Leichhardt, NSW, 2040
PO Box 45, Annandale, NSW, 2038
Ph: (02) 9552 2200 Fax: (02) 9552 1681
E-mail: info@federationpress.com.au
Website: http://www.federationpress.com.au

First edition   1998
Second edition   2004
Third edition   2008

National Library of Australia Cataloguing-in-Publication data:
    Discrimination : law and practice
    Author: Ronalds, Chris.

    3rd ed.
    Includes index.
    ISBN 978 186287 670 5 (pbk)

    Discrimination – Law and legislation – Australia. I.

342.94085

Typeset by The Federation Press, Leichhardt, NSW.
    Printed by Ligare Pty Ltd, Riverwood NSW

PREFACE

This book is designed as a reference tool and a handbook to assist in understanding the rapidly evolving field of Australian discrimination law.

The first edition of this book was published in 1998 and a second edition, co-authored with Rachel Pepper, was published in 2004. Since then, some major judicial decisions have required the preparation of a third edition to reflect the changes and developments in this important area of law. Rachel's professional commitments in 2007 were such that she was unable to contribute to the preparation of this edition.

Complaints about breaches of discrimination laws continue to be heard and often upheld by courts and tribunals. Applicants pursue remedies for decisions made about them or actions taken against them which they consider to be discriminatory.

It is often the case that, in working through such complaints, the decision-making processes of small firms and medium and large corporations are exposed to judicial scrutiny. Some decisions considered to be appropriate when first made have been found to be discriminatory when assessed against the standards imposed by the discrimination laws. Equally, some complaints have been dismissed following judicial review, as breaches of the discrimination laws have not been made out despite the genuinely held views of the applicants.

Today in Australia, the main grounds for discrimination complaints and litigation involve sexual harassment at work and disability in education. This is a different complaints profile to that in 1998 and reflects the changing nature of this area of the law.

I would like to thank my many friends and colleagues for their support and encouragement in producing this third edition, particularly Lindsay Cane, Hannah Binney, Sue Binney, Louise Goodchild, Tony McAvoy, Elizabeth Raper, Marena Manzoufas, Paul Stein, Barbara Adams and Harry Dixon.

I am again grateful to the Federation Press team who have provided prompt and useful advice and assistance, particularly Chris Holt, Kathy Fitzhenry and Diane Young. Notwithstanding their invaluable help, all errors and omissions are my responsibility.

Chris Ronalds SC
January 2008

In memory of my close friend and colleague, John Terry, whose untimely death on 9 May 1994 deprived us all of a wonderful wit and intellect as well as much fun and love. Gone but forever remembered, with the loss always deeply felt.

CONTENTS

Appendices:

TABLE OF CASES

TABLE OF CASES

TABLE OF STATUTES

1

BACKGROUND AND CURRENT POSITION

Overview

This book examines discrimination law and practice as it operates throughout Australia. It is a practical guide which looks at the law itself and then demonstrates the way it operates currently through the use of practical examples and decided cases.

It is designed to assist lawyers, equal opportunity and industrial relations practitioners, human resource managers and people involved in employment decisions as well as students and anyone with a general interest in the law and its effect.

Discrimination laws provide a series of rights, remedies and redress for certain, specified acts. These acts are made unlawful, that is, they are made a breach of the civil law.

A number of different grounds of unlawful discrimination are covered and these include sex, race, disability and age. A range of areas are included and the main ones are employment, education and the provision of goods and services. Harassment on various grounds is included and sexual harassment is the most common form of discrimination raised. There are some exceptions to the operation of all the laws and these have a limited impact on the practical working of the laws.

The person making a complaint is usually referred to as "the complainant" or "applicant" if the case proceeds to a court hearing and the person or corporation against whom the complaint is made is referred to as "the respondent".

There are Federal and State laws which follow a similar pattern of making certain acts of discrimination unlawful and then providing a mechanism for the redress of any breach of the law and a series of remedies when the breach is established. All States and Territories have discrimination laws and they vary in the grounds they cover, some of the areas brought within the operation of the law and the specific exceptions.

This book uses the Federal laws as the main focus as they operate nationally and also are a common benchmark for the State laws. The general principles underpinning the legislation and the legislated approach is common throughout Australia and this means that the general approach adopted in this book makes it relevant to any location and operative law.

Appendices A to D contain a series of tables which set out the similar provisions in the Federal and State laws and are designed to assist the reader to readily locate the law which operates within their jurisdiction at both the Federal and State level.

The impact of discrimination laws, especially in the areas of employment and education, continues to be an important component of corporate life in Australia and is one which has increasing consequence in the first part of the 21st century. As the principles of discrimination laws and their methods of operation become more widely recognised and accepted, the use of the laws will inevitably increase. One flow on from such laws is the demands on organisations to comply with the statutory requirements without the experience of a complaint being brought against them.

The long-term benefits of a planned approach to eliminating discrimination and harassment and promoting equal opportunity are clear. Such avenues need to be based on an understanding of the impact of the laws and their significance within the organisation. Positive steps to create an environment free of discrimination and harassment are a more productive use of resources than defending claims of breaches of the discrimination law. This will only occur where there is some in-depth appreciation of the potential of the laws and the way they work in relation to individuals and organisations. This book is designed to provide that information and to enable organisations to approach the topic with clarity and comprehension.

Most complaints arise in the employment area. The coverage and ramifications of the laws have required Australian companies to revise their human resources policies, provide internal grievance mechanisms and to recognise the legal rights of their employees to work in an environment free of discrimination and harassment. For large and medium sized companies, this has required the expenditure of resources on developing such policies and practices to conform with the requirements of the law and to avoid any legal liability.

The Australian approach to the elimination of discriminatory practices and acts is mainly through these laws. They are based on the identification of particular groups within the community which suffer disadvantage or detriment because of their membership of that particular group, such as women, Aboriginal people or people with a disability. The legal structure requires individuals to take action on their own behalf to remedy their individual situation.

This area of law is created only by statute and so it has a relatively short history in terms of the legal system. The first laws were passed in the mid-1970s and it was not until the early 1980s that there were some tribunal decisions which showed the impact of the laws and the way they could be used.

Since then, there has been a steady flow of judicial examination of the area of law. The High Court and the Federal Court, in particular, have played significant roles in the discussion of the fundamental issues and in developing the parameters and limitations on the operation of the law.

The future development of discrimination law will reflect the changing complexities of the market place and, in particular, the alterations to the arrangements of the workforce and the structure of employment relationships. As change is introduced, it is almost inevitable that there will be further disputes arising based on these laws.

The provision of these rights, remedies and redress will continue to provide an avenue for the resolution of disputes between different parties and the structure for achieving a negotiated outcome.

Historical background to legislation

The first discrimination law in Australia was a criminal law against race discrimination passed by the South Australian Parliament in 1966. There were only four prosecutions before it was replaced by a civil statute similar to the current models.

At a Federal level, the first national discrimination law was also aimed at race discrimination and was enacted by the Whitlam Labor Government in October 1975. The pioneering role of this statute is demonstrated in its different form when compared with the enactments of the 1980s and 1990s. The Act was substantially based on the *International Convention on the Elimination of All Forms of Racial Discrimination*. Major amendments to the *Racial Discrimination Act 1975* (Cth) were made in 1990 when the definition of indirect discrimination was inserted as s 9(1A) and in 1995 when the racial hatred provisions were included.

The initial focus on race discrimination reflected the international debate of the late 1960s generated by the social volatility in the United States relating to the lack of equality for Afro-Americans. By the earlier 1970s, the Australian public debate was around the rights of recently arrived migrants and particularly those who spoke English as a second language. There was little attention to the rights of Indigenous Australians within the parameters of the earlier equality deliberations.

The United Nations declared 1975 to be International Women's Year and the burgeoning feminist movement meant that the focus of the equality debate was moved to the role of women in Australian society, particularly in employment and to a lesser extent in education.

The Hawke Labor Government enacted the *Sex Discrimination Act* in 1984 after contentious community debate around the principles of eliminating discrimination against women. Opponents of the legislation forecast dire consequences to marriage, the family and the care of children which were not based on any realistic assessment of the role and function of such legislation and its coverage. There was a long and heated public and parliamentary debate during 1983, with significant unseemly personal attacks made on the responsible Minister, Senator Susan Ryan. The Act was substantially based on the *International Convention on the Elimination of Discrimination Against Women* which generated further opposition to the use of the external affairs power to provide a basis for domestic legislation.

Major amendments to the *Sex Discrimination Act* have included the addition of family responsibilities and revision of the definition of sexual harassment in 1992 and the revision of the definition of indirect discrimination in 1995.

In 1981, the Human Rights Commission was established and it handled race and sex discrimination complaints and ran related public education campaigns. It was replaced in 1986 with the *Human Rights and Equal Opportunity Commission Act* which has functions in relation to human rights, discrimination, community education and the handling of complaints. The portfolio Commissioners of Sex, Race and Disability had their functions substantially altered in 2000. Their previous complaint-handling functions were given to the President of the Commission and their main involvement was with the promotion of the issues generally within the community. The Aboriginal and Torres Strait Islander Social Justice Commissioner was created in 1993 with a single focus on Indigenous Australians. The HR&EOC addresses the statutory complaint-handling processes of race, sex and disability and the other grounds of sexual preference, religion, age, political opinion, trade union activity and medical record which have limited complaint processes. Since April

2000, enforceable decisions are made in the Federal Court and the Federal Magistrates Court.

The *Disability Discrimination Act* was enacted in 1992 by the Keating Labor Government following a government report on employment opportunities for people with a disability and broad consultations with community and business groups about the potential impact of such legislation. It followed some of the *Americans with Disabilities Act* approach with a defence of unjustifiable hardship available in certain circumstances. The United States of America led the way with disability discrimination laws following community agitation by injured veterans of the American-Vietnam War. The *Disability Discrimination Act* took an innovative approach by setting up a framework for the passage of disability standards which were to provide more comprehensive details on the requirements to eliminate discrimination against people with a disability.

Progress in the different States during the 1970s and 1980s to enact discrimination laws reflected the type of government in power. Labor Governments were generally more interested and active in the broader area of social policy reform and at redressing some areas of inequality in society. Conservative Governments were generally less committed to using the law as a means of social reform and were often critical of attempts to have parliaments establish the benchmarks for acceptable standards of behaviour and action in the workplace and other parts of the community.

South Australia was the first State to provide a legislative framework for eliminating discrimination against women when it enacted the *Sex Discrimination Act* in 1975. It followed with a new racial discrimination law in 1976 and a law for handicapped persons in 1981. A broader single law was passed in 1984. Once the leading State in terms of innovative approaches to the legislative options for eliminating discrimination, it has now been left behind as others States have statutes covering a broader range of grounds.

In 1977, New South Wales passed its first discrimination law which covered race, sex and marital status. Physical handicap was added as a ground in 1981 and intellectual handicap and homosexuality were added in 1982. The impairment grounds were replaced with the broader ground of disability in 1994. Further grounds have continued to be added to the NSW Act – racial vilification in 1989, compulsory retirement in 1990, age and homosexual vilification in 1993, transgender in 1996, carers' responsibilities in 2000 and breastfeeding in 2007. The first major sexual harassment case in Australia was heard as a sex discrimination case in New South Wales: *O'Callaghan v Loder (No 2)* [1983] 3

NSWLR 89. Sexual harassment was defined as a separate ground from sex discrimination in 1997 in New South Wales, which was a slow reaction to the 1984 Federal sexual harassment model.

Since October 1998, all NSW complaints have been referred to the Administrative Decisions Tribunal for hearing and determination. The NSW Law Reform Commission published an extensive review of the Act in November 1999 and, despite various government promises since, the long awaited new Act has still not been introduced into Parliament.

Victoria passed a similar law to New South Wales in 1977 which covered race, sex and marital status. The first major sex discrimination case was brought under this Act in 1979 when a woman pilot success-fully challenged her rejection for employment by one of the two national airlines. This case wound its way to the High Court and she eventually was employed as a commercial pilot: *Ansett Transport Industries (Operations) Pty Ltd v Wardley* (1980) 142 CLR 237. A broader Act was passed in 1995 covering race, sex, impairment, marital status and political or religious belief or activity. Parental status was added as a ground in 1997 and breast feeding, gender identity and sexual orientation were added in 2000. Since July 1998, all Victorian complaints have been heard by the Victorian Civil and Administrative Tribunal.

Western Australia enacted broad legislation in 1984. Queensland and the Australian Capital Territory followed in 1991 with broad legis-lation, as did the Northern Territory in 1992 and Tasmania in 1998. By 2003, all States and Territories have legislation which has a standard coverage in the major areas of race, sex and disability with different other options in areas such as religious and political activities, and sexual orientation and transgender status. See Appendix A for the full details.

Statutory approach to discrimination

Not all acts of "discrimination" are unlawful and hence in breach of a discrimination law. There are many acts which do not fall within the law as they are not based on a ground of unlawful discrimination or do not fall within a prescribed area.

The approach adopted in all Australian discrimination laws is the identification of specified conduct or decisions as an act of "unlawful discrimination". Before being able to ascribe the act as being both unlaw-ful and unlawful discrimination, a number of findings of fact and legis-lative interpretation must occur. One is that the ground of discrimination is identified and comes within a specified unlawful ground. Chapter 2 examines the various grounds of discrimination covered by the different laws, with a primary focus on sex, race and disability discrimination.

The next step involves determining whether there has been an act of direct discrimination or indirect discrimination, as defined. Chapter 3 analyses the various components of direct and indirect discrimination and the leading cases examining these statutory requirements.

Then the facts forming the basis of the complaint must come within a specified area. The area of employment is discussed in Chapter 4, education in Chapter 5, harassment in Chapter 6, vilification and racial hatred in Chapter 7, and other areas of discrimination in Chapter 8.

Chapter 9 examines the principles and relevant case law in the area of victimisation and the other acts of discrimination, including advertisements, incitement and offences. If the components of grounds, definition and area are met, then there is an act which can accurately be described as an act of "unlawful discrimination".

The next step is to ensure that the facts do not come within one of the exceptions. Chapter 10 addresses the defences and some exceptions which arise specifically in relation to respondents and Chapter 11 examines the general exemptions.

All Australian discrimination laws set up a conciliation approach to the resolution of a written complaint made by an individual or a group of individuals. The legislation is essentially reactive rather than pro-active and seeks to provide redress and a remedy when a certain situation has arisen. A person is required to provide a complaint to an independent statutory agency which then investigates and endeavours to conciliate the complaint. These processes are confidential between the parties and the agency. The focus is on trying to delineate the parameters of the complaint and ascertain whether any breach of the legislation can be identified. A resolution to the differences between the parties may include compensation, reinstatement or an apology and a change in policy or practice. The majority of complaints are resolved during the confidential conciliation phase by both sides reaching an agreed position and terminating the processes.

The conciliation processes are run by a government agency which has been created specifically for this purpose. These organisations usually also conduct community education programs and foster public debate around a range of relevant issues. Appendix E is a list of contact details for all agencies. Some complaints cannot be resolved through conciliation. These are the ones that then go before a court or a specially designed tribunal for a hearing and a decision and orders on whether there has been a breach of the law.

Chapter 12 examines the principles of conciliation and the statutory powers involved in bringing the parties together and structuring an agreement.

If that conciliation breaks down or is not possible, then the complaint is referred to a court or tribunal which conducts a hearing and makes a decision. These proceedings follow usual court processes and are open to the public and frequently are reported in the media. The courts or tribunals make enforceable orders after a hearing and a decision that the complaint is substantiated. Alternatively, a complaint is dismissed.

Chapter 13 examines the conduct of hearings and the way to conduct a matter during the various phases, including an appeal. Chapter 14 looks at the range of orders that may be made by the courts or tribunals operating federally and in each State.

Discrimination laws around Australia

There are five different Federal laws and laws in each State within the discrimination jurisdiction. These are outlined below. Detailed tables of comparison are at Appendix A to D.

Federal laws

There are four laws applying throughout Australia which proscribe discrimination by adopting a similar approach to each other and the State laws.

The *Racial Discrimination Act* 1975 (Cth) was the first Federal discrimination law enacted. The *Racial Discrimination Act* does not precisely follow the model of the other two Federal Acts as it includes a general provision which makes racial discrimination unlawful: s 9(1). It makes certain specified areas of discrimination unlawful on the ground of race.

The *Sex Discrimination Act* 1984 (Cth), the *Disability Discrimination Act* 1992 (Cth) and the *Age Discrimination Act* 2004 (Cth) are similar in approach and make discrimination on the specified grounds unlawful in a wide range of areas.

Decisions about unlawful discrimination under these Acts are made by the Federal Court or the Federal Magistrates Court.

The *Human Rights and Equal Opportunity Act* 1986 (Cth) ("*HR&EO Act*") follows a different model as it does not provide any rights which can be enforced through a complaints based system enforceable through the courts. It provides that a complaint on various specified grounds of discrimination can be made and if there is no resolution, it is able to be the subject of a report to be tabled in Parliament by the Attorney-General: *Secretary, Department of Defence v HR&EOC* (1998) 78 FCR 208.

While the HR&EOC has no power under that Act to make declarations, it can make recommendations. Those decisions are reviewable under the *Administrative Decisions (Judicial Review) Act* 1977 (Cth) in the Federal Court where the court can examine the questions of legal interpretation which arise from any Commission finding that there was an act or practice of discrimination and any recommendation that compensation or some other form of relief be adopted: *Commonwealth v Bradley* (1999) 95 FCR 218.

A declaration by the Federal Court that there has been a breach of the *HR&EO Act* does not have any real effect and cannot be done within the court's original jurisdiction: *Peacock v HR&EOC* [2002] FCA 984.

State laws

Each State has an Act which covers a variety of grounds and areas and the details are set out in Appendix A to D. They are all based on a similar general approach although there are three different models.

The name of each Act is:

- in New South Wales – *Anti-Discrimination Act* 1977;
- in Victoria – *Equal Opportunity Act* 1995;
- in Queensland – *Anti-Discrimination Act* 1991;
- in South Australia – *Equal Opportunity Act* 1984;
- in Western Australia – *Equal Opportunity Act* 1984;
- in Tasmania – *Anti-Discrimination Act* 1998;
- in the Australian Capital Territory – *Discrimination Act* 1991;
- in the Northern Territory – *Anti-Discrimination Act* 1992.

Choice of jurisdiction

As there is both a Federal and a State discrimination law in operation in many circumstances, a person has to decide which law to use before lodging a complaint. There can be ramifications flowing from such a choice which can be detrimental to later action.

Constitutional validity

The Federal discrimination laws all rely, to varying degrees, on the "external affairs" power of the Constitution for their validity. Section 51(xxix) of the Australian Constitution confers power on the Commonwealth Government to make laws "for the peace, order and good government of the Commonwealth" with respect to "external affairs". The High

Court has subjected this power to close scrutiny since the passage of the Constitution and the use and significance of the external affairs power has grown in the past 20 years.

The High Court has determined that it is fundamental to the Federal Government's capacity to conduct international relations that it has power to give effect to the obligations which arise in the course of those international relations. In *Polyukhovich v Commonwealth* (1991) 172 CLR 501 at 528, Mason CJ held "the grant of the legislative power with respect to external affairs should be construed with all the generality that the words admit and that, so construed, the power extends to matters and things, as well as relationships outside Australia".

The High Court's approach to the external affairs power recognises the need for the Federal Government to be legislatively capable of implementing or giving effect to any international obligations which it enters. The two landmark cases on the capacity of the Federal Government to give effect to its international obligations are *Koowarta v Bjelke-Petersen* (1982) 153 CLR 168 and *Commonwealth v Tasmania* (*Tasmanian Dams case*) (1983) 158 CLR 1 per Mason J at 124-4 and Deane J at 258. These principles were confirmed later in *Queensland v Commonwealth* (1989) 167 CLR 232 at 238.

It is clear that some earlier concerns about the constitutional validity of the Federal discrimination laws were unfounded. The High Court has held that the Federal *Racial Discrimination Act* 1975 is constitutionally valid through its reliance on the terms of the *International Convention on the Elimination of All Forms of Racial Discrimination*: *Viskauskas v Niland* (1983) 153 CLR 280; *University of Wollongong v Metwally* (1984) 158 CLR 447; *Gerhardy v Brown* (1985) 159 CLR 70; *Brandy v HR&EOC* (1995) 183 CLR 245. That Convention is the Schedule to that Act.

On the basis of those decisions, there appears little doubt that most, if not all, of the terms of the *Sex Discrimination Act* 1984 are validly based on the *International Convention on the Elimination of All Forms of Discrimination Against Women*. The Federal Court has upheld the constitutional validity of that Act in several decisions: *Aldridge v Booth* (1988) 80 ALR 1; *Secretary, Department of Foreign Affairs and Trade v Styles* (1989) 23 FCR 251; *Hall v A & A Sheiban Pty Ltd* (1989) 20 FCR 217.

On a similar basis, the terms of the *Disability Discrimination Act* 1992 were held by implication to be valid as the Act is based on several international treaties: *X v Commonwealth* (1999) 200 CLR 177. The Federal Court has held that the elimination of disability discrimination is an international concern and that the applications provisions make the

Act valid: *Soulitopoulos v La Trobe University Liberal Club* (2002) 120 FCR 584 at 599. The Federal Magistrates Court has held that access to accommodation for a person with a disability is a valid claim as being a matter of international concern: *O'Connor v Ross (No 1)* [2002] FMCA 210.

There has been no judicial consideration of the *Age Discrimination Act* by the High Court or Federal Court to date.

With all four Acts, there may be some provisions which potentially could be found not to be based on an international treaty and which have no other constitutional basis to support them. However, given the wide reach of the international treaties, this is unlikely. Also, the High Court has extended the operation of the external affairs power to matters of international concern which are reflected in the existence of an international duty in relation to a particular subject matter and the construction and operation the international community would attribute to the treaty: *Queensland v Commonwealth* (1989) 167 CLR 232 at 239-40.

The Federal Court has found that the Federal discrimination laws do not have extra-territorial effect and so cannot provide the foundation for a complaint where the situation occurred entirely overseas: *Brannigan v Commonwealth* (2000) 110 FCR 566 at 573.

Potential conflicts between Federal and State laws

There is a potential for conflict between the Federal discrimination laws and the various State laws as they are not precisely the same in wording or definitions, although the differences have diminished in recent years in some State laws. Some of the State laws have adopted a different approach to the Federal laws in the method of identifying the ground of discrimination and the separation of the grounds. This difference in approach seems to produce more semantic than substantive differences as the statutory formulae for the definitions, grounds and areas of discrimination and harassment remain close.

Section 109 of the Australian Constitution provides that where Federal law and a State law are inconsistent, then the Federal law prevails "to the extent of the inconsistency". One manner of determining the extent of the inconsistency is an assessment of whether the Federal Government intended to "cover the field" or whether there is any room for a potentially conflicting State law to operate: *Ansett Transport Industries (Operations) Pty Ltd v Wardley* (1980) 142 CLR 237; *University of Wollongong v Metwally* (1984) 158 CLR 447.

The possibility of the "cover the field test" in relation to inconsistency is addressed in the Federal discrimination laws through a mechanism which is a one way filter. If a person has lodged a complaint under a State law and they would have had a valid complaint under the Federal law, then they are not entitled to lodge a complaint under the Federal law: *Sex Discrimination Act* s 10. There is no similar provision in any of the State laws, so a person can initially lodge a complaint with the Federal agency and then transfer it to the State agency.

The potential limitation on a State to Federal transfer has been circumvented by some practical readings of the sections. If a person lodges a document with a State agency which is not valid under State law due to an exception which is not in the similar Federal law or for some other reason, then the general practice is to permit the document to be lodged under the Federal law and to then become a "complaint". This is a technical approach to an essentially practical problem.

Concerns that the law in this area would be deflected into lengthy constitutional and related battles and inconsistent decisions from different jurisdictions have not been realised. Interestingly, there are no major points of interpretation which have been adopted by the courts in different States. Minor differences in results have arisen due to some of the technical differences in the legislation.

Overall, each jurisdiction has been open to adopting precedents from other jurisdictions, giving rise to a reasonable consistency on issues of interpretation and application. Also, United Kingdom, Canadian and United States precedents have been used in some cases and have formed a fruitful basis for the development of related Australian precedents in different areas.

Equal opportunity and affirmative action

A different approach to the elimination of discrimination and the promotion of equality has been adopted in some areas which involves the implementation of equal opportunity or affirmative action programs. Such programs require the identification of barriers or disadvantages which prevent or impede members of a nominated group from progressing through an organisation at the same pace or on the same basis as others not in the nominated group. Most such programs arise within the employment context and are designed to eliminate or remove barriers and provide equal access and opportunity to all employees or potential employees in areas such as promotion, training and transfers. There are some in the education area addressing university entrance requirements.

These specific targeted programs address other structural issues which underpin the lack of real equal opportunity for particular groups such as women or Aboriginal people. They are commonly referred to as "affirmative action" or "equal opportunity" programs.

There are two different approaches to affirmative action or equal opportunity programs at a national level, one for the public sector and one for the private sector.

The legislation covering the private sector is the *Affirmative Action (Equal Employment Opportunity for Women) Act* 1986 (Cth) which covers companies with more than 100 employees, higher education institutions, community sector employers, non-government schools and group training companies. Each employer covered by the Act is required to submit an annual workplace program to the Equal Opportunity for Women in the Workplace Agency by 31 May each year. The requirement to lodge a public report may be waived for a period of up to three years if the Director so determines. The Agency has published a standard report form for employers to complete and prefers lodgement by email.

If an employer does not lodge a report or provide further information when requested, then the Director may name the employer in a report to Parliament. This can only occur after a period of 28 days notice has been given and the reasons for naming specified. Since 1 January 1993, an employer named in Parliament becomes ineligible for government contracts and some forms of industry assistance.

In relation to Federal public sector employment, government departments are covered by ss 10 and 18 of the *Public Service Act* 1999 (Cth) and statutory authorities by the *Equal Employment Opportunity (Commonwealth Authorities) Act* 1987. A similar scheme to that covering the private sector is in place.

New South Wales, South Australia, Western Australian and Victoria have established statutory schemes for the implementation of equal employment opportunities in State public sector employment.

Charter of rights

One important development in the framework of laws designed to protect and promote human rights is the introduction of a bill of rights or a charter of rights. Australia has no national law and is the only first world country without such a document either enshrined in the Constitution or passed as a Federal law. There is an ongoing debate about the potential for a charter of rights at a national level. Currently, there is an international jurisprudence of rights and remedies which is developing and Australia is not part of those developments. This means that increasingly Australia is out of step with the legal developments within a rights framework of similar Western countries. The Rudd Labor Government has a commitment to introducing a Charter of Rights by 2010. It is unlikely to involve any amendment to the Constitution and its extent, functions and enforceability are not yet clear.

Victoria and the Australian Capital Territory have both passed legislation aimed at providing a rights framework albeit with limited ambit.

The *Human Rights Act* 2004 (ACT) aims to protect some civil and political rights within the ACT. The Act requires all decision-makers, including politicians, bureaucrats, judges and tribunal members, to consider the terms of the Act when making a decision. The rights include equality before the law, protection from torture, protection of the family and children, and freedom of movement, thought, association and expression. There are provisions protecting the right to a fair trial, rights in criminal trials and compensation for wrongful conviction. The ACT Act has no operation in relation to Federal laws.

The *Charter of Human Rights and Responsibilities Act* 2006 (Vic.) seeks to protect some fundamental civil and political rights and freedoms including the right to vote, freedom of expression, protection from forced work, right to privacy, right to a fair trail and the protection of certain cultural rights including the cultural rights of Aboriginal people. Government departments are required to observe and comply with these rights when they propose a new law, make policies and provide services. When a new law is introduced into the Victorian Parliament, it must be accompanied by a Statement of Compatibility and, if the terms of the Charter are not met, then the reasons and rationale must be set out. The Charter does not provide a new set of legal remedies by providing the basis to commence legal action. It may be raised in litigation which is directed at other matters and a breach of the Charter can be part of the application or a defence to a claim. Its primary focus is on the planning side of government delivery of services rather than providing a proactive basis to commence litigation to challenge Victorian government decisions. The Charter has no operation in relation to Federal laws.

2

GROUNDS OR ATTRIBUTES OF DISCRIMINATION

All Australian discrimination laws are based on the concept of a "ground" or an "attribute" of unlawful discrimination.

Chapter 1 sets out the details of the laws which operate currently in Australia and this chapter addresses the primary issue of the identification of the basis for a discriminatory act.

What is a "ground" or "attribute"?

The term "ground" or "attribute" refers to the main identifier which is the basis or part of the basis of the act of discrimination. Only conduct or decisions which come within a specified ground are able to have access to the complaint mechanisms and redress provided in discrimination laws.

"Ground" is the term used in the Federal legislation and in New South Wales, South Australia and Western Australia. "Attribute" is the term used in Victoria, Queensland, Tasmania, the Australian Capital Territory and Northern Territory.

While the Queensland, Australian Capital Territory and Northern Territory Acts use the term "attribute" in the sections defining the coverage of the Act, the heading to the Part itself uses the term "ground". They appear to be making some sort of distinction but the basis for it is unclear and, on the face of it, the existence of any difference is not readily apparent.

To save repetition and for ease of reading and reference, the term "ground" is used throughout this chapter and the entire book to mean "ground" and "attribute".

Each ground set out in a statute is discussed separately below.

Federal approach

There are currently four Federal Acts based on different grounds of discrimination and different international instruments form the basis for their constitutional validity. The primary four grounds are race, sex, disability and age. ·

There are other grounds in the Federal area which are specified in the *Human Rights and Equal Opportunity Commission Act* 1986 (Cth) and which may be the subject of a complaint for investigation only. There is no access to any remedies for the complainant other than a report to Parliament.

State approach

The discrimination laws enacted by the various State governments have adopted a different approach to the Federal Government by covering a number of different grounds of unlawful discrimination in the one statute. In some States, such as New South Wales and Victoria, grounds have been added over the years and hence the coverage of the legislation has been gradually increased.

Specified grounds

Each of the separate grounds included in a discrimination law is set out below.

"Sex"

The primary focus of the *Sex Discrimination Act* 1984 (Cth) is sex discrimination, particularly discrimination against women. The ground of sex is included in all State legislation and provides one of the main bases for complaints. The pattern of complaints indicates that the vast majority of complaints of sex discrimination are lodged by women.

Women have brought many complaints on the ground of sex discrimination and the majority, and the most significant, have been in the area of employment. This reflects the continuing employment patterns of women in lower paid employment and in certain lower status jobs.

The issue of sexual harassment is dealt with separately in the various laws, although in some complaints there may be allegations of sexual harassment and sex discrimination arising from the same facts: *Hall v A & A Sheiban* (1989) 20 FCR 217 (see Chapter 6).

There have been some complaints by men alleging sex discrimination. Men have claimed sex discrimination:

- for being dismissed for wearing an earring when the female staff were allowed to wear jewellery: *Bree v Lupevo Pty Ltd* (2003) EOC ¶93-267;
- for failing to obtain a position as a male midwife: *Askey-Doran v Fremantle Women's Health Centre* (2001) EOC ¶93-116;
- in Family Court proceedings in the context of proceedings relating to parenting orders or child support: *Mackie v Tay* (2001) EOC ¶93-175, *Maher v Commonwealth (Child Support Agency)* (2001) EOC ¶93-140;
- in the course of seeking an exemption from a course while enrolled at university: *Dudzinski v Griffith University* (2000) EOC ¶93-094.

"Marital status"

One ground of unlawful discrimination is marital status. It is one of the few grounds of discrimination that is not immutable, that is, an individual's marital status may vary during their life and they may have more than one marital status at any time.

The *Sex Discrimination Act* and all State laws prohibit discrimination on the ground of marital status. Marital status is defined as meaning the status or condition of being:

(a) single;

(b) married;

(c) married but living separately and apart from one's spouse;

(d) divorced;

(e) widowed; or

(f) the de facto spouse of another person.

This definition applies only to heterosexual relationships as the term "married" and "spouse" cover relationships between men and women only and should be given the ordinary current meaning according to Australian usage: *Secretary, Department of Social Security v SRA* (1993) 43 FCR 299. This decision was recently upheld and applied in the Family Court case of *Attorney-General (Cth) v Kevin and Jennifer* (2003) 172 FLR 300, which concerned the status of a marriage between a post-operative transsexual male, who at birth was registered as female, and a woman. The court held that the marriage was valid because at the relevant time the couple were married as a man and a woman, the court finding that the post-operative transsexual male was a "man" for the purpose of the *Marriage Act* 1961 (Cth).

A "de facto spouse" is defined as living with a person of the opposite sex on a bona fide domestic basis although not legally married to that person.

In relation to the ground of marital status, Black CJ has observed:

> Marital status is defined by s 4(1) of the Act to mean (not to include) any one of six conditions … In this context it is clear that, in the furtherance of the object of eliminating so far as possible discrimination on the ground of marital status in the area of employment and elsewhere, s 6(1) looks to the way in which the discriminator treats or would treat a person of *any* different marital status to that of the aggrieved person. Given the objects of the Act it could hardly provide otherwise. (*Commonwealth v HR&EOC (Dopking No 1)* (1993) 46 FCR 191 at 195)

The potential use of the marital status provisions was narrowed considerably by the New South Wales Court of Appeal in 1984. A woman was denied a job because her husband worked for a competitor and because of concerns on the part of her potential employer that she may inadvertently disclose confidential information. The Court of Appeal held that there was no discrimination based on marital status as it arose through the identity or situation of her spouse and not from her marital status in a general sense: *Boehringer Ingelheim Pty Ltd v Reddrop* [1984] 2 NSWLR 13. The basis of the decision was that the individual complainant had the characteristics identified as coming within the definition, rather than a group of persons.

The New South Wales Court of Appeal side-stepped this decision in a later decision involving the rejection of Gai Waterhouse's application to the Australian Jockey Club for a trainer's licence: *Waterhouse v Bell* (1991) 25 NSWLR 99. The court found that "corruptibility at the hands of one's husband is a characteristic attributed, or generally imputed, to all married women" and it was necessary to ascertain "the ground of the impugned decision".

The court held that the basis of the Australian Jockey Club's decision to reject her application was solely because she was married to Robbie Waterhouse and "she was liable to be corrupted by him" and "the conclusion is inescapable that [Gai Waterhouse] was denied a licence because she was married to a dominating rogue and not because she was thought to have personal character deficiencies" (at 114-15).

There have been a series of decisions by the Federal Court and the HR&EOC on some seminal interpretation issues concerning this ground. The decisions arose from a complaint of unlawful discrimination on the ground of marital status concerning housing benefits available to a soldier transferred to a new location by his employer, the Australian

Defence Force, when others similarly transferred, who were married and accompanied by their family members, were able to obtain benefits. It was held that the policy did not involve either direct or indirect discrimination on the basis of marital status: *Commonwealth v HR&EOC* (1991) 32 FCR 468; *Dopking No 1* (1993) 46 FCR 191; *Commonwealth v HR&EOC (Dopking No 2)* (1995) 63 FCR 74.

The ground of "marital status" does not include discrimination on the basis of homosexuality. Therefore in *Wilson v Qantas Airways Ltd* (1985) EOC ¶92-141, it was held that an airline which operated a roster system under which married and de facto couples could be rostered on together was not unlawfully discriminating against a same sex couple on the basis of marital status when they were denied access to this system because they were not legally married or in a de facto relationship. A similar decision was reached in *Nolan v Repatriation Commission* (2003) EOC ¶93-258.

"Pregnancy or potential pregnancy"

A separate ground of discrimination is "pregnancy" and in the *Sex Discrimination Act* "potential pregnancy" is also covered. "Potential pregnancy of a woman" is defined in s 4B as including a reference to:

(a) the fact that the woman is or may be capable of bearing children; or

(b) the fact that the woman has expressed a desire to become pregnant; or

(c) the fact that the woman is likely, or perceived as being likely, to become pregnant.

Dismissal from employment when a woman either informs the employer that she is pregnant or her pregnancy becomes physically obvious remains a regular basis for complaint (see Chapter 4 for case illustrations).

"Breastfeeding"

Breastfeeding is a recently added separate ground of discrimination at a Federal level under the *Sex Discrimination Act* and in New South Wales, Queensland, Victoria, Tasmania and the Northern Territory.

"Family responsibilities, family status, parenthood and responsibilities as a carer"

The *Sex Discrimination Act* was amended in 1992 to include a new ground of discrimination, that of "family responsibilities", which applies in the context of an employment relationship only. All State Acts now cover this ground and the coverage is significantly wider than the operation of the Federal law, as all areas are covered.

The term is defined in s 4A of the *Sex Discrimination Act*, in relation to an employee, as meaning "responsibilities of the employee to care for or support:

(a) a dependent child of the employee; or

(b) any other immediate family member who is in need of care and support".

"Child" is defined as including an adopted child, a step-child or an ex-nuptial child. "Dependent child" is defined as meaning a child who is wholly or substantially dependent on the employee. "Immediate family member" includes a spouse and an adult child, parent, grandparent, grandchild or sibling of the employee or the spouse of the employee. "Spouse" includes a former spouse, a de facto spouse and a former de facto spouse.

These definitions mean that a person in a homosexual relationship is not covered by the family responsibilities provisions in relation to their relationship with their partner but are in connection with their relationship with any dependent child.

One of the leading cases under this ground of unlawful discrimination is *Hickie v Hunt & Hunt* (1998) EOC ¶92-910, where it was held that the complainant had been indirectly discriminated against on the basis of sex, the act of discrimination by the employer, a firm of solicitors, was based on the complainant's inability to work full time after her return from maternity leave due to her family responsibilities. (See Chapter 4 for a more detailed discussion of this ground in an employment context.)

"Sexual harassment"

The growth of a specific law covering sexual harassment means that it is not strictly a separate ground of unlawful discrimination but a self-contained area of discrimination. However, given the continuing focus on sexual harassment as a major issue for women in employment, and a significant cause of complaint, it can be considered technically as a separate ground (see Chapter 6 for a more detailed discussion of this ground).

The inclusion of the term "sexual harassment" in the *Sex Discrimination Act* was the first time that the words had been used in a legislative formula anywhere in the world. There are now also specific provisions in all State laws.

There is a statutory definition of "sexual harassment" in the *Sex Discrimination Act*, which states that a person sexually harasses another person if:

(a) the person makes an unwelcome sexual advance, or an unwelcome request for sexual favours, to the person harassed, or

(b) engages in other unwelcome conduct of a sexual nature in relation to the person harassed.

"Conduct of a sexual nature" is defined as including "making a statement of a sexual nature to a person, or in the presence of a person, whether the statement is made orally or in writing": *SD Act* s 28A(2).

Sexual harassment can take many different forms. It can be obvious or indirect, physical or verbal. For example:

- touching, patting or fondling;
- staring or leering;
- sexually suggestive comments and jokes;
- persistent invitations or requests for sex;
- showing lewd pictures, posters or cartoons;
- sending lewd or pornographic words or images by email;
- altering computer photographs to insert the head of a work colleague into a lewd or pornographic photograph and then circulating it,
- unnecessary familiarity, such as deliberately brushing up against someone.

Sexual harassment can also involve indecent exposure, sexual assault or obscene telephone calls or letters.

"Race"

All the Acts use different definitions of the term "race" and some of the State legislative definitions are wider than the *Racial Discrimination Act* 1975 (Cth). Section 9(1) of that Act includes a general provision which makes racial discrimination unlawful.

The Federal definition mirrors the definition of "racial discrimination" in Article 1.1 of the *International Convention on the Elimination of All Forms of Racial Discrimination*. This arises as the Act itself is designed to give effect to the Convention, which provides the constitutional basis for the legislation: *Koowarta v Bjelke-Petersen* (1982) 153 CLR 168 at 221. The Convention states that the term "race" means:

> any distinction, exclusion, restriction or preference based on race, colour, descent or national or ethnic origin which has the purpose or

effect of nullifying or impairing the recognition, enjoyment or exercise, on an equal footing, of human rights and fundamental freedoms in the political, economic, social, cultural or any other field of public life.

All the State discrimination laws proscribe discrimination on the ground of race.

"Race" is defined in the New South Wales Act as including "colour, nationality, descent and ethnic, ethno-religious or national origin". The Victorian and Queensland Acts define "race" as including "colour", "descent or ancestry", "nationality or national origin", "ethnicity or ethnic origin". The Victorian Act includes a further definition of "if 2 or more races are collectively referred to as a race – (i) each of those distinct races; (ii) that collective race".

There has been some judicial consideration of some of the terms used in these definitions. The most contentious term has been "national origin". The interpretation to be preferred is a broad one and is not confined to a person's current citizenship or connection with a sovereign state but covers a person's race or descent:

> Of course, in most cases a man has only a single "national origin" which coincides with his nationality at birth in the legal sense and again in most cases his nationality remains unchanged throughout his life. But "national origins" and "nationality" in the legal sense are two quite different conceptions and they may well not coincide or continue to coincide. (*Ealing London Borough Council v Race Relations Board* [1972] AC 342 at 365)

The definition in *Ealing* has been adopted and applied in Australia: see, for example, *Macabenta v Minister for Immigration and Multicultural Affairs* (1998) 90 FCR 202 at 211; *AB v New South Wales* (2005) 194 FLR 156, *Bropho v Western Australia* [2007] FCA 519 at [303.

The term "ethnic origin" has been judicially considered in New Zealand and England and more recently in Australia. The New Zealand Court of Appeal held that Jews in New Zealand formed a common ethnic group within the meaning of the race discrimination legislation. The court held:

> A group is identifiable in terms of its ethnic origin if it is a segment of the population distinguished from others by a sufficient combination of shared customs, beliefs, traditions and characteristics derived from a common or presumed common past, even if not drawn from what in biological terms is a common racial stock ... They have a distinct social identity based not simply on group cohesion and solidarity but also on their beliefs to their historical antecedents. (*King-Ansell v Police* [1979] 2 NZLR 531 at 543)

This wide interpretation was adopted by the House of Lords in their finding that Sikhs were "a group of persons defined by reference to ethnic groups who must possess some characteristics of a race, namely group descent, a group of geographical origin and a group history": *Mandla v Dowell Lee* [1983] 2 AC 548 at 569. It has also been adopted in Australia, particularly in the context of determining whether Jewish people in Australia comprise a group of people within an "ethnic origin" for the purposes of the *Racial Discrimination Act* 1975 (Cth): *Miller v Wertheim* [2002] FCAFC 156 at [14] and *Jones v Scully* (2002) 120 FCR 243 at 272. In the latter case it was held that Jewish people in Australia were a group of people with an "ethnic origin" because they saw themselves as a distinct community bound by common customs and beliefs, having a common language and sharing common characteristics (at [112]).

"Racial hatred" or vilification

The *Racial Discrimination Act* prohibits offensive behaviour based on racial hatred (see Chapter 7 for a more detailed discussion). That Act provides:

> It is unlawful for a person to do an act, otherwise than in private, if:
> (a) the act is reasonably likely, in all the circumstances, to offend, insult, humiliate or intimidate another person or a group of people; and
> (b) the act is done because of the race, colour or national or ethnic origin of the other person or of some or all of the people in the group.

Section 18C(2) defines when an act is not performed in private and s 18C(3) defines "public place". Section 18D provides for exemptions for artistic work, work for an academic or scientific purpose, and fair and accurate reporting.

The laws in most other jurisdictions now make racial vilification or racial harassment and incitement unlawful: *Commissioner of Police v Estate of Russell* (2002) 55 NSWLR 232.

Racial or race-based harassment

There are no specific statutory provisions to make racial or race-based harassment unlawful other than in Western Australia (where such provisions are contained in the State's *Criminal Code*). However, the direct discrimination provisions cover acts of harassment which are racially based, such as abuse which is racial in content, or assaults which are directed at an individual on the basis of their race.

"Disability"

Discrimination on the ground of disability was added to the Federal stable of discrimination laws in 1992, although the commonly used earlier term "impairment" had been a ground of discrimination in all existing State laws since the early 1980s. The *Disability Discrimination Act* 1992 defines "disability", in relation to a person, as:

(a) total or partial loss of the person's bodily or mental functions; or

(b) total or partial loss of a part of the body; or

(c) the presence in the body of organisms causing disease or illness; or

(d) the presence in the body of organisms capable of causing disease or illness; or

(e) the malfunction, malformation or disfigurement of a part of the person's body; or

(f) disorder or malfunction that results in the person learning differently from a person without the disorder or malfunction; or

(g) a disorder, illness or disease that affects a person's thought processes, perception of reality, emotions or judgment or that results in disturbed behaviour;

and includes a disability that:

(h) presently exists; or

(i) previously existed but no longer exists; or

(j) may exist in the future; or

(k) is imputed to a person.

All State laws include disability and have similar definitions to that in the *Disability Discrimination Act*. An applicant must adduce evidence to prove that they have a disability and the nature and extent of the disability where that is relevant to the claim: *Wecker v University of Technology, Sydney* [2007] NSWSC 927.

The meaning of the term "disability" in the context of the *Disability Discrimination Act* came under judicial scrutiny by the High Court in *Purvis v New South Wales (Department of Education and Training)* (2003) 217 CLR 92.

The case concerned Daniel Hoggan who had been suspended and later excluded from a high school due to his aggressive and violent behaviour. Daniel suffered from a range of disabilities which manifested in aggressive behaviour such as hitting or kicking. An initial issue before the court was the interpretation of the definition of "disability" in the Act:

was Daniel's disability to be identified as the disorder from which he suffered, the disturbed behaviour that resulted or a combination of both.

The court noted that, unlike the *Sex Discrimination Act* and the *Racial Discrimination Act*, where the central purpose of those Acts was to require that people not be treated differently as difference in race or gender ought to be an irrelevant consideration (at [198]), by contrast "disability discrimination legislation necessarily focuses upon a criterion of admitted difference" (at [199]). The court went on to note three aspects of the definition (at [209]-[212]): first, that the definitions of disability in paras (a)-(g) are not exclusive of each other. So a disability can fall into one or more of those paragraphs. Secondly, that effect must be given to the whole definition. Accordingly, Daniels's disability could not be identified by reference to physiological changes, but was more correctly described as a particular kind of brain malfunction. Thirdly, that to focus only on the cause of Daniel's bad behaviour to the exclusion of the bad behaviour itself would confine the operation of the Act by excluding attributes of the disabled person which makes that person different in the eyes of others (at [212]).

Accordingly, the High Court in *Purvis* has given expansive definition to the term "disability", a definition that includes both cause and effect. A wide range of disabilities is covered: *Williams v Commonwealth* [2002] FMCA 89.

As can be seen from the discussion above, the definition of "disability" is wide and includes all obvious categories of disability, such as physical disability and intellectual disability, and extends to other conditions such as people who are HIV positive or have AIDS-related conditions and people with attention deficit disorder. Indeed the definition is so wide that it has been interpreted to include illicit drug addiction: *Marsden v HR&EOC* [2000] FCA 1619. As a result of that decision, some jurisdictions have amended their disability discrimination law to render lawful discrimination on the grounds of disability in the workplace by reason of an addiction to a prohibited drug: see, for example, s 49PA(2) of the *Anti-Discrimination Act* 1977 (NSW); *Carr v Botany Bay Council* [2003] NSWADT 209.

In New South Wales it is also unlawful to vilify someone on the basis of their HIV/AIDS status: see Part 4F of the *Anti-Discrimination Act* 1977.

"Physical features"

In Victoria, direct and indirect discrimination on the grounds of physical features is prohibited under the *Equal Opportunity Act* 1995 (Vic). The term "physical features" is defined to mean a person's height, weight, size or other bodily characteristic. This ground is both unique and very flexible and would cover certain physical characteristics that would not necessarily be caught by other grounds of unlawful discrimination such as disability. Discriminatory remarks about a person's body hair could amount to unlawful discrimination under this ground: *Fratas v Drake International Ltd* (2000) EOC ¶93-038. Derogatory comments about a person's weight could also be a breach: *Hill v Canterbury Road Lodge Pty Ltd* [2004] VCAT 1365. Tattoos could be a "physical feature" (*Jamieson v Benalla Golf Club Inc* (2000) EOC ¶93-106) and so to refuse to employ someone because they had tattoos could infringe this provision.

"Age"

Age discrimination was made unlawful by Federal legislation from June 2004 and this made it consistent with all State and Territory legislation. Age discrimination refers to discrimination on the basis of chronological age. "Age" is defined in the *Age Discrimination Act* to include "age group": s 5.

Most of the complaints and litigation have been on events affecting older persons. However, there has been a growing awareness of the capacity of the legislation to protect young people at work, especially where there has been some harassment of them because they are apprentices or the most junior employee. The basis of the discrimination complaint is that if the person were not young, that is, of a certain chronological age, then the less favourable treatment in the workplace would not have arisen. Such complaints cover incidents of verbal harassment and intimidation as well as physical assaults. Previously considered as skylarking and rites of passage, especially in blue collar workplaces, it is clear that this type of behaviour towards young, and often vulnerable, workers is not acceptable and constitutes a breach of the age provisions.

As there was no earlier Federal age discrimination legislation, most cases of age discrimination have been brought under industrial relations legislation. In *Qantas Airways v Christie* (1998) 198 CLR 280, the issue before the High Court was whether the complainant, an airline pilot, could be lawfully dismissed because he was age 60. Section 170DF(1)(f) of the then *Industrial Relations Act* 1988 (Cth) stated that an employer could not terminate an employee's employment for reasons that included age. While it was acknowledged that the employment had been terminated because of his age, the High Court found for the employer on the basis that, as certain countries prohibited pilots who were over the age of 60, the complainant could no longer perform the inherent requirements of his employment. Consequently, the employer was covered by a specific exception to the prohibition.

All State laws prohibit discrimination on the ground of age and most also prohibit compulsory retirement on the ground of age. Some examples of where a complaint of age discrimination has been successfully made out include:

- applicants for positions as flight attendants were found to have been discriminated against on the ground of their age when not offered employment: *Virgin Blue Airlines Pty Ltd v Stewart* [2007] QSC 075;

- an employer who had dismissed two skilled and experienced storemen on the basis that there was "insufficient work owing to a down turn in trade", only to shortly afterwards employ two younger and inexperienced men to replace them, had unlawfully discriminated against the dismissed employees on the ground of age: *Lightening Bolt Co Pty Ltd v Skinner* [2002] QCA 518.

Age discrimination was alleged by the mother of a gifted student who claimed discrimination by the education authorities due to the younger age at which her child achieved certain results usually achieved by an older primary school student. The complaint was not made out on certain factual grounds: *Malaxetxebarria v Queensland (No 2)* (2007) 95 ALD 89.

Other grounds

Sexuality

There is no discrimination law at a Federal level which provides any enforceable rights in relation to any ground of discrimination based on sexuality. The majority report of the Senate Legal and Constitutional Affairs Committee *Report on Inquiry into Sexuality Discrimination*, AGPS, December 1997, recommended that the Federal Parliament pass a Sexuality and Gender Status Discrimination Bill but this recommendation has never been implemented.

It is, however, unlawful to discriminate against someone on the ground of their sexuality in all State jurisdictions across Australia.

The State laws have taken differing approaches. In New South Wales, the ground is identified as "homosexuality". In Victoria and Queensland, the ground is identified as "lawful sexual activity". In South Australia, the ground is identified as "sexuality" which is defined as meaning "hetero-sexuality, homosexuality, bisexuality or transsexuality".

In the Australian Capital Territory, the ground is identified as "sexuality" which is defined as "heterosexuality, homosexuality (including lesbianism) or bisexuality". In the Northern Territory, the ground is identified as "sexuality" which is identified as meaning "the sexual characteristics or imputed sexual characteristics of heterosexuality, homosexuality, bisexuality or transsexuality". In Western Australia and Tasmania the ground is identified as "sexual orientation".

In New South Wales it is also specifically unlawful to vilify someone on the basis of their homosexuality or perceived homosexuality.

Transsexuality

A separate ground in New South Wales and Victoria ("gender identity") or included within the definition of "sexuality" or "sexual orientation" in all other jurisdictions now means that discrimination on the grounds of transsexuality is unlawful: *Burton v Houston* [2004] TASSC 57, *PW v Royal Prince Alfred Hospital* (EOD) [2007] NSWADTAP 36. In New South Wales, it is also specifically unlawful to vilify a person on the ground that they are a transgender person.

Religious belief or activity

Discrimination on the ground of religious belief or activity is made unlawful in most States. In New South Wales and South Australia, the ground is not covered. In New South Wales it has been held that the addition of the words "ethno-religious" to the definition of "race" did not extend the Act to cover discrimination on the ground of religion. Consequently, it was found that the Act did not cover a claim that Jewish children in public schools were discriminated against by the holding of Christmas and Easter activities: *A obo V & A v Department of School Education* [1999] NSWADT 120.

The Victorian Act defines "religious belief or activity" as meaning "(a) holding or not holding a lawful religious belief or view, (b) engaging in, not engaging in or refusing to engage in a lawful religious activity". There are similar definitions in Western Australia, Queensland, Tasmania, the Australian Capital Territory and Northern Territory.

There have been several cases which looked at the operation of this ground: *Queensland v Mahommed* [2007] QSC 018, *Catch the Fire Ministries Inc v Islamic Council of Victoria Inc* (2006) 235 ALR 750 and *Kapoor v Monash University* (2001) 4 VR 483.

"Religion" is included in the definition of "discrimination" in the *Human Rights and Equal Opportunity Commission Act* 1986. Consequently, if a complaint is made, the Commission may investigate it and endeavour to settle it between the parties and, if this is unsuccessful, then a report on the complaint may be made to Parliament. This means that the enforceable remedies available under the State laws are not available in the Federal arena in relation to religion.

There is also afforded a limited guarantee of religious freedom, at least insofar as the Commonwealth is concerned, by virtue of s 116 of the Constitution. That section prohibits, amongst other things, the Commonwealth from prohibiting the free exercise of any religion. The provision had been narrowly construed by the High Court and is not often employed.

Political belief or activity

Another ground is discrimination on the ground of political belief or activity (this is to be contrasted with industrial or trade union activity). In New South Wales and South Australia, this ground is not covered. In some jurisdictions, some measure of protection in afforded under the relevant industrial laws: see, s 659 of the *Workplace Relations Act* 1996 (Cth) (see Chapter 15).

The Victorian Act defines "political belief or activity" as meaning "(a) holding or not holding a lawful political belief or view, (b) engaging in, not engaging in or refusing to engage in a lawful political activity". There are similar definitions in Western Australia, Queensland, Tasmania, the Australian Capital Territory and Northern Territory.

The term "political" activity or belief has been the subject of judicial scrutiny in various States. Essentially the courts have determined that a person holds a political belief or engages in political activity when they express an opinion or pursue courses of action with a view to changing or influencing government. These can include the holding of republican views as opposed to monarchist views: *Lindisfarne R & SLA Sub-Branch v Buchanan* (2004) 80 ALD 122. Accordingly, the Queensland Tribunal held that the State Government had unlawfully discriminated against an employee on the basis of her political belief in terminating her employment because of her political affiliation with the ALP: *Byrne v Queensland* (1999) EOC ¶93-010.

"Political opinion" is included in the definition of "discrimination" in the *Human Rights and Equal Opportunity Commission Act* 1986 (Cth). Consequently, if a complaint is made, the Commission may investigate it and endeavour to settle it between the parties and, if this is unsuccessful, then a report on the complaint may be made to Parliament. This means that the enforceable remedies available under the State laws are not available in the Federal arena in relation to political opinion.

Trade union activity

In Victoria, Queensland, Tasmania, the Australian Capital Territory and Northern Territory, the concept of membership or non-membership of a trade union has been added as a ground of discrimination. In some States, the ground is defined as being "trade union activity": *Bennett v Human Rights and Equal Opportunity Commission* (2003) 134 FCR 334. In others, it has been defined as "industrial activity".

The Victorian Act defines "industrial activity" as meaning "(a) being or not being a member of, or joining, not joining or refusing to join, an industrial organisation; (b) participating in, not participating in or refusing to participate in a lawful activity organised or promoted by an industrial organisation". It includes both present and past industrial activity: *Thorne v Council of Northern Melbourne Institute of TAFE* (2000) EOC ¶93-068.

Pursuant to ss 659(2)(b), 664 and 665 of the *Workplace Relations Act* 1996 (Cth), an employer may not dismiss a person for membership of a trade union or participation in trade union activities. The penalties for breaching this provision are harsher than those applying to unfair dismissal and the employer carries the onus of proof to establish that the dismissal did not occur for that reason. This provision is designed to meet Australia's international treaty obligations in relation to the protection of the rights of employees (see Chapter 15).

Criminal record

Discrimination on the grounds of an irrelevant or spent conviction is unlawful in the Northern Territory, Western Australia (*Spent Convictions Act* 1988) and the ACT only. Laws have been enacted in other jurisdictions to permit certain criminal records (those that are not serious) to lapse after a period of time. Such laws, while not contained within the rubric of anti-discrimination legislation, are nevertheless aimed at preventing discrimination on the basis of a prior criminal conviction.

Federally, s 85ZV of the *Crimes Act* 1914 (Cth) prevents an organisation taking into account or disclosing an individual's prior criminal conviction under Federal law if the conviction is more than 10 years old for adult convictions and five years old for juvenile convictions, and where certain other criteria have been fulfilled.

Associate

Most jurisdictions recognise that a person may be discriminated against not on a ground that they personally possess or have, but due to their association or connection with a person who does possess or have, that ground. In some State laws, the extension of all grounds to an associate has led to some absurd statutory interpretation results and to the provisions being essentially unworkable. This is due to the attempt to transfer the personal characteristic of which the person complains, such as their race or disability, onto their associate, without any of the defining characteristics.

The New South Wales Act defines the term "associate" as meaning "(a) any person with whom the person associates, whether socially or in business or commerce, or otherwise; and (b) any person who is totally or mainly dependent on, or a member of the household of, the person". The Victorian Act extends the definition of "attributes" to include "personal association (whether as a relative or otherwise) with a person who is identified by reference to any of the above attributes". There are similar definitions in other jurisdictions.

3

DEFINITIONS OF DISCRIMINATION

All discrimination legislation in Australia has separate definitions for direct discrimination and indirect discrimination and it is important from the outset to characterise any alleged act of unlawful discrimination as either direct or indirect discrimination (see Chapter 2). The tests for each vary considerably.

Direct discrimination arises where the conduct in question is "directly" grounded upon the complainant's status or a characteristic appertaining generally or generally imputed to the complainant's status, for example, his or her gender, and where the complainant is treated less favourably than someone without such a characteristic. Indirect discrimination is a mechanism for examining the impact of policies and practices which on their face appear to operate in a neutral or non-discriminatory manner but which have a disproportionate detrimental impact on persons of the status of the complainant and which are unreasonable. The latter identifies systemic discrimination and targets the factors that lead to a result which disadvantages one particular group.

Most cases brought in Australia are based on direct discrimination as opposed to the lesser utilised and often more difficult to prove indirect discrimination provisions.

This chapter analyses the components of direct and indirect discrimination and the role of the discriminatory ground where there is more than one reason for a particular act.

See Appendix A for reference to the specific sections in the Federal and State discrimination laws. See Chapter 2 for a discussion of the different grounds or attributes of unlawful discrimination and the coverage of the various Acts. See Chapters 4 to 8 for the various areas of unlawful discrimination covered by the legislation.

Separate definitions

It is unclear as to whether or not the two definitions of direct and indirect discrimination are "mutually exclusive" as has been previously suggested. In *Waters v Public Transport Corporation* (*Waters' case*) (1991) 173 CLR 349 at 393, the High Court came to the view that they were mutually exclusive. Likewise, in *Australian Medical Council v Wilson* (*Siddiqui's case*) (1996) 68 FCR 46 at 55, the Federal Court said "such an approach is consistent with the language of the provisions, their legislative history and the preponderance of authority". However, in *Minns v New South Wales* [2002] FMCA 60, the Federal Magistrate noted the Federal Court's view in *Siddiqui* and held that this statement did not mean that the same set of facts could not ground both a claim in direct and indirect discrimination or that the complainant had to make an election (at [245]). It is now relatively common for the same set of facts to be pleaded in the alternate as both direct and indirect discrimination.

The concept of "reasonable" which is explicit in the definition of indirect discrimination is absent and hence irrelevant to any consideration of the definition of direct discrimination.

Direct discrimination

The basis of the definition of direct discrimination is that of a comparison between the aggrieved person or the person making the complaint ("the complainant") and some other person.

All Australian statutes, except the *Racial Discrimination Act* 1975 (Cth), have a similar definition of direct discrimination and all are based on the same formula although there is different wording in some parts of the definitions.

The definition in relation to the ground of sex in s 5(1) of the *Sex Discrimination Act* is:

> For the purposes of this Act, a person (in this subsection referred to as the "discriminator") discriminates against another person (in this subsection referred to as the "aggrieved person") on the ground of the sex of the aggrieved person if, by reason of –
>
> (a) the sex of the aggrieved person,
> (b) a characteristic that appertains generally to persons of the sex of the aggrieved person; or
> (c) a characteristic that is generally imputed to persons of the sex of the aggrieved person,
>
> the discriminator treats the aggrieved person less favourably than, in circumstances that are the same or are not materially different, the discriminator treats or would treat a person of the opposite sex.

Section 9(1) of the *Racial Discrimination Act* provides that:

> It is unlawful for a person to do any act involving a distinction, exclusion, restriction or preference based on race, colour, descent or national or ethnic origin which has the purpose or effect of nullifying or impairing the recognition, enjoyment or exercise, on an equal footing, of any human right or fundamental freedom in the political, economic, social, cultural or any other field of public life.

While the courts have accepted that s 9(1) applies the concept of direct discrimination, it is still open to debate whether s 10 provides for both direct and indirect discrimination or whether indirect discrimination is not covered: see, for example, *Bropho v Western Australia* [2007] FCA 519 at [298]-[292].

There are various components to the definition of direct discrimination which are discussed separately below.

"Ground" or "attribute"

All discrimination laws specify a particular ground or attribute which must be demonstrated as the primary basis for an action (see Chapter 2): *Australian Medical Council v Wilson* (*Siddiqui's case*) (1996) 68 FCR 46 at 58.

"Characteristic"

All the definitions of direct discrimination extend beyond the nominated ground of discrimination to cover a "characteristic" imputed or appertaining generally to persons of or with the nominated ground.

This extension of the definition is sometimes described as attempting to address "stereotyping" of a particular group of persons on the basis of actual or implied distinguishing or idiosyncratic traits: *Boehringer Ingelheim Pty Ltd v Reddrop* [1984] 2 NSWLR 13 at 18. In *Commonwealth v HR&EOC* (*Dopking No 1*) (1993) 46 FCR 191, Wilcox J noted that this extended definition was:

> presumably inserted to prevent the circumventions that would otherwise occur where discriminators justified their conduct by reference to a characteristic (actual or implied) of persons of a particular marital status, rather than by reference to the marital status itself. Parliament may also have been concerned with discrimination based on stereotyping. (at 207)

It is necessary for complainants to be able to precisely identify and adequately describe the characteristic upon which they seek to rely. Also, they will need to produce some evidence in support of a claim that the characteristic is one that "appertains generally" or is "imputed" to the group in which the complainant seeks to demonstrate membership. In *Thomson v Orica Australia* (2002) 116 IR 186, the Federal Court defined these terms broadly in stating that (where the impugned conduct was founded upon a female taking maternity leave) (at [168]):

> The capacity or ability to become pregnant is obviously a characteristic that appertains generally to women. What attends pregnancy, that is, the characteristics of pregnancy, can thus, perhaps without doing violence to the language of s 5, and recognising the remedial nature of the statute and the width and purpose of the Convention, be seen as characteristics that appertain generally to women. If, as here, an employer treats a female employee less favourably than a male employee in equivalent circumstances by reason of (in part) the fact that the employee took maternity leave, can this be seen as connected with the employee's female sex? It is not difficult to answer that question in the affirmative. Likewise, if an employer hired men rather than women in order to avoid a perceived extra cost in providing for maternity leave, the relevance of 'potential pregnancy' in s 7 would be obvious, but such conduct could also be seen to be undertaken by reason of a characteristic that appertains to women, but not men. I do not think that the word 'generally' in subs 5(1) and subs 7(1) means 'with few or no exceptions'. It could be limited to be a weaker adverb denoting 'for the most part' or 'extensively'; or it may also include the notion of 'in a general sense'. (See generally Oxford English Dictionary.) I think the word encompasses both these latter two senses in this context. So read, the taking of maternity leave can be seen as a characteristic that appertains in a general sense to women, or extensively to women. Thus, I would conclude that the applicant has demonstrated unlawful discrimination for the purposes of para 5(1)(b) and para 14(2)(a), para 14(2)(b), para 14(2)(c) and para 14(2)(d). In para 5(1)(c) the notion of 'generally imputed' means, it seems to me, 'for the most part' or 'extensively'. That is, some characteristic that is imputed (not always, but extensively or usually) to females. To impute is to 'attribute' or 'ascribe'. The above analysis would also support a conclusion of unlawful discrimination based on para 5(1)(c).

The court held that the taking of maternity leave was a characteristic that appertains generally to women who are pregnant.

It is not necessary to establish that the identified characteristic exists in every case but it must be established that it generally exists or operates. The basis of comparison using a characteristic is with a person with that characteristic and a person of a different specified ground, such as sex or marital status. "In other words, the comparison is not made with a person having a characteristic that appertains generally to or is imputed to persons of another marital status; it is made with a person of a different marital status": *Dopking No 1* at 204-5.

"Less favourable treatment"

One of the crucial components of the definition of direct discrimination is that of "less favourable treatment". This is the basis of the comparison. The South Australian Act uses the word "unfavourably" and this covers the same concept.

The classic statement of the concept is:

> The words "less favourably" ... requires a comparison of the treatment in the actual and in an hypothesised case ... A "detriment" concept of discrimination has hitherto been adopted ... The motives, reasons or suggested justifications of the detriment are irrelevant, if it can be shown that there is differentiation of treatment, which results in detriment to the person affected. (*Haines v Leves* (1987) 8 NSWLR 442 at 471)

The identification of the less favourable treatment requires a factual inquiry as to the treatment received: *Commonwealth v Humphries* (1998) 86 FCR 324 at 333B.

In *Dopking No 1*, when examining the "less favourable" criteria, Wilcox J said that the "concept underlying this element is detriment; the aggrieved person being treated in a manner less favourable than that accorded with someone of a different ... status" (at 210). Accordingly, in *Thomson*, it was held that the complainant was treated less favourably than a male employee in equivalent circumstances by reason of the fact that she took maternity leave, the capacity or ability to become pregnant being a characteristic that appertains generally to women.

A denial of a benefit can amount to a detriment but not where the benefit would not have been provided in any event to someone of a different status from that of the complainant: *New South Wales (Department of Education) v HR&EOC and Purvis* (2001) 186 ALR 69 at 81 (issue not specifically addressed by the later High Court *Purvis* decision).

"By reason of", "on the ground of", "on the basis of" or "because"

The requirement for an act of direct discrimination is that there be an identifiable causal link between the ground of discrimination alleged and the decision or action complained about. Establishing the existence of that causal link is frequently the most crucial element in any case.

The *Sex Discrimination Act* uses the term "by reason of". The New South Wales and Western Australian Acts use the term "on the ground of". The Queensland, Victorian and Tasmanian Acts use the term "on the basis of". The *Disability Discrimination Act* and the South Australian and Australian Capital Territory Acts set up an even simpler link by using the words "because of".

Essentially, while these all establish a similar test, subtle variations of some significance do occur. There have, for example, been differences of opinion expressed about the meaning of phrases such as "on the ground of" and "by reason of": *Creek v Cairns Post Pty Ltd* (2001) 112 FCR 352 at 357-9. For a discussion on the use of the term "based on" and relevant authorities, see *Macedonian Teachers' Association of Victoria Inc v HR&EOC* (1998) 91 FCR 8 at 24-41.

The phrase "by reason of" in the sex discrimination definition in the *Sex Discrimination Act* has been interpreted in the following way:

> In my opinion the phrase "by reason of" in s 5(1) of the SD Act should be interpreted as meaning "because of", "due to", "based on" or words of similar import which bring something about or cause it to occur. The phrase implies a relationship of cause and effect between the sex (or characteristic of the kind mentioned in s 5(1)(b) or (c)) of the aggrieved person and the less favourable treatment by the discriminator of that person. (*HR&EOC v Mt Isa Mines Ltd* (1993) 46 FCR 301 at 321-322, cited with approval in *Thomson v Orica* at [158]-[161])

In *Waters v Public Transport Corporation* (1991) 173 CLR 349, Mason CJ and Gaudron J considered that the term in the Victorian Act meant that the treatment was "based" on the nominated ground of discrimination. "A material difference in treatment that is so based sufficiently satisfies the notions of 'on the ground of' and 'by reason of'" (at 359).

In looking at claims of race discrimination, the Federal Court has held in a series of cases that the words "by reason of", in the context of the *Racial Discrimination Act*, "require practical application of causation principles explained in *March v E & MH Stramare Pty Ltd* (1991) 171 CLR 506 whilst at the same time according due recognition to the beneficial purpose and objects of the RDA. The ambit of the expression 'by reason of' is not confined to absence or limited extent of the enjoyment of the persons first mentioned in the section, but must extend right through to the point at which the section starts to do its deeming work": *Macabenta v Minister for Immigration* (1998) 90 FCR 202 at 213 and *Commonwealth v McEvoy* (1999) 94 FCR 341 at 353.

With respect to the racial vilification provisions of the *Racial Discrimination Act*, the relevant causative phrase is "because of" and has been held to require consideration of the reason or reasons for which the relevant act was done: *Hagan v Trustees of Toowoomba Sports Ground*

Trust (2000) 105 FCR 56 at [23]. The words in the context of those provisions have been interpreted to mean "whether 'anything suggests race as a factor in the respondent's decision to publish' the work in question": *Jones v Scully* (2002) 120 FCR 243 at 273.

"*Circumstances ... same or are not materially different*"

The less favourable treatment must be based on the "circumstances" which must be "the same" or "not materially different". This means that there must be a sufficient degree of similarity or common features or factors to form the basis of an appropriate comparison. The identification of the circumstances which are to form the basis of the comparison is an essential component of the statutory formula for direct discrimination as a whole.

The prohibited ground can form part of the materially different circumstances. The HR&EOC has described the approach as:

> It would fatally frustrate the purposes of the Act if the matters which it expressly identifies as constituting unacceptable bases for differential treatment could be seized upon as rendering the overall circumstances materially different, with the result that the treatment could never be discriminatory within the meaning of the Act. (*Sullivan v Department of Defence* (1992) EOC ¶92-421 at 79,005)

This approach has been cited with approval by several Federal Court judges when considering the various components of direct discrimination: *Dopking No 1* at 194, 201, 209; *Mt Isa Mines case* at 327. As Wilcox J described it in *Dopking No 1*: "To the extent that the Commonwealth argues in this case that there is a material difference between single people and married people in that the former tend not to have 'family' whereas the latter do, the difference is the proscribed discrimination itself" (at 209).

> The words ... "in circumstances that are the same or are not materially different" are not in my opinion directed to the differences between men and women. If differences between men and women are capable of being material for the purposes of [the definition of direct discrimination] then the effect of those words would remove from the ambit of discrimination many cases of less favourable treatment occurring by reason of sex. (*Mt Isa Mines case* at 105)

In *Purvis v New South Wales (Department of Education and Training)* (2003) 217 CLR 92, the complainant argued that the expression "circumstances that are the same or are not materially different" in s 5(1) and (2) of the *Disability Discrimination Act* meant the exclusion of all the circumstances that constituted the disability in question. Only then would the comparator be in the same position as the person with the disability. The majority of the High Court rejected this approach, In their joint judgment Gummow, Hayne and Heydon JJ held:

> It may readily be accepted that the necessary comparison to make is with the treatment of a person without the relevant disability. Section 5(1) makes that plain. It does not follow, however, that the "circumstances" to be considered are to be identified in the way the appellant contended. Indeed, to strip out of those circumstances any and every feature which presents difficulty to a disabled person would truly frustrate the purposes of the Act. Section 5(2) provides that the relevant circumstances are not shown to be materially different by showing that the disabled person has special needs. The appellant's contention, however, went further than that. It sought to refer to a set of circumstances that were wholly hypothetical – circumstances in which no aspect of the disability intrudes. That is not what the Act requires.
>
> In requiring a comparison between the treatment offered to a disabled person and the treatment that would be given to a person without the disability, s 5(1) requires that the circumstances attending the treatment given (or to be given) to the disabled person must be identified. What must then be examined is what would have been done in *those* circumstances if the person concerned was not disabled. The appellant's argument depended upon an inversion of that order of examination. Instead of directing attention first to the *actual* circumstances in which a disabled person was, or would be, treated disadvantageously, it sought to direct attention to a wholly *hypothetical* set of circumstances defined by excluding all features of the disability. (at 160, emphasis in original).

The High Court specifically noted that such an interpretation, albeit more restrictive than that proffered by the complainant, prevented the different treatment of persons with disability. The legislature had not sought in the *Disability Discrimination Act* to provide for equality of treatment. Rather, the test for direct discrimination requires a comparison with a person without the particular disability but otherwise in the same position in all material respects as the complainant. The question to ask is two-fold: first, how in the particular circumstances of the complainant would the alleged discriminator have treated a person without the particular disability? Secondly, if the treatment to the complainant was less favourable than the treatment that would have been given to a person without the disability, the issue then becomes – was this because of the disability or was it for some other reason (at 161).

The courts applying the *Purvis* decision have dismissed many disability discrimination claims as the basis of the comparator could not be established and the evidence demonstrated that any person without a disability behaving in the same manner would have been treated in the same way. This outcome includes education and employment cases: *Forbes v Australian Federal Police (Commonwealth)* [2004] FCAFC 95; *Fetherston v Peninsula Health* [2004] FCA 485; *Power v Aboriginal Hostels Ltd* [2004] FMCA 452.

Motive, malice, consciousness and intention

Debate still exists as to whether or not it is necessary for the discriminator to knowingly or actively commit an act of discrimination or whether it can be an unconscious or unintended result of a decision or an action. In many States, though not all, discrimination laws specifically provide that motive is irrelevant. All Federal laws are silent on this question.

In English jurisprudence there are two schools of thought on this issue. These have been summarised by Lockhart J in *Mt Isa Mines* at 321-2 and referred to in *Thomson* at [160]. There is the view expressed in *Birmingham City Council v Equal Opportunities Commission* [1989] 1 AC 1155, that intention or motive is not a necessary component of unlawful discrimination. However, a later contrary view was expressed in *James v Eastleigh Borough Council* [1990] 1 AC 751, to the effect that a respondent's reason for doing an act was also relevant and not just the causative effect of the act.

In Australia, the position remains equally unclear. In *Waters' case*, Mason CJ and Gaudron J, referring to the grounds in the Victorian Act, "status" and "private life", held:

> It would, in our view, significantly impede or hinder the attainment of the objects of the Act if [the definition of direct discrimination] were to be interpreted as requiring an intention or motive on the part of the alleged discriminator that is related to the status or private life of the person less favourably treated. (at 359)

This is the more orthodox view, though it is by no means a uniform one (*cf Australian Iron and Steel Pty Ltd v Banovic* (1989) 168 CLR 165 at 175-7). In the *Mt Isa Mines case*, Lockhart J expressed a different opinion that more accurately reflects the approach taken when determining the relevant factors in complex matters. He stated:

> The intention of the defendant is not necessarily irrelevant. The purpose and motive of the defendant may also be relevant ... Thus, in

some cases intention may be critical; but in others it may be of little, if any, significance. The objects of the [Sex Discrimination] Act would be frustrated, however, if sections were to be interpreted as requiring in every case intention, motive or purpose of the alleged discriminator ... The search for the proper test to determine if a defendant's conduct is discriminatory is not advanced by the formulation of tests of objective or causative on the one hand and subjective on the other as if they were irreconcilable or postulated diametrically opposed concepts ... This task may involve the consideration of subjective material such as the intention or even motive, purpose or reason of the alleged discriminator; but its significance will vary from case to case ... If an objective test requires the exclusion of the intention, state of mind, purpose, reason or motive of the alleged discriminator then it offends the language of the section itself and in addition offends common sense. It seems obvious to me that the search for the reason for or ground of the decision or conduct of the alleged discriminator must take the inquiry into the state of his mind as well as an analysis of his own acts. (at 326, approved in *Thomson* at [161])

In the decision of *Purvis*, the majority of the High Court did not decide the question, but stated that:

> For present purposes, it is enough to say that we doubt that distinctions between motive, purpose or effect will greatly assist the resolution of any problem about whether treatment occurred or was proposed "because of" disability. Rather, the central question will always be – *why* was the aggrieved person treated as he or she was? If the aggrieved person was treated less favourably was it "because of", "by reason of", that person's disability? Motive, purpose, effect may all bear on that question. But it would be a mistake to treat those words as substitutes for the statutory expression "because of". (at [236])

Objective not subjective assessment

When determining whether a particular set of circumstances come within the statutory formula that defines direct discrimination, the facts must be assessed on an objective basis to ascertain their existence or operation: *Boehringer Ingelheim Pty Ltd v Reddrop* [1984] 2 NSWLR 13. Many complainants make a subjective assessment of their circumstances and then pursue their complaint through the process with little pause to put the facts alleged on a broader or objective basis. Such complaints are bound to fail as the complainant is unable to discharge their onus of proof (see Chapter 13).

No test of reasonableness

As there is no intention or motive required to establish an act of discrimination, it follows that no explanation or test of "reasonableness" is applicable in relation to direct discrimination.

Real or hypothetical comparator

A real person does not have to exist for the basis of comparison of treatment – it can be a hypothetical person.

If there is no real person to whom the complainant compares herself or himself, then an objective test will be applied to ascertain whether on the basis of all the information available, it can be concluded that the decision was a discriminatory one and hence unlawful.

If a complaint is based on characteristics which are asserted to appertain or be imputed generally to the complainant, then the imputed characteristic must be taken into account in conceiving the comparator: *IW v City of Perth* (1997) 191 CLR 1.

Conclusion

The definition of direct discrimination further requires a causal nexus that establishes that the complainant was treated in a particular way because of the ground of discrimination identified. The criteria in the definition of direct discrimination must mesh together to demonstrate a decision or action and then a result which is a detriment to the complainant and is on the basis of the proscribed ground of discrimination.

Act done for two or more reasons

In the earlier history of discrimination laws, there was some dispute about whether the identified act of unlawful discrimination needed to be the only reason, a substantial or dominant reason or merely one of a number of equal reasons. This dispute has been resolved by the incorporation in all laws of the general proposition that the discrimination need be just one reason for the act. This provision applies only to the definition of direct discrimination.

Section 8 of the *Sex Discrimination Act* provides that the doing of an act referred to in any of the definitions of direct discrimination on a specified ground:

> includes a reference to the doing of such an act by reason of 2 or more matters that include the particular matter, whether or not the particular matter is the dominant or substantial reason for the doing of the act.

The only legislation with a different approach is the *Age Discrimination Act* where s 16 requires that age must be the dominant reason for doing the unlawful act.

Indirect discrimination

The definition of indirect discrimination is complex and requires a substantially different approach to presenting the factual material in a complaint than with complaints of direct discrimination. While not suggesting that direct discrimination claims are easy or straightforward to establish, the propositions to be asserted are in distinct categories and do not raise the range of circumstances which are essential to address in an indirect discrimination case.

Indirect discrimination requires a detailed examination of the facts of a situation to ascertain whether the operation of the requirement or condition appears on the face of it to be neutral and applies equally to all persons, but in fact disadvantages a particular group of nominated persons such as women.

The point of provisions attacking indirect discrimination was described by Sackville J in *Siddiqui's case*:

> [It] is to prevent individuals from the effect of apparently neutral conditions or requirements, which in fact operate in a manner that discriminates against particular groups the members of which have characteristics in common (such as race or national origin). A particular individual within a group subjected to discriminatory practices often will have some chance of complying with the offending condition or requirement. The chances of compliance may depend on how the condition is administered, or on whether the individual is able to overcome the practical obstacles placed in his or her path by the invidious condition or requirement. (at 79-80)

General definition

The definition of indirect discrimination is similar in all laws except the *Sex Discrimination Act* and the *Age Discrimination Act*.

Section 6 of the *Disability Discrimination Act* defines indirect discrimination as:

> For the purposes of this Act, a person ("discriminator") discriminates against another person ("aggrieved person") on the ground of a disability of the aggrieved person if the discriminator requires the aggrieved person to comply with a requirement or condition

(a) with which a substantially higher proportion of persons without the disability comply or are able to comply; and

(b) which is not reasonable having regard to the circumstances of the case; and

(c) with which the aggrieved person does not or is not able to comply.

The components of this definition have been subjected to close judicial scrutiny on various occasions. The provisions are discussed below.

Sex Discrimination Act definition

The *Sex Discrimination Act* was amended in 1995 and the indirect discrimination provisions were extensively redrafted to overcome some of the difficulties which had emerged when the High Court and the Federal Court endeavoured to interpret the provisions: for example, *Waters' case, Australian Iron and Steel Pty Ltd v Banovic* (1989) 168 CLR 165, the two *Styles' cases* (1989) 23 FCR 251 and (1988) 84 ALR 408.

These changes partly followed the proposals made in the report of the House of Representatives Standing Committee on Legal and Constitutional Affairs, *Half Way to Equal* (AGPS, 1992). When introducing the amendments, the Attorney-General stated that the previous provisions had proven "complicated and difficult to apply in practice". Also, he indicated that they had "been criticised for being overly technical, legalistic and complex": *Hansard (HR)*, 28 June 1995 at 2460.

Given the identified difficulties, the other two Federal enactments have not been amended at the same time nor have they since been brought in line with the *Sex Discrimination Act* and so retain the former definition. This inconsistency in approach is even more inexplicable in light of the definition of indirect discrimination in the *Age Discrimination Act*, which follows the definition in the *Sex Discrimination Act*.

The major difference in the *Sex Discrimination Act* and the *Age Discrimination Act* compared with the other Federal legislation is that the reasonableness test is defined and the burden of proof is transferred to the person who did the act rather than the person complaining about the act. This reversal of the onus of proof means that the employer must establish that where an act of indirect discrimination is established, it was reasonable.

Indirect sex discrimination is defined in s 5(2) of the *Sex Discrimination Act* as:

> For the purposes of this Act, a person (the "discriminator") discriminates against another person (the "aggrieved person") on the ground of the sex of the aggrieved person if the discriminator imposes, or

proposes to impose, a condition, requirement or practice that has, or is likely to have, the effect of disadvantaging persons of the same sex as the aggrieved person.

There is a similar provision in s 6(2) on the ground of marital status and s 7(2) on the ground of pregnancy or potential pregnancy.

Section 7B of the *Sex Discrimination Act* sets out the factors to be taken into account when determining whether a condition, requirement or practice that is, or is likely to have, the disadvantaging effect is reasonable in the circumstances and these include:

(a) the nature and extent of the disadvantage resulting from the imposition, or proposed imposition, of the condition, requirement or practice; and

(b) the feasibility of overcoming or mitigating the disadvantage; and

(c) whether the disadvantage is proportionate to the result sought by the person who imposes, or proposes to impose, the condition, requirement or practice.

Development of case law

There are several significant cases which have addressed the interpretation of the indirect discrimination provisions.

In *New South Wales v Amery* (2006) 226 ALR 196, The High Court closely examined the various components of the indirect discrimination definition and the way it applied to a claim by female casual school teachers that their pay rates were adversely affected by their gender as their family responsibilities prevented them from becoming permanent teachers as they were restricted in where they could offer to teach. The majority of the High Court found that the definition was not made out. The court found that the exclusion of the female casual teachers arose because the Department complied with the terms of the relevant industrial award and elected not to make over-award payments to the casual teachers. As a consequence, they were not acting unreasonably. The court found that it was the categorisation of the teacher as casual or permanent that give rise to the essential difference and that they could not all be treated as just "teachers". The descriptor did not properly meet the correct terms of their employment.

Gleeson CJ held, in relation to describing the "requirement or condition":

The "requirement" was, at all levels of the litigation, said to be "the requirement to have permanent status". The requirement to have permanent status was said to be a condition of access to the higher level of salary scales. However, if it is necessary to identify what the department does that imposes that requirement (that is to say, the conduct of which the department, as opposed to parliament, or the Industrial Relations Commission, is the perpetrator), it must be, as Beazley JA said, that the department adheres to a policy and practice of paying teachers in accordance with the award. The department has the legal capacity to make over-award payments if it wants to. It could change its policy so as to pay supply casuals whose teaching has, in the sense considered by the tribunal, the same work value as that of permanent teachers, above the award. It is difficult to imagine that if, in practice, it did so, it could restrict the over-award payments to female supply casuals, but that is another question. The department could, if it wished, make over-award payments. It is in that sense that, as was held in the tribunal, the appeal panel, and the Court of Appeal, it requires teachers to comply with a condition of having permanent status (with all the statutory incidents of that status, including deployability) in order to have access to the higher salary levels from which casual teachers are excluded. It is to the requirement, so understood, that the test of reasonableness is to be applied. It is not "the system" that is under scrutiny; it is the conduct of the department within the system. No doubt, from the personal viewpoint of the respondents, they are employed by the government. They may not distinguish between the role of the New South Wales Parliament in legislating about the teaching service and the role of the department in implementing the legislation. The distinction, however, is legally significant. It is the department that is the alleged perpetrator of discrimination, and it is the conduct of the department that is in question. (at 203)

Gummow, Hayne and Crennan JJ held:

The distinction between permanent and non-permanent teachers in the teaching service is a feature of the structure of the workforce employed in that service. That structure was not adopted by decision or practice of the department. It was imposed by the [Teaching Service] Act. The pay scales set by the award and the practice, adopted by the department, of not extending to its supply casual teaching staff over-award payments were an incident of the management of that structure.

Not every such incident may be described as being a requirement or condition, compliance with which is required either in the terms on which employment in the teaching service is offered or in the terms or conditions of employment afforded by the department. For the reasons given above, the so-called requirement of permanence which the respondents sought to impugn was not such a requirement or condition within the meaning of the AD Act. (at 216)

In NSW, a significant indirect discrimination case concerned a claim by five female librarians for access to motor vehicles with private use rights which were provided by their employer to other employees on the same level of seniority who were predominantly male: *Wollongong City Council v Bonella* [2002] NSWADTAP 26, *Bonella v Wollongong City Council* [2001] NSWADT 194.

In *Finance Sector Union v Commonwealth Bank of Australia* (1997) EOC ¶92-889, a restructure of the Bank's entire retail banking staff was held by the HR&EOC to be indirect discrimination. This arose through the failure to offer retrenchment to some workers who were on extended leave. Mainly women were affected as they were on leave for childbirth and childcare purposes. They were denied access to an opportunity to express interest in retrenchment and hence the opportunity for a significant payout. The Bank gave them four weeks to return to work but this was not sufficient time to organise childcare so the condition imposed on all persons on extended leave had a disproportionate impact on women. This decision was overturned by the Full Federal Court: *Commonwealth Bank case* (1997) 80 FCR 78. The crucial element was the application of the "reasonableness test" to the facts and found that a relevant consideration was the guarantee of a comparable job on their return to work.

The *Dopking* litigation involved a complaint of marital status discrimination against the Australian Defence Force on the conditions of entitlement to certain housing allowances, where the distinction was based on members with or without a family. The claim of indirect discrimination was eventually dismissed: *Commonwealth v HR&EOC* (*Dopking No 2*) (1995) 63 FCR 74. This followed earlier decisions of the Full Federal Court in *Dopking No 1*, an appeal from a single judge (1991) 32 FCR 468 addressing the issues of direct discrimination.

In *Waters' case* (1991) 173 CLR 349, the Victorian legislation was examined in a claim by people with a disability that the removal of conductors from some trams and the introduction of "scratch tickets" for use on public transport was an act of direct and indirect discrimination. The judges gave detailed reasons and held that, as a matter of law, the facts as alleged could amount to indirect discrimination.

The hiring practices, threats of retrenchment and then the retrenchment of the respondent were the basis of the consideration by the High Court of the indirect discrimination provisions in the New South Wales Act in *Australian Iron and Steel Pty Ltd v Banovic* (*AI&S case*) (1989) 168 CLR 165.

A woman journalist unsuccessfully claimed that the failure to select her for an overseas posting by her employer was an act of indirect sex discrimination: *Secretary, Department of Foreign Affairs and Trade v Styles* (*Styles' case*) (1989) 23 FCR 251. A second attempt to establish direct and indirect discrimination in her employment was similarly unsuccessful; after a lengthy hearing with detailed evidence the HR&EOC dismissed the complaint: *Styles v Commonwealth* (1995) EOC ¶92-706.

"Requirement or condition"

The initial step in the analysis for an indirect discrimination claim is the identification of the "requirement" or "condition" which forms the basis of the decision or action being challenged. The 1995 amendments to the *Sex Discrimination Act* added the word "practice", apparently for abundant caution rather than any noted lack of coverage with the other two words. While the requirement or condition ought to be broadly construed (*Department of Foreign Affairs v Styles* and *Waters*), the nomination is a crucial question of fact and care needs to be exercised to ensure it is properly identified and described: *AI&S* at 185.

The Full Federal Court examined the indirect discrimination provisions in relation to the provision of education for a hearing-impaired student who needed an Auslan interpreter to participate in the class: *Catholic Education Office v Clarke* (2004) 138 FCR 121. Sackville and Stone JJ held:

> If a term or condition of admission to an educational institution simply defines the nature of the institution, or the educational services provided by that institution, it may well not constitute a "requirement or condition" for the purpose of s 6 of the DD Act. If, for example, a business college admits only persons who undertake to study accountancy in the first year of the course, this may be a term or condition on which it is prepared to admit a person as a student for the purposes of s 22(1)(b) of the DD Act, but not necessarily a requirement or condition for the purposes of s 6.
>
> Several additional propositions relevant to the present case can be derived from *Waters v Public Transport Corp*. First, the identification of the services provided by the alleged discriminator, for the purposes of s 24(1)(b) of the DD Act, is a question of fact ... So, too, is the question of whether the alleged discriminator has imposed a requirement or condition on persons wishing to use the services ...
>
> Second, the expression "requirement or condition" in s 6 of the DD Act should be construed broadly to include any form of qualification or pre-requisite, although the actual requirement or condition should be formulated with some precision ... In this respect, the legislation should be given a generous interpretation and an alleged

discriminator should not be permitted to evade the statutory prohibition or indirect discrimination by defining its services so as to incorporate the alleged requirement or condition …

Third, an alleged discriminator may be found to insist on compliance with a "requirement or condition" within s 6 even though the requirement or condition is not explicitly imposed. It is sufficient for the requirement or condition to be implicit in the conduct which is said to constitute discrimination.

Identifying the pool

One part of the process of establishing an indirect discrimination claim is the identification of the pool with which the person seeks to compare themselves. Correct identification of the pool is essential to eventually sustaining a claim.

The landmark *AI&S case* established that the term "proportion" does not mean merely numerical comparison. The identification of the pool and the constituent qualities of the pool are the crucial issues. In looking at s 24(3) of the then New South Wales Act, Deane and Gaudron JJ held:

> The more difficult question concerns the identification of the groups of men and women which will enable the proportions of complying men and women to be calculated … s 24(3)(a) requires an exercise which will ascertain whether sex is significant to compliance with the condition or requirement in question. It may be expected … that the base groups which are appropriate to that exercise will vary according to the context in which the condition or requirement is imposed. That being so, there is no warrant for reading s 24(3)(a) as invariably requiring the calculation of proportions by reference to the general male and female populations. Equally, there is no warrant for reading s 24(3)(a) as excluding that calculation if it will reveal the significance, if any, of sex to compliance … The determination of the appropriate base group will ordinarily involve the making of findings of fact … A decision to select particular base groups involves a question of law. (at 178-9)

Dawson J in the *AI&S case* stated:

> But a proportion must be a proportion of something, so that it is necessary to determine the appropriate grouping or pool within which to calculate the proportions which are to be compared. (at 187)

Putting it in a marginally different context but still within the same principles, Heerey J in *Siddiqui's case* held:

> The comparison is not strictly speaking between two groups in the sense of separate independent entities but rather between a subgroup (the complainant's group) within a larger group (all who face the same term, condition or requirement) ... It is clear that the base group is a group which is affected by the term, condition or requirement in question ... the particular section of the public "upon whose lives the impact of the relevant requirement or condition has to be measured". (at 63-4)

In the *Commonwealth Bank case,* Sackville J drew together four general principles which he held applied:

- the base groups appropriate to particular cases will vary, according to the context;
- the selection of the base group should be calculated to reveal the significance, if any, of sex to compliance;
- the decision to select a particular base group involves a mixed question of fact and law; and
- the Federal Court on an application for review does not make its own assessment of the base groups, but considers whether the group chosen is too broad or too narrow, by a process akin to determining whether relevant considerations were taken into account or relevant considerations were not taken into account. (at 42)

"Substantially higher proportion"

After identifying the pool, then a calculation needs to be made to ascertain whether the members of the pool not in the identified group form a substantially higher proportion of the pool than members from the identified group, such as persons with a disability or persons of a specific gender.

One of the overwhelming difficulties with the proof of indirect discrimination is that it can require complex statistical or other technical evidence to establish the claim. This can mean that great attention to the details of the pool and the proportion of those who can or cannot comply with the requirement or condition can take a significant proportion of hearing time if a complicated analysis is required. The task of establishing the appropriate proportionality also requires evidence to establish the membership of pool and the membership of the identified group. While this may be a relatively straightforward task in relation to a sex discrimination claim, it will require more complex statistical evidence in a race or disability complaint.

"Does not or is not able to comply"

One component of the definition of indirect discrimination is that the person "does not or is not able to comply" with the requirement or condition which has been imposed.

This is generally a practical factual matter and not a matter of hypothesis; however, the fact that the requirement or condition is not yet operational does not mean that the complainant cannot comply with it: *Waters v Rizakalla* (1990) EOC ¶92-282. It requires a determination on whether the identified requirement or condition was in fact complied with at the relevant time: *Siddiqui's case* at 62. The phrase "can comply" includes "at least a case of inherent inability to comply": *Siddiqui's case* at 80. For example, a solicitor's inability to comply with a requirement to work full time thereby resulting in her losing most of her practice and consequently not having her contract renewed as a partner, was one with which a substantially higher proportion of men than women were able to comply. This was held to be indirect discrimination: *Hickie v Hunt and Hunt* (1998) EOC ¶92-910.

Concept of "not reasonable"

One of the main points of debate is the concept of "not reasonable" and the factors which make up any analysis of the pertinent facts, including the process of identifying which facts are themselves pertinent.

For all the words devoted to the topic, the legislative phrase "which is not reasonable having regard to the circumstances of the case" has been repeatedly held to mean just what it says, that is, *all* the circumstances must be taken into account. The basic proposition was set out in *Styles' case* as "the test of reasonableness is less demanding than necessity but more demanding than a test of convenience" (at 263).

A majority in *Waters' case* established that the meaning of "reasonable" in the equivalent Victorian Act provision meant "not reasonable in all the circumstances", as Mason CJ and Gaudron J held:

> [R]easonable in that paragraph must mean reasonable in all the circumstances. If "reasonable" is not limited by the concept of "discrimination", there is nothing else in the Act to limit the considerations to be taken into account in reaching a decision on that issue. (at 365)

According to Brennan J, consideration must first be given to whether it is reasonable to impose the requirement or condition "in order to perform the activity or complete the transaction" (at 378). Secondly, regard must be had to whether the transaction or activity can be performed without imposing a requirement that is discriminatory (at 378). Relevant factors to be taken into account as part of the exercise of considering the relationship of the requirement to the transaction or the activity include (at 378):

1. The effectiveness of the requirement;
2. The efficiency of the requirement;
3. The convenience of the requirement; and
4. The cost of not imposing the discriminatory requirement or substituting another requirement.

Further, Brennan J held that:

> In considering reasonableness, the connection between the requirement or condition and the activity to be performed or the transaction to be completed is an important factor … But even where the imposition of the particular requirement or condition is appropriate and adapted to the performance of the relevant activity or the completion of the relevant transaction, it is necessary to consider whether performance or completion might reasonably have been achieved without imposing so discriminatory a requirement or condition. (at 378-9)

This accords with the view expressed by Bowen CJ and Gummow J in the appeal in *Styles' case* that one of the factors to be taken into account is "the nature and extent of the discriminatory effect" ((1989) 23 FCR 257 at 263).

Therefore, in *Travers v New South Wales* [2001] FMCA 18, it was held that while it might have been reasonable for a school to require the students in a particular class to utilise the toilet in another building, it was unreasonable to require a student in that class who had a disability involving serious incontinence problems to do so when there was an available toilet just outside the door. "All the available circumstances" included, but were not limited to, the needs of the particular disabled student.

By contrast, in *Minns v New South Wales* [2002] FMCA 60, it was held that various schools' decision to suspend and/or expel a student who suffered from, among other disabilities, Asperger's syndrome, attention deficit hyperactivity disorder and conduct disorder, and who could not comply with school disciplinary policies, was reasonable having regard to the circumstances of the case, namely, that the policies were designed for the benefit of all students and staff attending those schools.

The factors to be taken into account in construing the test of reasonableness in all of the circumstances are to be widely collected: see Mason CJ and Gaudron J in *Waters* at 365.

A mere distinction or difference, even if it amounts to unlawful discrimination, is not sufficient to meet the test of "not reasonable".

In *Dopking No 2*, Lockhart J identified the divergence as:

> Application of this test in the present matter, according to s 6(2) of the [*Sex Discrimination*] Act, required the Commission, first, to examine the reasons in favour of the condition, and secondly, to weigh those reasons against the nature and extent of the discriminatory effect of the condition. The conclusion of discrimination within s 6(2) of the Act can be reached only where the Commission determines that, in all the circumstances, the difference of treatment between members without a family and members with a family is not reasonable. An examination of the Commission's reasons shows that, essentially, the Commission was of the view that the condition did discriminate between members of the Defence Force with a family and those without a family, and therefore, that it was unreasonable ... the Commission's reasoning was based on the presumption that any difference of treatment between members of the Australian Defence Force with a family and a member without a family was prima facie discriminatory, and therefore unreasonable, irrespective of any material difference in the needs and circumstances of each category of member. (at 82-3; this approach has been supported in the *Commonwealth Bank case* at 11-12)

In relation to the evidence to be adduced, the views of the complainant as to some material will be subjective and while they may provide some assistance to determine the nature, extent and effect of the act alleged to be discriminatory, "ultimately, the test must be an objective one, applied by the Commission after considering all the material facts": *Dopking No 2* at 83.

This also accords with the opinion expressed by Bowen CJ and Gummow J in *Styles' case*, cited with approval in *Waters' case*, where the Full Federal Court held:

> [T]he test of reasonableness is less demanding than one of necessity, but more demanding than a test of convenience ... The criterion is an objective one, which requires the court to weigh the nature and extent of the discriminatory effect, on the one hand, against the reasons advanced in favour of the requirement or condition on the other. All circumstances of the case must be taken into account. (at 263; again adopted in the *Commonwealth Bank case* at 12-13)

Sackville J in the *Commonwealth Bank case* summarised the correct legal position as "since the test is objective, the subjective preferences of the aggrieved persons cannot be determinative of the reasonableness of the impugned condition or requirement". In identifying the factors and the role they play in determining the reasonableness, he continued:

The presence of a logical and understandable basis is a factor – perhaps a very important factor – in determining the reasonableness or otherwise of a particular condition or requirement. But it is still necessary to take account of both the nature and extent of the discriminatory effect of the condition or requirement (in the sense in which the authorities interpret that concept) and the reasons advanced in its favour. A decision may be logical and understandable by reference to the assumptions upon which it is based. But those assumptions may overlook or discount the discriminatory impact of the decision. Depending on the circumstances, such a decision might be legitimately characterised as not reasonable, having regard to the circumstances of the case, within the meaning of s 5(2)(b) of the *SD Act 1984* ... the question is not simply whether the alleged discriminator could have made a "better" or more informed decision. The issue is that posed by the legislation, namely, whether the requirement is not reasonable having regard to the circumstances of the case. (at 34-5)

Conclusion

Despite the apparent difficulties in meeting the statutory criteria for indirect discrimination, the definition has a useful role to play in the law. The use of the provision will become more common as its implications are more widely realised. With changes to the structures of the labour market, and an increase in flexibility in employment conditions, it may be envisaged that more complex matters will be scrutinised in complaints of indirect discrimination.

A complainant will need to be able to adduce evidence "about the nature, extent and effect of the alleged discriminatory treatment, an exercise which it was required to do in accordance with *Styles* and *Waters*": *Dopking No 2* at 84. This evidence may be detailed and only available from the respondent through the use of a carefully worded summons. The basis of comparison to establish the pool and the proportion of people who can comply with the identified requirement or condition requires factual material and the various components to be presented to a court or tribunal in a clear and accessible manner.

Future discrimination

In some limited circumstances, it may be possible to challenge an action or decision before it is made or implemented. For example, it has been used in disability complaints in the area of access to new buildings before their completion or at the planning and consent stage: *Cocks v Queensland* (1994) EOC ¶92-612.

4

EMPLOYMENT DISCRIMINATION

All discrimination laws cover a range of employment relationships. Employment continues to be the largest cause of complaints of discrimination. This chapter covers all employment relationships and the exceptions which are specific to the area of employment.

The relationships covered in this chapter are applicants for employment, employees, commission agents and contract workers. Also covered are trade unions, partnerships, qualifying bodies and employment agencies.

The most frequent employment discrimination complaints arise from the standard employment relationship between an employer and an employee. However, the operation of some anti-discrimination legislation may not be limited to persons in common law employment relationships. It may extend to police officers despite the particular nature of their employment relationship: A minister of religion, albeit governed by matters that are spiritual, can nevertheless be employed under a contract of employment: *Ermogenous v Greek Orthodox Community of SA Inc* (2002) 209 CLR 95.

See Appendix B for reference to the specific sections in the Federal and State discrimination laws covering employment. See Chapter 2 for a discussion of the different grounds or attributes of unlawful discrimination and the coverage of the various Acts. See Chapter 3 for a discussion of the definitions of direct and indirect discrimination. "Ground" is used throughout the chapter for clarity and incorporates the same concept as the term "attribute" or "on the basis of", which is used in some legislation.

Acts of harassment may be acts of discrimination also. For a more detailed discussion of those issues, see Chapter 6.

Applicants for employment

All the discrimination laws make it unlawful to discriminate on the specified grounds in the various methods used in selecting applicants for employment. On grounds such as disability, it is often this gateway to employment which provides the most substantial barrier to entering the labour market.

Section 14(1) of the *Sex Discrimination Act* is reflected across the other discrimination laws.

> It is unlawful for an employer to discriminate against a person on the ground of the person's sex, marital status, pregnancy or potential pregnancy –
>> (a) in the arrangements made for the purpose of determining who should be offered employment;
>> (b) in determining who should be offered employment; or
>> (c) in the terms or conditions on which employment is offered.

"Arrangements"

The arrangements made include all the administrative and related steps which are crucial to the selection and appointment process. They include the wording of advertisements, the interviewing processes, the selection processes and any related procedures. In *Virgin Blue Airlines Pty Ltd v Stewart* [2007] QSC 075, the Queensland Supreme Court held that older applicants for the position of flight attendant had been treated less favourably than younger applicants on the ground of their age. The statistical evidence of the age of the workforce and an analysis of the "flawed working of the selection process" formed the basis of that determination.

Interview questions

Questions asked during an interview can give rise to a valid complaint of unlawful discrimination. Inappropriate questions, for example, pertaining to an applicant's marital status or whether or not she or he has any children may ground a complaint of unlawful discrimination.

Similarly, the same processes and procedures for assessing applications and making the various decisions along the path to determining the successful applicant for a position should be the same or of a sufficiently similar nature that no difference in any objective sense can be demonstrated.

A causal connection must be established between the failure to obtain an interview or the job interviewed for and the alleged ground or attribute said to found the unlawful discrimination.

Determining who should be employed

The various decision-making processes leading to the final determination of the identity of the person who is to be offered employment will vary depending on the nature of the employer. Small employers may have a minimal number of applicants with no detailed application procedures. Large employers, including both private and public sector employers, may have detailed application procedures. These may include processes for the completion of application forms, formal culling processes including the requirements for the selection committee to meet and discuss the application, develop a short list and then make arrangements for interviews. Regardless of the actual processes adopted, the entire procedure must be free of any discrimination on any of the grounds covering the employer in question.

Employers can assume that across Australia they are all covered by the discrimination laws relating to sex, disability, race and age and there are additional grounds of unlawful discrimination operating in each State (see Appendix A). The fundamental requirement is that each applicant should be judged on their merits as an individual and not on the basis of some assumptions made about their capacities or experience. Similarly, preference cannot be given to one person based on their gender, race, age or lack of any disability because of stereotyped views about certain groups of people and their capacities or potential abilities.

If interviewing a person with a disability for a position, it is essential to openly discuss with the person any lack of capacity they may or may not have. To make a decision that a person is not suitable for a position on the basis of assumptions and guesses about their capacity will be open to challenge as a discriminatory decision. Therefore, in *X v Commonwealth* (1999) 200 CLR 177, it was ultimately held that to refuse to employ a soldier in the defence forces because of his positive HIV status amounted to unlawful discrimination on the grounds of disability, although an exception operated in those particular circumstances.

A decision to offer a person employment usually means that there is a simultaneous decision not to offer employment to another person or persons, also applicants for the position. This decision-making and appointment process is the subject of review if a complaint is made. It is not usually the role of any court or tribunal to determine whether an individual would necessarily have been appointed to a position. The only issue is whether the process was in some way infected by a discriminatory approach adopted by the decision-makers involved with that selection process. That "infection" could be either through an openly stated policy which has some discriminatory effect or through the operation of unstated but prevailing discriminatory employment practices, including the mechanisms for assessing and recognising work and previous experience.

Flaws in the selection process or some part of it may emerge where there is a selection committee which is required to make a recommendation to a larger body or a more senior person within the organisation and the required ratification or approval is not forthcoming. Then a process which has applied all the components of the merit test for all applicants throughout may be overturned on the basis of a discriminatory decision by a different individual or group of individuals, some or all of whom were not involved in the selection process. At that point, a complainant may be able to identify the existence of a discriminatory decision made at an identifiable point by certain individuals which has resulted in the person not being offered employment.

Where an employer can demonstrate that the circumstances of each appointment provide an explanation which is inconsistent with discriminatory attitudes or practices then the complaint must fail.

A complainant can face insurmountable difficulties when seeking to examine a selection process as the sheer weight of the number of applicants and interviewees and the lack of documentation may mean that she or he is not able to establish a sufficient objective factual basis to sustain a complaint of unlawful discrimination, despite a personal belief that the failure to be appointed was an act of unlawful discrimination by the employer.

Terms or conditions of offer

Where an employer decides to employ a person, then they are required to offer non-discriminatory terms or conditions of employment. This includes the full range of benefits available from employment.

For example, if a woman was employed at a lower salary level than her equivalent male colleagues or was not given the same components of a salary package such as a car or medical benefits, and this difference arose because of her gender, then the employer would be committing an act of unlawful discrimination on the ground of sex: see, for example, *Wollongong City Council v Bonella* (EOD) [2002] NSWADTAP 26 discussed below (access to motor vehicles with private use rights).

Unlawful discrimination against an employee

Once a person is employed, then their employer is required to provide them with a non-discriminatory work place and environment and this covers all components of the work environment.

Section 14(2) of the *Sex Discrimination Act* is reflected across the other discrimination laws.

> It is unlawful for an employer to discriminate against an employee on the ground of the employee's sex, marital status, pregnancy or potential pregnancy –
> (a) in the terms or conditions of employment that the employer affords the employee;
> (b) by denying the employee access, or limiting the employee's access, to opportunities for promotion, transfer or training, or to any other benefits associated with employment;
> (c) by dismissing the employee; or
> (d) by subjecting the employee to any other detriment.

An employee may have rights pursuant to the Federal or State industrial relations laws as well as the discrimination laws and, in some instances, there may be certain parts of the overall employment package which can only be addressed by another court, commission or tribunal. While the choice of legislation will depend on the facts and circumstances, the desired outcome of the employee may be the most important component in the selection of jurisdiction.

During the course of employment

For a complainant to sustain an employment complaint, they must be able to demonstrate that the alleged discriminatory conduct came within the normal or usual course of their employment. Any decision or action must arise within the context of the employment relationship or be directly related or linked to it to give rise to any basis for a complaint.

If an event occurred outside work hours and away from work premises even though it arose between work colleagues or a supervisor and staff, there is no automatic assumption that it comes within the context of the employment relationship. The essential nexus between the employee and the employer must be established.

Terms or conditions of employment

The terms or conditions of employment cover a wide range of matters and include all the components of the employment relationship, including the working environment itself. These terms are not restricted to matters contained in any contract of employment, but include "benefits and concessions" and "demands and requirements" from the employer to the employee: *Allders International Pty Ltd v Anstee* (1986) 5 NSWLR 47 at 55.

In *New South Wales v Amery* (2006) 226 ALR 196, the High Court held that the actual category and type of employment must be properly identified as the indicator of the terms or conditions of employment of the complainants. An indirect sex discrimination claim failed as the women were casual teachers and this dictated their terms or conditions of employment as governed by the relevant award. They were not employed just as "teachers" and so were unable to gain access to higher wages available to permanent teachers.

If there is some other explanation for a difference such as varying pay rates between a female complainant and the men who occupied the position immediately before and after her, then it may be found that there was no act of sex discrimination. For example, where the differential in the hourly rate of pay relates to the job and the level of qualifications required or used rather than the gender of the person in the job, then a sex discrimination complaint will not be made out. Similarly, if in relation to the failure to provide a benefit such as a car to a person there is some reasonable explanation which is unrelated to the ground of discrimination alleged by a complainant, then the employer will be found not to have committed an act of unlawful discrimination.

However, in the absence of any reasonable explanation, the conduct may be unlawful. In *Bonella v Wollongong City Council* [2001] NSWADT 194, it was held that an employer had discriminated against five of its female employees, who were librarians, with regard to the use of company vehicles. Company vehicles with private use rights were allocated to 75% of male assistant managers but only 50% of female assistant managers. The NSW Tribunal found that the allocation of motor vehicles with private rights constituted a condition that the Council afforded to some employees. Private use was a benefit and accordingly the Council had discriminated against its female assistant mangers on the grounds of sex. On appeal, the Tribunal's decision was upheld: *Wollongong City Council v Bonella* EOD [2002] NSWADTAP 26.

Promotion

Decisions in relation to the promotion of employees can be contentious matters as individual employees may consider themselves the most suitable person for an available promotion as they have certain perceptions of the colleagues with whom they work. A failure to obtain a promotion can cause various professional and personal reactions and cause a search for an identified reason. Public sector employers and some private sector employers have clear policies in relation to the principles of promotion and the methods of assessing individual employees.

Other employers may have a relatively closed process. This can mean employees are unaware of individual promotion positions until a person is selected and informed.

The method adopted by an employer is required to be non-discriminatory. The more open and accountable a process, the more likely that employees passed over in a particular situation will be able to satisfy themselves that the process was non-discriminatory. For an employee to be able to demonstrate a breach of the legislation, she or he must demonstrate that the reason for the failure of an employer to promote her or him on that occasion was based at least in part on the ground of discrimination. If that is not able to be shown, then the complaint will fail.

Where an employer has given reasons for the failure to appoint or promote, "the complainant must cast sufficient doubt on the credibility of the reasons expressly given in order to ground the inference that some extraneous and unlawful factor was in operation": *Bailey v Australian National University* (1995) EOC ¶92-744 at 78,546.

In *Hills v South Australia* (2002) 82 SASR 102, the SA Supreme Court found that the appropriate comparator in a direct discrimination claim where the police force had not promoted an officer with a disability was between officers who were eligible for promotion with a physical impairment which made them unfit for operational duties and eligible police officers without such a disability.

To make a finding of discrimination in promotion, it is not necessary for the court or tribunal to find that the person would have been promoted except for the discrimination. It is only necessary for a finding that the person was treated in a way that breached the discrimination laws at some point in the selection processes, for example, in the interviews or the selection for short listing.

Transfer

In some employment situations, opportunities to transfer into another position or to another work site with the same employer is an essential pre-requisite to the broadening of experience which an employee needs to be considered for promotion or other positions with the employer. Consequently, it can be important for individual employees that a non-discriminatory transfer system is followed and that a person is considered fully on their merit and not on any of the proscribed grounds of discrimination.

An employer is entitled to require an employee to transfer to another position within the workplace, including when there are other arrangements being made such as a general restructure of the workplace or where the firm or organisation itself physically relocates: *Gardiner v New South Wales WorkCover Authority* [2003] NSWADT 184.

Training

Access to training can lead to further opportunities for an employee in the workplace and the discrimination laws require that the decision-making processes to determine which employees, if any, are to be offered training opportunities by the employer must be conducted in a non-discriminatory manner.

Training opportunities can arise in two ways. The first is the provision of access to internal training opportunities provided to a number of employees. The second is the payment of external training courses, either one-off arrangements such as the attendance at seminars or the reimbursement of costs associated with longer courses, such as tertiary education or higher degrees. Such reimbursement usually only occurs where the course being undertaken has some immediate relevance to the job of the employee and will lead to an increase in skills and expertise for the employee and be of some consequent benefit to the employer.

The increasingly professional approach to management itself means that many employers provide management training for selected employees, either internally or externally. These courses may become an essential step to any promotion. Access to such courses can have long-term benefits to an individual employee and can have a significant impact on their employment opportunities.

An employer can place reasonable requirements on an employee that they undertake internally provided training as part of their contract of employment. To do so is not an act of discrimination unless the person chosen for the training and any other changes is selected, even partially, on one of the grounds of discrimination, such as sex, disability or national origin: *Thompson v Courier Newspaper Pty Ltd* [2005] NSWADT 49.

Benefits associated with employment

There is a general "catch all" coverage for "benefits" associated with employment, which would cover any other matter provided by an employer not covered by the more specific wording. It has a wide meaning and is not restricted to the other matters listed in the paragraph – promotion, training and transfer – and is not limited to the legal entitlements of an employee: *R v Equal Opportunity Board; ex parte Burns* [1985] VR 317.

Case law

There are a plethora of cases relating to the impact of the law on the rights of employees to work in an environment free from harassment and discrimination. The more significant ones are discussed elsewhere in this chapter and in other chapters (see Chapter 6). Some examples of recent case law where discrimination in employment was found include where:

- an employer committed an act of direct discrimination on the ground of pregnancy when he dismissed a recent recruit because she told him she was pregnant and requested maternity leave, not for poor work performance as he had argued: *Dare v Hurley* [2005] FMCA 844;

- a man who suffered both attention deficit disorder and a major depressive illness was demoted and then eventually dismissed on the ground of his disability as the employer failed to properly assess his medical certificates and he was using available leave to cover his absences: *Ware v OAMPS Insurance Brokers Ltd* [2005] FMCA 664;

- a fire fighter was subjected to over 28 years of ongoing discrimination after he lost one eye and was kept in non-operational positions and denied opportunities for promotion or training: *Commissioner of Fire Brigades (NSW) v Lavery* [2005] NSWSC 268.

Some cases have failed as the court or tribunal has not accepted that the act of discrimination occurred as alleged or was on the ground of discrimination as alleged. Some of these are:

- a claim of disability discrimination in relation to a failure to re-employ a police officer after her contract expired and also for the material provided to the panel reviewing the process and making recommendations was rejected by the Full Federal Court as the series of decisions was not made on the ground of her depressive illness but because there was an irretrievable breakdown in the employment relationship including a three-year absence from work. A claim that there was a failure to provide adequate counselling or rehabilitation was rejected as having been decided on other reasons including advice that she did not have a serious disability: *Forbes v Australian Federal Police (Commonwealth of Australia)* [2004] FCAFC 95;

- a medical practitioner with a diabetes-related visual impairment failed to establish that his termination was a breach of the disability law when his employer required him to attend an assessment of his visual acuity but he failed to co-operate and permit the specialist to report back to his employer; and so his dismissal was not because of his disability but because of his failure to co-operate: *Fetherston v Peninsula Health* [2004] FCA 485;

- a solicitor failed to gain two promotions and claimed the selection panels' decisions were race discrimination as he was an Indian and so there were "conspiracies by members of two selection panels not to appoint the appellant to a position for which he was well qualified for reason of his race, and to give false explanations as to the reasons for his non-appointment. These are extremely serious charges to make. The case sought to be made was not one of a subconscious motivation, but of consciously improper conduct". The Full Federal Court affirmed the decision below and dismissed the claim as not having been made out: *Sharma v Legal Aid (Qld)* (2002) 115 IR 91, application for special leave refused;

- a lesbian dismissed for discussing her sexuality openly with clients contravening a board directive was not indirect discrimination on the ground of sexual orientation as the policy was reasonable and in the interests of the clients: *Bock v Launceston Women's Shelter Inc* [2005] TASSC 23.

A long running series of cases brought by Aboriginal people who lived on reserves in far north Queensland when they were paid under-award payments over many years by the Lutheran Church based on grants paid by the Queensland Government has been held by the Full Federal Court to have been race discrimination as it only occurred because of the race of the applicants: *Baird v Queensland* [2006] FCAFC 162.

Dismissal from employment

It is axiomatic that dismissal from employment is usually an extremely significant and distressing event for an employee. This reaction is increased if there are no appropriate warnings or other procedures in place and it is not related to any misconduct or other behaviour of the employee. If no reason or no adequate reason is provided to an employee, then they will have a natural inclination to search for an acceptable explanation.

To establish a claim of discrimination in dismissal, the causal link between the ground and the act of dismissal must be demonstrated. Where an employer is restructuring the entire workplace or some identified part of it, then the dismissal of a person whose job has become redundant in that general process may not be an act of discrimination: *Cosma v Qantas Airways Ltd* (2002) 124 FCR 504.

Of course, an employer is not prevented from dismissing an employee who happens to be pregnant or have some other specified attribute or characteristic as long as there is no causal connection between the dismissal and the pregnancy or alleged ground of discrimination, such as where there are genuine concerns about the employee's capacity to work effectively and efficiently. In *Penwill v National Jet Systems Pty Limited* [2002] FCA 5, it was held that a flight attendant was dismissed not because of her physical or mental disability but because of her history of repeated lateness.

Where the causal connection is established then the employer will, subject to any available defences, be liable. In *Barghouthi v Transfield Pty Ltd* (2002) 122 FCR 19, it was held that when an employer dismissed an employee who suffered a back injury while working for a previous employer, this was unlawful as the employer had not sought to explore alternative job opportunities for the employee within the organisation.

In relation to dismissal on the basis of alleged disability, an employer cannot disregard a medical opinion that the employee is fit to return to work: *Hobbs v Anglo Coal (Moranbah North MGT) Pty Ltd* [2004] QADT 28. However, the converse situation is equally applicable, that is, where a doctor assesses the employee as not fit for duty, then an employer is entitled to rely on the assessment as long as the identified disabilities prevent the worker from performing their job duties.

Constructive dismissal

"Constructive dismissal" is a term often used and often misunderstood. The original test which had been applied in Australia was:

> If the employer is guilty of conduct which is a significant breach going to the root of the contract of employment, or which shows that the employer no longer intends to be bound by one or more of the essential terms of the contract, then the employee is entitled to treat himself as discharged from any further performance. If he does so, then he terminates the contract by reason of the employer's conduct. He is constructively dismissed. (*Western Excavating (ECC) Ltd v Sharp* [1978] QB 761 at 769)

More recently, the term has been given a purposive and expansive construction to include a wide range of changes in employment conditions of the employee. It is not necessary, for example, that there be a total cessation of employment by the employee where there is a significant downgrading of job duties and a new contract is effectively in place.

A person who leaves their employment because of acts of discrimination or harassment against them by their employer or for which the employer is vicariously responsible may be able to claim constructive dismissal and come within the concept of dismissal. The Federal Court defined the concept as:

> Constructive dismissal is an unlawful termination of the contract of employment in circumstances where the employee leaves, without an express act or enunciation of "dismissal" by the employer. It will be taken to be a dismissal (hence the word "constructive") if the employer has behaved towards the employee in a way that entitles the employee to treat the employment as at an end. (*Thomson v Orica Australia Pty Ltd* (2002) 116 IR 186 at 226)

Constructive dismissal can also arise where an employer alters the terms or conditions of employment in such a manner that the change itself arose due to a prohibited ground, such as the pregnancy of the worker, and the employee is unable to accept the negative alterations or downgrading to their work and so leaves: *Thomson v Orica*.

On some occasions, a complaint of constructive dismissal may be pursued as an unfair dismissal claim under the appropriate industrial relations law (see Chapter 15).

Detriment

The concept of "detriment" in relation to employment arises where the employer subjects an employee to a negative effect, such as a move to an inferior position, a reduction in pay or a denial of overtime available to others.

Returning from maternity leave

A series of cases has looked at the issue of the employer's responsibilities when a woman is returning from maternity leave. A constructive dismissal claim may arise where there is no position for the woman to return to or where the duties are downgraded or varied significantly so that she can properly consider that she has been dismissed. Some cases are where:

- an employee returning to work from maternity leave was given different duties and responsibilities from those she performed before her departure, effectively resulting in a demotion. The person who had taken over her position while she was on leave remained in that position after she returned, contrary to the expectations of the employee. No rational explanation was given by the company for failing to return her to her old position. This was so notwithstanding that the employer's "Family Leave Policy" stated that employees granted family leave had the right to return to their previous position or, if this no longer existed, to a comparable position. The Federal Court found that the employer had engaged in unlawful discrimination on the basis of pregnancy and that the employee was entitled to treat herself as constructively dismissed at common law and, therefore, the employer had, in breach of contract, wrongfully dismissed the employee: *Thomson v Orica Australia Pty Ltd* (2002) 116 IR 186;

- the Federal Court held on appeal that a woman who was denied a new contract and subjected to a series of detrimental actions leading to her constructive dismissal after taking her legitimate entitlements to carer's leave was discrimination on the ground of family responsibilities but not sex discrimination: *Commonwealth v Evans* (2004) 81 ALD 402;

- the demand from a female manager that she be given a part-time job on return from maternity leave was not sex discrimination as there were no part-time work opportunities available at her level and she had been offered work at a lower level but she had rejected that offer: *Kelly v TPG Internet Pty Ltd* (2003) 176 FLR 214;

- a pregnant flight attendant was discriminated against on the ground of pregnancy when her employer refused to allow her access to her accrued sick leave when she refused an offer of lower paid ground-based work and instead placed her on unpaid maternity leave while a claim of constructive dismissal was dismissed as a refusal to provide part-time work at a particular time was not made out as she continued to work and her access to part-time work related to the availability of part-time positions and not her sex or her family responsibilities: *Howe v Qantas Airways Ltd* (2004) 188 FLR 1;

- a female solicitor, who was an equity partner in a firm for a fixed term, was subjected to sex discrimination when she returned from maternity leave to work part time but following a partnership performance appraisal was refused further partnership in the practice, as the negative partnership appraisal was a result of the removal and reallocation of a large portion of her practice during her absence on maternity leave: *Hickie v Hunt & Hunt* (1998) EOC ¶92-910.

Commission agents

A commission agent is in a different form of employment relationship with the principal than that between an employer and employee. It is unlawful to discriminate on any of the specified grounds when engaging a commission agent.

It is unlawful to discriminate on any of the specified grounds against a commission agent by a principal in the terms or conditions afforded, by denying or limiting access to any benefits, including opportunities for promotion, transfer or training or by terminating the engagement or by subjecting the commission agent to any other detriment.

A Chinese insurance agent claimed race discrimination when he was not promoted and then terminated, alleging that agents of other races were treated more favourably. On appeal, the NSW Tribunal found that the failure to promote and the termination decision were based on his failure to meet targets and build a team and not because he was Chinese: *Lin v American International Assurance Company (Australia) Pty Ltd* (EOD) [2007] NSWADTAP 9.

Contract workers

A "contract worker" is defined as meaning a person who does work for another person under a contract for services. The more usual form of employment relationship discussed above is commonly referred to as a contract of service or a contract of employment. Determining the correct categorisation of the relationship has frequently turned on an application of the "control test": *Stevens v Brodribb Sawmilling Co Pty Ltd* (1986) 160 CLR 16 at 24; *Hollis v Vabu Pty Ltd* (2001) 207 CLR 21. The common law indicia can be incorporated into an assessment of a statutory definition, such as in discrimination laws: *Australian Timber Workers' Union v Monaro Sawmills Pty Ltd* (1980) 29 ALR 322.

The difference can be important for a potential complainant and for a respondent as the contract worker provisions are narrow, especially in their coverage of applicants for work. If a person was not given an interview and the reason appeared to be discriminatory, it is doubtful that they could sustain a complaint of discrimination within the terms of the Federal laws at least as they would not come within the terminology of "contract worker" and none of the provisions would apply. There is no obvious reason for this distinction.

As the restructuring of the labour market continues, it can be anticipated that there will be an increase in the proportion of employment arrangements entered into under a contract for services.

Trade unions and employers' organisations

The *Sex Discrimination Act,* the *Disability Discrimination Act* and the *Age Discrimination Act* and the State discrimination laws make it unlawful for an organisation registered under the *Workplace Relations Act* 1996 (Cth) to discriminate on a proscribed ground. While this covers both trade unions and employers' organisations, the main issue which has arisen is in relation to trade unions. Trade unions can be exposed to liability either on their own or jointly with an employer when there are entrenched work practices which may operate in breach of discrimination laws.

Admission to membership

It is unlawful for a trade union or an employers' organisation to discriminate on any of the prescribed grounds by refusing or failing to accept an application for membership, or in the terms and conditions of admission to membership: *Sex Discrimination Act* s 19(1).

Before the sex discrimination laws, there were some unions which refused to permit women to be employed at individual worksites and so become eligible to apply to become members of the relevant union. On occasions, management and unions worked together to keep women out of particular jobs or worksites, especially where there was a closed shop arrangement. The mining unions were the most vocal in continuing their refusal to admit women as members and there are vestiges of those attitudes still in operation. The *Racial Discrimination Act* covers the right to join trade unions only.

Members

Section 19(2) of the *Sex Discrimination Act* makes it unlawful for a trade union or employers' organisation to discriminate on a prescribed ground by:

(a) denying or limiting a member's access to any benefit provided by them;

(b) depriving the member of membership or varying the terms of the membership; or

(c) subjecting the member to any other detriment.

The *Racial Discrimination Act* and all State discrimination laws have similar provisions.

Unless a trade union treats all members equally, then it could be in breach of the discrimination laws. This treatment covers the procedures for dealing with complaints made about other members or non-members who are co-workers. The level and degree of support and assistance offered by the union to its members when there is some form of conflict between individual union members can also be challenged and reviewed.

The way the union deals with a discrimination complaint made to management and the union jointly or to the union initially can raise a number of difficult issues in terms of practical handling and long-term relationships at the worksite. Where there are allegations of sexual harassment or discrimination by a woman member against one or several male members, the potential for an on-going conflict is clear unless the union intervenes effectively from an initial stage. It may be that the interests of the union, the individual members and the managers are inimical and if they do not interfere they may be found liable: *Horne v Press Clough Joint Venture and MEWU* (1994) EOC ¶92-556, ¶92-591 and *Djokic v Sinclair* (1994) EOC ¶92-643.

Partnerships

It is unlawful to discriminate on any of the specified grounds in inviting any person to join a proposed partnership or an existing partnership and access to the benefits of a partnership, expulsion from the partnership or any other detriment. It is made unlawful for a partnership to discriminate on any of the specified grounds.

Qualifying bodies

It is unlawful for qualifying bodies to discriminate on any of the specified grounds of discrimination. These include bodies or authorities which "confer, renew, extend, revoke or withdraw an authorisation or qualification" that is required to practise a profession or carry on a trade.

Employment agencies

Employment agencies are also covered and it is unlawful for an agency to discriminate in the provision of its services on any of the specified grounds of discrimination. An agency may be covered as "permitting" discrimination or harassment when it refers a client to an employer when they are aware of previous complaints against that employer: *Elliott v Nanda* (2001) 111 FCR 240.

Local government

In some State laws, specific provision has been made to cover local government. It is unlawful for any member or members of council when acting, whether alone or together, in their official functions to discriminate on any of the specified grounds against another member.

These sections were included when a series of cases found that there was a lack of coverage of the discrimination laws towards local councillors when acting in their capacity as councillors and making decisions such as "hire and fire" decisions for staff and planning and development decisions.

It is unlikely that the councillors would be agents for the council itself and that consequently any vicarious liability would arise.

Employment-related matters

Matters concerning employment-related issues such as superannuation and insurance also have varied coverage. Superannuation will usually come within the terms and conditions of employment and is covered by a range of exemptions. Superannuation, the administration of Commonwealth laws and programs and requests for information are discussed in Chapter 8 and the exemptions for superannuation and insurance are discussed in Chapter 11.

Exceptions

There are some exceptions to the discrimination laws which apply only in the employment area or to some parts of the employment process only. These are discussed below.

The broader exemptions which apply more generally to areas and grounds are discussed in Chapter 11.

Genuine occupational qualification

One exemption which was originally seen as being a powerful mechanism to avoid the impact of discrimination laws was the exemption for a genuine occupational qualification. Despite the controversy surrounding its inclusion in early discrimination laws, it is seldom utilised.

Section 30 of the *Sex Discrimination Act* covers applicants for employment only and provides an exemption where the duties can only be performed by a woman or a man for decency or privacy reasons, body searches, living on the employer's premises or where people of the other sex are usually undressed apply to the position in question. There are similar provisions in all State laws.

A standard for a certain level of visual acuity was found not to be a genuine occupational qualification but an arbitrary standard that could operate unreasonably and that did not apply to a serving officer, indicating that it was not an "occupational" requirement: *Commissioner of Fire Service v Seaton* (1996) EOC ¶92-839.

There were two parts of the job duties of a group worker in a maximum security detention centre for boys aged 16 to 18 which it was accepted women could not do, and they were to maintain the privacy of the boys. Consequently, women could not supervise boys in the showers or toilets and not participate in strip searches: *Bowie v Director-General of Community Services of WA* (1990) EOC ¶92-320.

Disability specific exemptions

In the disability discrimination laws, there are exceptions which relate to the capacity and inherent requirements to perform the job duties and also whether there is "unjustifiable hardship" on an employer. Unjustifiable hardship is discussed in Chapter 11 as it applies to other areas as well as employment.

Inherent requirements for job

All the disability discrimination laws recognise that there are some situations which may arise for some people with some disabilities where they are unable to carry out the job due to the inherent requirements of the job.

Section 15(4) of the *Disability Discrimination Act* provides that in limited circumstances it is not unlawful for an employer to fail to determine that a person with a disability should be offered employment or to dismiss a person if they are unable to carry out the inherent requirements of the job or if in order to carry out the requirements, they would require services or facilities not required by persons without the disability, the provision of which would impose an unjustifiable hardship on the employer.

The factors to be taken into account when an employer or potential employer makes the decision include:

- the person's past training, qualifications and experience relevant to the particular employment,
- if the person is already employed, their performance as an employee,
- all other relevant factors that it is reasonable to take into account.

The third specified factor is extremely wide and could cover a range of situations, depending on the duties to be performed and the disability and the effects of the disability.

This exemption is limited in its coverage and so does not cover the terms or conditions of employment or access to the benefits of employment. There is no exemption for the employer in those situations.

The employer must show, through appropriate evidence, the inherent requirements of the job, the nature and conduct of the job and the methods of performing it, the inability of the person with a disability to be able to perform the inherent requirements of the job and show that the person, with or without any reasonable accommodation to meet their particular needs, would be unable to perform the job such as to justify the failure to employ the person or the dismissal of the person.

Several important decisions on the interpretation of this exception have been handed down. Consideration was initially given to the term in an industrial relations context in *Qantas Airways Ltd v Christie* (1998) 193 CLR 280 (see Chapter 15). *Christie's case* stands for the proposition that the legal capacity to perform employment tasks is, or at all events can be, an inherent requirement of employment. It states that, in determining what the inherent requirements of a particular employment are, it is necessary to take into account the surrounding context of the employment and not merely the physical capability of the employee to perform a task unless by statute or agreement that context is to be excluded. Thus, the inherent requirements of a particular job go beyond the physical capacity to perform the employment.

In *Christie's case* an airline pilot flew over many countries which excluded from their airspace aircraft flown by pilots over the age of 60. An employed pilot sought to extend his employment past his 60th birthday. Qantas refused to extend his employment on the ground that, amongst others, it was an inherent requirement of the job that he be aged less than 60 in order to be available for world-wide service. This argument was accepted by the court. Gaudron J in the High Court stated:

> A practical method of determining whether or not a requirement is an inherent requirement, in the ordinary sense of that expression, is to ask whether the position would be essentially the same if that requirement would be dispensed with. (at 295 [36])

This approach was confirmed in a case brought by an insulin-dependent diabetic employed as a communications and information systems controller who was involved in combat-related duties as he was likely to be involved in working with a person involved in combat: *Commonwealth v Williams* (2002) 120 IR 186. His disability discrimination claim was dismissed.

Coverage of the exemption for inherent requirements of the job was examined in a case concerning the dismissal of an HIV-infected soldier because of his HIV-positive status and his inability to "bleed safely": *X v Commonwealth* (1999) 200 CLR 177. In that case, the High Court applied the reasoning in *Christie* and found the essential question was whether or not the soldier posed a real risk to other soldiers and persons and whether that risk could be nullified or eliminated by the provision of services or facilities which could be provided and which did not constitute a justifiable hardship to the employer. McHugh J observed that:

> Whether something is an "inherent requirement" of a particular employment for the purposes of the Act depends on whether it was an "essential element" of the particular employment. However, the inherent requirements of employment embrace much more than the physical ability to carry out the physical tasks encompassed by the particular employment ... Employment is not a mere physical activity in which the employee participates as an automaton. It takes place in a social, legal, and economic context. Unstated, but legitimate, employment requirements may stem from this context. It is therefore always permissible to have regard to this context when determining the inherent requirements of a particular employment ... The inherent requirements of a particular employment go beyond the physical capacity to perform the employment. (at 187-8)

His Honour concluded that it was permissible to have regard to the risks to the health and safety of others when considering the inherent requirements of employment (at 191-2).

Gummow and Hayne JJ stated, in the context of the facts in *X's case*, that the inquiry about what are the inherent requirements of the particular employment should:

> begin by identifying the terms and conditions of service which revealed what the Army required of the appellant, not only in terms of tasks and skills, but also the circumstances in which those tasks were to be done and skills used. From there the inquiry would move to identify which of those requirements were inherent requirements of the particular employment ... Only when the inherent requirements of the employment have properly been identified can one ask whether *because* of the employee's disability the employee was *unable* to carry out those requirements ... But the requirements that are to be considered are the requirements of the particular employment, not the requirements of the employment of some identified type or some different employment modified to meet the needs of a disabled employee or applicant for work ... We consider that an employee must be able to perform with reasonably safety to the individual concerned and to others with whom that individual will come in contact in the course of employment. (at 209-10)

In *Cosma v Qantas Airways Limited* (2002) 124 FCR 504, the Full Federal Court held that the expression "particular employment" in s 15(4) of the *Disability Discrimination Act* referred to the actual employment which the employee is required to perform pursuant to the original contract of employment and any variations. The employer raised the defence in response to a claim for disability discrimination by a porter on ramp service duties who had injured his shoulder. The employee's application was dismissed on the basis that there was no question of the employee performing the inherent requirements of the job because of his shoulder injury. The employee, having been specifically employed to carry things as a porter, could no longer carry out the inherent requirements of the job.

Identification of the capacity or ability of the person to do the job duties must be based on an objective standard and not on a general impression, unfavourable to the person with a disability, without taking into account the factors which would be present for any person, such as new equipment and a new environment which requires time for all new employees to adapt.

The assessment process of whether a person can perform the inherent requirements of the job must be conducted fairly and not on the basis of any perceived notions about the outcome or not conducted at all because of some views about the person, their disability and the negative impact that the disability may have on their capacity.

In an appeal against a decision to dismiss the defence that an applicant to join the police force who had a visual disability and so could not safely perform the inherent requirements of the job, the NSW Tribunal held:

> Although it is desirable for an employer to have accurately identified the inherent requirements before refusing to offer employment to an applicant with a disability, their failure to do so does not mean that they are prevented from relying on the defence in proceedings before the Tribunal ...
>
> In order to make out the defence in s 49D(4) [of the NSW Act] an employer is required to adduce evidence at the hearing which is sufficient to satisfy the Tribunal that, as a matter of fact at the time the employer refused the person's application:
>
> - the applicant would have been unable to carry out the inherent requirements of the particular employment because of his or her disability; and
> - that in order to carry out those requirements the applicant would have required services or facilities that it would impose an unjustifiable hardship on the employer to provide.

The employer must also adduce evidence that these two conclusions have been reached taking into account the applicant's past training, qualifications and experience relevant to the particular employment and, if the person is already employed by the employer, the person's performance as an employee, and all other relevant factors that it is reasonable to take into account. (*Commissioner of Police, NSW Police v Zraika* [2005] NSWADTAP 1 at [17], [37]-[38])

In *Vickers v Ambulance Service of NSW* [2006] FMCA 1232, an employment application was not further processed after the applicant undertook a medical assessment for a trainee ambulance officer and was identified as having insulin-controlled diabetes. The employer failed to make out the inherent requirements defence as the evidence was that the short time needed to ingest sufficient glucose and the heightened awareness of the applicant meant that there was no valid reason for his application not to proceed as his disability did not pose a significant risk to the health and safety of himself or other.

Some cases where the defence of inherent requirements for the position has failed and the employee has succeeded include where:

- an assistant manager on probation was terminated when the employer wrongly concluded that he was suffering from depression and so was unable to do the job. The court found he was able to perform the inherent requirements of the position as he was able to do the duties and so his termination was disability discrimination: *Power v Aboriginal Hostels Ltd* [2004] FMCA 452, see also an earlier appeal to the Federal Court: *Power v Aboriginal Hostels Ltd* (2003) 133 FCR 254;

- an employer sought to rely on medical evidence to prevent an employee from returning to work when he wanted to after a delicate knee operation, it was held that merely because the medical evidence said that the employee could not squat did not mean that the employee could not perform the inherent requirements of the job. The employer had failed to pay sufficient regard to the employee's evidence that he could kneel to perform his employment and, therefore, the defence was rejected: *Cargill Australia Ltd v Higginson* [2002] NSWADTAP 20;

- a disabled post office employee who required a stool to sit on during the course of performing her job and who could not lift parcels of more than 5 kilograms at a time was not incapable of meeting the inherent requirements of her employment as she was still capable of serving customers at the shop counter: *Daghlian v Australian Postal Corporation* [2003] FCA 759.

Breach of employment contract

The Federal Court and the Federal Magistrates Court have the power under the "associated" jurisdiction to hear matters that arise from the same sub-stratum of facts as the principal proceedings: s 32 *Federal Court of Australia Act 1976* (Cth) s 18; *Federal Magistrates Act 1999* (Cth). In employment discrimination cases, this frequently gives rise to additional claims for breaches of the employment contract.

While the basis of the discrimination claim may not be made out, a breach of contract may be sustained on the same facts. The comparator for a direct discrimination claim may fail, but the criteria to demonstrate a breach of an implied term of the employment contract by destroying or damaging the trust and confidence between an employer and an employee may be made out. If there are policies such as grievance and complaint handling, sexual harassment or maternity leave entitlements and these are breached by the employer, then a breach of the implied term may be demonstrated: *Thomson v Orica Australia Pty Ltd* (2002) 116 IR 186 at 226.

In *Goldman Sachs JBWere Services Pty Ltd v Nikolich* [2007] FCAFC 120, the Full Federal Court found that a part of a specific policy was incorporated into the contract of employment that the employer "would take every practicable step to provide and maintain a safe and healthy work environment for its employees". The majority of the Full Federal Court found that there was a breach of the policy and hence of the contract, the breach caused injury and so the employee was entitled to damages for that breach. Marshall J found that there was no need for the employee to actually sign the policy for it to be incorporated expressly into the employment contract, nor did the ability of the employer to unilaterally vary the policy from time to time remove the clause from the contractual obligations of the employer (at [121]-[122]).

There must be evidence to show that there has been a breach of the contract such as the implied term and not just that the company was following its policies and its decisions were reasonable within the general context of the decision-making processes such as selecting who would be made redundant based on the skills of the staff and the work priorities: *Sheaves v AAPT Limited* [2006] FMCA 1380.

Pay equity issues

The issue of pay equity or equal remuneration for work of equal value remains an evolving issue within the employment discrimination area. The capacity of discrimination law or the industrial relations system to deliver pay equity to women in the current economic and labour market conditions requires a detailed analysis beyond the reach of this book.

The Human Rights and Equal Opportunity Commission's publication, *The Equal Pay Handbook*, provides some information on the principles of equal remuneration for work of equal value and its application in the Australian labour market.

5

EDUCATION DISCRIMINATION

Recently, the elimination of discrimination across the education system has been directed mainly at two issues – disadvantage of Aboriginal people and people with a disability. Educating students with a disability continues to be a growing area of conflict between the rights of the children and young people with a disability to be appropriately educated and the resources of the education system to provide access to appropriate education.

The conflict between the rights of certain students to gain an appropriate education and the resources of the system to provide that education is the basis for these ongoing debates. The content of curriculum and its relevance to particular students have been given some emphasis in relation to the particular needs of some Aboriginal students including education in Indigenous languages.

In the area of the educational access for girls and for boys, there has been considerable debate on issues such as encouraging girls to consider a broad range of subjects when selecting their courses, especially to include technical, scientific and mathematical subjects, and encouraging boys to stay on at school. The retention rates for girls into the later years of high school have now passed those of boys and there has been some policy responses to address these differences.

The provisions in relation to education in discrimination laws are set out below. See Appendix B for specific reference to the sections in State and Federal legislation. See Chapter 2 for a discussion of the different grounds of unlawful discrimination and the coverage of the various Acts. See Chapter 3 for a discussion of the definitions of direct and indirect discrimination. "Ground" is used throughout the chapter for clarity and incorporates the same concept as the term "attribute" or "on the basis of", which is used in some State legislation.

Coverage

All Acts except the *Racial Discrimination Act* cover the entire spectrum of the education system. "Educational authority" means a person or body administering an educational institution. "Educational institution" is defined as meaning a school, college, university or other institution at which education or training is provided. Accordingly it does not cover a residential college where accommodation only is provided: *Worsley-Pine v Kathleen Lumley College* [2001] FCA 818.

The *Racial Discrimination Act* does not specifically cover education and the provisions in relation to goods and services or the general s 9 provision should be referred to as the basis for any complaint about education: *Sinnapan v Victoria* (1994) EOC ¶92-611.

The Act derives part of its constitutional basis from the *Convention on the Elimination of All Forms of Racial Discrimination*. Article 5(e)(v) defines civil rights to include economic, social and cultural rights which in turn includes "the right to education and training". Article 7 provides that parties adopt "immediate and effective measures, particularly in the fields of teaching, education ... with a view to combating prejudices which lead to racial discrimination and to promoting understanding, tolerance and friendship among nations and racial or ethnic groups".

The *Disability Discrimination Act* 1992 (Cth) covers State Government education departments as well as other educational institutions such as tertiary institutions: *Sluggett v Flinders University* [2003] FCAFC 27. Federal sex and race discrimination laws cover universities, the State TAFE colleges and school education departments.

The *Disability Discrimination Act* was amended in 2005 as part of the process to include the *Disability Standards for Education 2005* (see Chapter 11). The definition of "education provider" was inserted which extended the coverage to "an organisation whose purpose is to develop or accredit curricula or training courses used by" educational authorities or educational institutions. Any State independent agencies which set curriculum and conduct the school system's public examinations are covered under separate provisions as they provide a "service": *VN on behalf of VO v Office of the Board of Studies NSW* [2006] NSWADT 106.

Admission as a student

The terms of the *Sex Discrimination Act* covering the admission of a student are similar to all the other legislation except the *Racial Discrimination Act*. It provides that it is unlawful to discriminate on the specified ground:

(a)   by refusing or failing to accept the person's application for admission as a student; or

(b)   in the terms or conditions on which it is prepared to admit the person as a student.

The principal time when admission arises as a controversy is when children with a disability endeavour to enrol at a mainstream school rather than at a special school. Therefore, where a school refused to accept the enrolment of a child with spina bifida in kindergarten, the school was held to have unlawfully discriminated against the child on the ground of disability: *Hills Grammar School v HR&EOC* (2000) 100 FCR 306.

Likewise, to deny students seeking admission to educational institutions access to the same resources or classes based on a particular attribute, such as gender, as those attending an equivalent institution may amount to unlawful discrimination: *Haines v Leves* (1987) 8 NSWLR 442 where it was held that to deny females at an all girl school the opportunity of studying industrial arts whereas students at an equivalent boys school were permitted to study this subject as an elective, amounted to discrimination of the grounds of sex.

When a profoundly deaf student was about to enter high school and the school refused to provide adequate Auslan interpreters for him and did not welcome such interpreters on a volunteer basis organised by his parents into the school, the Full Federal Court found that this was an act of disability discrimination: *Catholic Education Office v Clarke* (2004) 138 FCR 121.

In addressing the concept of positive discrimination in education, Sackville and Stone JJ held:

> The reasoning in the joint judgment in *Purvis* does not support the proposition that the appellants appeared to be urging, namely that the DD Act should be construed so as to preclude any requirement that an educational authority "discriminate positively" in favour of a disabled person. The concept of "positive discrimination" is itself of uncertain scope and does not provide a sure guide to the construction of the statutory language, in particular to s 6 of the DD Act. As McHugh J remarked of a comparable provision, arguments based on any concept of discrimination outside the statutory definition are not legitimate aids to the construction of the term "reasonable": *Waters v Public Transport Corp* at CLR 400 ... In any event, it is not appropriate to approach the task of statutory construction from a pre-determined position which rules out a particular result regardless of the language used by parliament. There is no substitute for analysing the words of the enactment, having regard to the stated objectives of the legislation and the statutory context: *IW v City of Perth* (1997) 191 CLR 1 at 12 per Brennan CJ and McHugh J. (at 141)

A student with Romanian national origin was denied access to a NSW selective school as admission was only available to Australian citizens or persons with permanent residence. The Federal Magistrates Court dismissed a claim of discrimination on the ground of race as no breach of s 9 of the *Racial Discrimination Act* was established: *AB v New South Wales* (2005) 194 FLR 156.

A gifted student sought early enrolment in high school. This was refused partly on the basis of her lack of social maturity compared with students several years older than her. This was held to be a reasonable view of the education department when they refused the application and offered an alternate study arrangement and so no discrimination on the ground of age was found: *Malaxetxebarria v Queensland* (2007) 95 ALD 89.

The *Disability Discrimination Act* 1992 (Cth) has an exception for "unjustifiable hardship" if avoidance of disability discrimination in the admission process would impose an unjustifiable hardship on the education provider: ss 11, 22(4). There are similar exceptions in the State laws.

The *Sex Discrimination Act* contains an exception for single-sex institutions and for institutions other than tertiary institutions where the education or training is provided only or mainly for students of the opposite sex to the sex of the applicant. The State Acts have similar exceptions for all the grounds covered by those statutes.

The *Disability Discrimination Act* contains an exception for educational institutions established wholly or primarily for students with a particular disability enabling them to refuse admission to a person who does not have that particular disability. There are similar exceptions in New South Wales, South Australia, Western Australia and the ACT. Accordingly, specialist schools providing educational opportunities for students, for example students with hearing impairments or with visual impairments, can continue to operate without challenge from a person without that particular disability. A student with multiple disabilities could be admitted if the specified disability was one of their disabilities.

The *Age Discrimination Act* contains an exception for admission to educational institutions established wholly or primarily for students above a particular age. State laws provide various exceptions for age discrimination in relation to entry into educational institutions. There is a lack of uniform provisions and different approaches have been adopted.

Students

The terms of the *Sex Discrimination Act* covering students participating in the education system are similar to all the other legislation except the *Racial Discrimination Act*.

The *Sex Discrimination Act* provides that it is unlawful to discriminate on the specified ground by denying the student access, or limiting the student's access, to any benefit provided by the educational authority, by expelling the student and by subjecting the student to any other detriment.

In *Purvis v New South Wales (Department of Education and Training)* (2003) 217 CLR 92, the High Court found in favour of a school who expelled a Year 7 student who was brain damaged with consequential behavioural problems. The Full Federal Court below found that because a student not suffering from this disability would have been similarly punished it could not be said that the actions of the school were based on the student's disability but were based on his conduct and that therefore the school's actions were soundly based and not unlawful discrimination. The High Court affirmed this finding on appeal. The main focus of the decision was on the definition of direct discrimination (see Chapter 3).

In another case involving an indirect discrimination claim by a profoundly deaf student seeking education to be provided in Auslan, the Full Federal Court found for the student that there had been acts of disability.

> It is true that, for at least the early part of the claim period leading up to 30 May 2002, she was too young to have been seriously disadvantaged by not being taught in Auslan. However, by the end of that period she was over 4 years old. It is hardly necessary to say that this is an impressionable age, and one that is generally regarded as of considerable importance developmentally.
>
> The evidence ... strongly suggested that Tiahna had already been detrimentally affected by having been denied Auslan assistance in the period leading up to 30 May 2002. It was at least implicit, and, arguably, explicit as well, that she would be further disadvantaged in years to come, as a result of having been denied that assistance during the claim period. The early learning years are plainly vital to later educational development. Tiahna's long-term disadvantage, to which the experts alluded, was simply that she might ultimately be denied the opportunity to achieve her full potential. On the facts of Tiahna's case, the detriment that she sustained would plainly be regarded as "serious".
>
> Finally, in order to avoid any misunderstanding, it should be stressed that Tiahna's case is not a test case. The judgment of this court does not establish that educational authorities must make provision for Auslan teaching or interpreting for any deaf child who desires it. It does not establish that Auslan is better than signed English as a method of teaching deaf children. It does not determine that an educational authority necessarily acts unreasonably if it declines to provide Auslan assistance...

We have concluded that [the trial judge] erred in his construction of the "not able to comply" component of s 6(c). His Honour's own findings ought to have led him to conclude that Tiahna was relevantly "not able to comply" with the requirement or condition that she be taught in English, without the assistance of Auslan. In our view, it is sufficient to satisfy that component of s 6(c) that a disabled person will suffer serious disadvantage in complying with a requirement or condition of the relevant kind, irrespective of whether that person can "cope" with the requirement or condition. A disabled person's inability to achieve his or her full potential, in educational terms, can amount to serious disadvantage. In Tiahna's case, the evidence established that it had done so. (*Hurst v Queensland* (2006) 151 FCR 562 at 584-5)

In *Devlin v Education Queensland* [2005] FCA 405, the Federal Court found that the failure to provide a deaf student with an Auslan interpreter in the classroom was an act of disability discrimination. A TAFE student failed to make out an indirect discrimination claim for the provision of Auslan services and the Federal Magistrates Court found:

The particular limitation on hours and the effect of that limitation on Mr Ferguson's enjoyment of the benefits provided by TAFE are there set out. The applicant was clearly conscious when framing his complaint that the facts of his case were not those in Clarke; he had not been refused interpretation, he had completed the course. He felt he should have been able to do this in less time had he been given sufficient hours. The finding of this court is that in those years during which he asserted he could have completed the course if sufficient hours were provided – 1997-2001 – four complete years, he received all the interpreting assistance which he could usefully handle. In so far as later years are concerned the finding is that Mr Ferguson was indisposed or because of employment unable to undertake any course over and above the one subject he did complete in 2002. Only in 2003 could it be said that he might have benefited from extra hours properly allotted to him. The failure to provide the needs analysis meant that his needs and ability to use the hours was not identified. But the failure does not establish his complaint, which relates to earlier years. (*Ferguson v Department of Further Education Employment Science and Technology (SA)* [2005] FMCA 954 at [34])

A disabled student who was not subject to the normal discipline policy because of his special needs was suspended and then excluded due to inappropriate behaviour that gave rise to serious concerns by the school about their duty of care to other students and to staff. A claim for direct discrimination was not made out as the Federal Magistrates Court found that a comparator without a disability but exhibiting the same behaviours and not subject to the discipline policy would have been excluded also: *Tyler v Kesser Torah College* [2006] FMCA 1.

A TAFE student failed to establish any of the multiple assertions in a race and sex claim about her treatment while a student: *Obieta v New South Wales Department of Education and Training* [2007] FCA 86.

A university student who was provided with course material in normal font on white paper needed to convert it into coloured paper with an enlarged font so she could read it. She failed to establish an indirect discrimination claim as she did convert most of the material and so she could comply with the requirement for most material and, when she could not, the university provided equipment to convert it and a specialist disability officer to assist and so it was reasonable for them to impose the requirement: *Hinchliffe v University of Sydney* [2004] FMCA 85.

A school needs to have an informed understanding of the medical condition and special needs of a student with a disability. The school needs to take reasonable steps to meet the special needs of the student: *Krenske-Carter v Minister for Education* (2003) EOC ¶93-256.

It may not be unlawful to exclude a person of one gender from participating in competitive sport where the physical strength or stamina of the competitors is critical. Therefore while it would probably be unlawful to exclude a female student from participating in a dressage competition on the grounds of gender, it may be lawful to exclude a female student from an all male softball team: *Jernakoff v WA Softball Association (Inc)* (1999) EOC ¶92-981.

In Victoria, there is a specific exception which provides that an educational authority may set and enforce reasonable standards of dress, appearance and behaviour for students, having taken account of the views of the school community in setting the standards. No other laws have a similar exception. Accordingly, different rules or policies about appearance, dress or behaviour based on the students' gender could be open to challenge.

The provision of a curriculum which does not discriminate between girls and boys is now an accepted principle in the delivery of education. Mere difference in the available curriculum is insufficient to fall within the definition of direct discrimination as there must also be a detriment to the complainant. This was identified when a girls' school offered domestic science and the neighbouring boys' school offered technical subjects which were not available at the girls' school. The complainant successfully linked her educational alternatives with her future employment prospects and these were accepted by Street CJ in the New South Wales Supreme Court as "a legitimate and proper consideration": *Haines v Leves* (1987) 8 NSWLR 442 at 460. One element considered crucial in analysing her detriment was that she had not been advised previously of the reduced options available to her and so she had not been able to take any steps to avoid the disadvantage the curriculum ultimately offered her.

The discrimination laws make harassment of students by staff or other students unlawful: *Huang v University of NSW* [2005] FMCA 463. Such conduct can be the responsibility of the educational institution.

Policies on sexual and racial harassment need to be in place to provide an avenue of complaint and resolution if such events occur. The policies need to clearly establish the position and perspective of the institution and any possible outcome for breaching the policy.

Most schools now have adopted "zero tolerance" policies against harassment and discrimination with strong disciplinary measures for any breach of the policy. Complaints of sexual, racial and homophobic abuse and harassment have been made by teachers and students have been suspended, expelled or asked to move to another school in response to these complaints.

Policies need to address all forms of harassment, with the main focus on sexual and racial harassment and harassment on the ground of homosexuality. Research suggests that in a minority of schools there are some students who harass, abuse and bully individual students whom they consider are homosexual. Such an isolated student could complain about discrimination on the ground of homosexuality or sexuality in all States. Their complaint could properly be against the school or the government department responsible for administering schools for failing to provide them with a safe educational environment. The concept of "detriment" in the education provisions of the discrimination laws could cover any such harassment that resulted in a hostile educational environment. Liability could be further demonstrated if the student had complained within the school and no attempt or no effective attempt was made to have those responsible for the harassment cease their activities.

The difficulties facing educational institutions in endeavouring to control the behaviour and actions of their students has been recognised as a factor in assessing liability for discrimination but is not of itself sufficient to avoid liability if discrimination is established. However, if the discipline is related to the student's behaviour and not any unlawful ground of discrimination then no liability will lie.

The *Disability Discrimination Act* 1992 (Cth) has an exception for "unjustifiable hardship" if avoidance of disability discrimination against a student would impose an unjustifiable hardship on the education provider: ss 11, 22(4). There are similar exceptions in the State laws.

Expulsion

The terms of the *Sex Discrimination Act* covering students participating in the education system are similar to all the other legislation except the *Racial Discrimination Act*. The *Sex Discrimination Act* provides that it is unlawful to discriminate on the specified ground by expelling a student as does the *Disability Discrimination Act* and the *Age Discrimination Act*.

Disciplinary measures taken by a school against a group of Aboriginal students were challenged as discriminatory: *Carson v Minister for Education of Queensland* (1989) 25 FCR 326. Given the long-term detriment which can arise for students when they are suspended or expelled from school, it is essential that all appropriate steps are taken by the principal or other decision-makers. These steps need to be based on procedural fairness towards the students (*CF v New South Wales* [2003] NSWSC 572 at [10]) and not on assumptions or stereotypical views about certain students.

However, discrimination law does not condone or permit abuse, harassment or assault of teachers or other students – to whom educational institutions owe a duty of care (*New South Wales v Lepore* (2003) 212 CLR 511) – by a student, particularly where such conduct could amount to a breach of the criminal law: *Purvis v New South Wales (Department of Education and Training)* (2003) 217 CLR 92 at 161-162. However, it may provide a basis to challenge any response to such actions which is not the same for all students. There have been complaints from students with a disability that the response of teachers to any negative situation in which they are involved can be stronger than towards students without a disability. In some instances, it has been claimed that other students harassed, abused and even assaulted the student with a disability and, when his tolerance broke and he responded in like terms, he was the one subjected to disciplinary measures. This would be a "detriment" to that student within the education provisions of discrimination laws and the less favourable treatment would be on the ground of his disability.

The combination of age and disability discrimination has been the focus of some complaints arising from students with a disability being excluded from school once they turn age 18 (see below).

The *Disability Discrimination Act* 1992 (Cth) has an exception for "unjustifiable hardship" if avoidance of disability discrimination by not expelling a disabled student would impose an unjustifiable hardship on the education provider: ss 11, 22(4). There are similar exceptions in the State laws.

Curriculum or training courses

The *Disability Discrimination Act* was amended in 2005 and a specific provision inserted that makes it unlawful for an education provider to discriminate on the ground of disability by developing curricula or training courses with content that will exclude a person with a disability or subject them to any other detriment or by accrediting curricula or training courses having such content: s 22(2A).

Special measures

The four Federal discrimination laws contain exceptions for special measures in the area of education. This approach is also adopted in all the State laws also.

The exceptions recognise that the impact of past discriminatory policies and practices may need equal opportunity or affirmative action policies and programs to eliminate the impact of the past and to provide extra emphasis or focus for a particular disadvantaged group. The High Court examined the concept and the principles underpinning the adoption of special measures in *Gerhardy v Brown* (1985) 159 CLR 70 (see Chapter 11).

The *Disability Discrimination Act* contains a provision for the Attorney-General to formulate standards in education. Now that the *Disability Standards in Education 2005* are in operation, it is unlawful to breach the Standards. Compliance with the Standards is a defence to a complaint of unlawful disability discrimination (see Chapter 11).

Disability issues

The main focus of complaints about admission of a student arise when a school refuses to admit a student with a disability: see, for example, *Hills Grammar v HR&EOC* (2000) 100 FCR 306. This refusal can be for various reasons, including lack of physical access for a student with a mobility aid such as a wheelchair, lack of suitable support mechanisms such as teacher's aides or an inappropriate curriculum. Similar issues arise when a student is excluded or suspended after a period in a mainstream school typically for behavioural problems caused by a disability: see, eg, *Purvis v New South Wales (Department of Education and Training)* (2003) 217 CLR 92 and *Minns v New South Wales* [2002] FMCA 60.

The State Government departments that run schools have policies on the integration of children with a disability into mainstream schools. All continue to run some special schools for some children with a disability. These are sometimes stand-alone facilities or are separate facilities within the general area of a mainstream school.

The debate about the continued existence of special schools and the need for all children with a disability to be integrated into mainstream education continues. At times it is highly contentious and bitter as parents struggle to obtain a premium education for their child with a disability. This often brings them into conflict not only with education administrators responsible for resource allocation and policy administration, but also with individual teachers who are required to manage classroom situations that can be demanding when a student with behavioural difficulties or with special needs is present.

Admission and exclusion raise the same issues as in some instances a student with a disability has been admitted for a time to a mainstream school and then further attendance is denied and the defence of unjustifiable hardship is raised by the school (which was rejected by the court in *Hills Grammar*). The cases indicate that, while the general principle of the elimination of discrimination is the starting point, a reasonable balance between the rights of the student with a disability and the rights of other students and the employment duties of teachers and others involved with the student need to be taken into account. For example in *Krenske-Carter v Minister for Education* (2003) EOC ¶93-256, the school in question was held to have indirectly discriminated against a student who had chronic lupus diseases affecting her immune system. A lack of understanding by staff at the school as to the student's special needs had resulted in her being treated in the same fashion as other children despite her special needs. It was found that the school had failed to take reasonable measures to meet the student's special requirements arising out of her disability.

There are many issues that need to be recognised and reconciled if an individual student with a disability is to enter and remain in the mainstream education system. It is unrealistic to adopt the position that all students must have access to any school they select. There are some students with a disability who, because of the nature and effects of their disability, will never be able to participate in a classroom situation and obtain any educational benefit. Other methods of educating such a student need to be provided by the education system and for optimum opportunity, these may not be able to be provided in a mainstream classroom. This position is recognised within the statutory exception of "unjustifiable hardship" (see below and Chapter 10).

Some of these issues were highlighted in the contrasting decisions of *L v Minister for Education for Queensland* (1996) EOC ¶92-787 and *Hills Grammar*. In *L*, various actions and decisions involving a seven-year-old student with an intellectual impairment were found to be acts of unlawful discrimination but were covered by the defences of unjustifiable hardship and an action authorised by another Act. The Queensland Tribunal found that her suspension was on the basis of behaviours that were characteristic of a child with her disability and could not be treated as divorced from it. These included regurgitation and toiletting problems, lack of concentration and noise making and an inability to participate in the classroom educational program because of the development gap between L and the other students. Her teachers gave evidence that she was learning very little in the withdrawal area at the back of the class where she was supposed to be working on her individual education program.

These competing interests were examined by the HR&EOC and the Federal Court in *Hills Grammar v HR&EOC* (2000) 100 FCR 306. *Hills Grammar* concerned the case of a student seeking admission into a kindergarten of a private school. The child had spina bifida. The school rejected her application for admission on the grounds that accommodating her needs would result in an unjustifiable hardship to the school. At first instance the HR&EOC rejected the school's defence and held that they had unlawfully discriminated against the child on the grounds of disability. This was upheld on appeal by the Federal Court

The decision embraces the principle that cost alone is insufficient as a criterion to measure whether conduct that is on its face discriminatory is justified. Rather the balancing act is far more complex and the needs of the particular student, other students, the school in question and the wider community must be examined. The result is a much more appropriate outcome for a student with a disability. Therefore, a school that refused to allow a student to attend an all day school excursion because she was in a wheelchair which could have posed a safety risk in relation to her travel arrangements was held to have unlawfully discriminated against her: *I v O'Rourke* (2001) EOC ¶93-132.

Similarly, in *Travers v New South Wales* [2001] FMCA 18 it was held that while it might have been reasonable for a school to require the students in a particular class to utilise the lavatory in another building, it was unreasonable to require a student in that class who had a disability giving rise to serious incontinence to do so when there was an available toilet just outside the classroom door. Failure to provide a key to the close but locked toilet was discrimination.

Where the disability results in behavioural problems courts and tribunals are generally less inclined to find the balance tipped in favour of the student. This no doubt reflects the perceived disruptive impact that such behaviour has on the other students and staff, particularly where the student is violent.

In *Purvis*, Gummow, Hayne and Heydon JJ Held:

> Secondly, in a case like the present, the construction we have descri-
> bed allows for a proper intersection between the operation of the Act
> and the operation of State and federal criminal law. Daniel's actions
> constituted assaults. It is neither necessary nor appropriate to decide
> whether he could or would have been held criminally responsible for
> them. It is enough to recognise that there will be cases where criminal
> conduct for which the perpetrator would be held criminally responsible
> could be seen to have occurred as a result of some disorder, illness or
> disease. It follows that there can be cases in which the perpetrator
> could be said to suffer a disability within the meaning of the Act.
>
> It would be a startling result if the Act, on its proper construction,
> did not permit an employer, educational authority, or other person
> subject to the Act to require, as a universal rule, that employees and
> pupils comply with the criminal law. Yet if the appellant's submission
> is right, the "circumstances" to which s 5(1) refers can include no
> reference to disturbed behaviour (even disturbed criminal behaviour)
> if that behaviour is a characteristic of, or consequence of, the actor's
> disability. Understanding the operation of the Act in this way would
> leave employers, educational authorities, and others subject to the
> Act, unable to insist upon compliance with the criminal law without in
> some cases contravening the Act. (at 161-162)

There is an exception in the Victorian Act which further reflects such an
assessment process as it permits discrimination on the ground of impairment if "the person could not participate or continue to participate in, or
derive or continue to derive substantial benefit from, the educational
program even after the provision of the special services or facilities".

The provision of resources and the constraints of the available
budgets of educational institutions and their administering bodies will
continue to give rise to occasional conflicts. It is inevitable that this will
occur as there will always be financial limitations on the availability of
special equipment or extra staffing.

Discrimination legislation is designed to ensure that the attempts at
striking a balance are carried out on a proper basis and are not merely the
negative reaction of decision-makers based on stereotyped views about
children with a certain disability and their capacities to benefit from a
mainstream education. Each decision must be made on the basis of the
individual student and their specific needs.

School closures

There has been some consideration of the special issues which arise
specifically in the design of curriculum and more generally in the

delivery of educational services to disadvantaged groups, especially for Aboriginal students. The closure of schools which cater mainly or specifically for Aboriginal students has been challenged in the Northern Territory and Victoria as acts of unlawful discrimination on the grounds of race: *Aboriginal Students' Support and Parent Awareness Committee, Traeger Park Primary School, Alice Springs v Minister for Education, Northern Territory* (1992) EOC ¶92-415.

The closure of a secondary college offering an alternative curriculum for Aboriginal students in Melbourne was subject to close judicial scrutiny. Eventually, race discrimination was made out and the Victorian Equal Opportunity Board made orders that had the effect that the school had to be re-opened: *Victoria v Sinnapan (No 2)* (1995) EOC ¶92-663 (VSC), *(No 3)* (1995) EOC ¶92-698 and *(No 4)* (1995) EOC ¶92-699. The school was re-opened.

This long judicial battle demonstrates the potential for discrimination legislation to provide a forum for disadvantaged or otherwise alienated groups to challenge government decisions which fundamentally affect them, without which they would have no opportunities or limited opportunities to demonstrate their opposition.

Private schools

There is a general exception to the education provisions in the *Sex Discrimination Act* for educational institutions established for religious purposes.

In the New South Wales Act, there is an exception to the sex, transgender, marital status, disability, homosexuality and age discrimination provisions in the area of education for a "private educational authority".

In the Queensland Act, there is an exception for non-State school authorities to discriminate on all grounds except race and impairment. Also, educational institutions for students of a particular religion or a general or specific impairment are exempt.

There are some other more narrow exceptions in the other State laws which exempt some educational institutions of a private nature in regard to some of their operations.

6

HARASSMENT

All discrimination laws make harassment unlawful and define it differently from discrimination. The most common cause of complaint is sexual harassment of women by men. Despite many years of publicity about sexual harassment cases, there continues to be a steady stream of complaints and court decisions.

This chapter focuses on sexual harassment in employment as it is a major area of complaint. It examines in less detail the provisions for sexual harassment in other areas and other forms of harassment.

A single act of harassment is sufficient to give rise to a complaint. There does not need to be a "continuous or repeated course of conduct": *Hall v A & A Sheiban Pty Ltd* (1989) 85 ALR 503 at 514-15, 532. This means that if a person makes a lewd suggestion or inappropriately touches a person on one occasion only, then a breach of the harassment law may have occurred. A single incident may result in lower damages than if there has been ongoing conduct over a lengthy period. However, an employer is required to respond to a single incident in the same way as if a long series of events are the subject of a complaint and to take the matter as seriously and respond as promptly as with other complaints.

Alternatively, the conduct can occur over a lengthy period and on occasions can involve more than one perpetrator. In cases where a woman employee is subjected to inappropriate printed material being left at her worksite or put on her computer without her knowledge or consent, then it may involve several of her work colleagues joining together to commit the various acts of harassment.

One common factor in some sexual harassment complaints is that there is an escalation of the behaviour over a period, sometimes as a direct response to the victim's requests to cease the harassment. An employer's vicarious liability can increase if the victim complains to management about her situation and there is no effective and appropriate intervention on her behalf so that the behaviour ceases immediately.

It is an essential element of sexual harassment that there be conduct of a sexual nature or sexually related as objectively determined by a test of matters that would be viewed by the general community as being sexual or sexually related. This can include banter and comments with sexual innuendo or with specific sexual content but put within a general context: *Cate v International Flavours and Fragrances (Aust) Pty Ltd* [2007] FMCA 36 at [28]-[34], [77].

In some circumstances, the employer has terminated the harasser's employment once the harassment has been investigated and established as having occurred: *GrainCorp Operations Limited v Markham* (2003) EOC ¶93-250 (see Chapter 15).

An employer will only be vicariously liable for the acts of sexual harassment of an employee where it can be demonstrated that the acts occurred during the course of employment and were directly and relevantly related to it. An employer will not automatically be liable for all acts of harassment which occur between employees (see Chapter 10). If employees engage in social interactions away from the workplace and which the employer played no role in organising, then it is unlikely that the employer would be liable. If there was no direct connection with the workplace and there was no subsequent link back to the workplace, such as any detriment if the harasser was rebuffed, then any liability of the employer would be clouded with uncertainty. If it occurred at a work event such as a Christmas function organised and paid for by the employer which occurred during usual work time, then potential liability for the employer increases.

There is an obligation on an employer to investigate any allegations of harassment made by an employee against a co-worker. That investigation should be prompt and impartial and conducted by a person with experience in this area. Sometimes an external investigator is appointed or an internal person with sufficient distance from all those involved may be able to perform the task. Any report is made to senior management for their decisions. To ensure procedural fairness, it is essential that any allegations are put in a complete form to the alleged harasser so they know the full facts put against them and are able to properly answer them: *McAleer v University of Western Australia* [2007] FCA 52.

The Sex Discrimination Commissioner's publication, *20 Years on – The Challenges Continue – Sexual Harassment in the Australian Workplace*, provides an overview of the nature and reporting on sexual harassment since the enactment of the *Sex Discrimination Act* in 1984.

The nature and degree of proof for sexual harassment claims were reviewed in the NSW Supreme Court in a challenge to an employer's decision to terminate a sexual harasser where it was held:

An allegation of sexual harassment plainly involves a serious allegation and the consequences of an adverse finding against an employee in disciplinary proceedings are potentially grave indeed. Such a finding impugns the integrity and reputation of a person subject to such a finding. Sexual harassment under State legislation is unlawful: Anti-Discrimination Act 1977 (NSW), ss 22A and 22B(6). It is plain that in proceedings such as here in question where allegations of sexual harassment made by one employee against another is in issue, the *Briginshaw* standard applies ...

The decision itself does evidence and reflect an appreciation by the Board of the seriousness of the allegations and the need to consider, in particular, issues such as the following:

(a) witness credibility and reliability;

(b) corroboration of the complaint of sexual harassment;

(c) consistency and lack of consistency in evidence;

(d) an evaluation of delay in reporting the harassment to the complainant's husband;

(e) the basis or lack of basis for the plaintiff's perception of a conspiracy against him;

(f) the investigatory process employed and the need for due process. (*Duhbihur v Transport Appeal Board* (2005) 149 IR 126 at [66], [71])

Defining "harassment"

While most attention has focused on the development of the law on sexual harassment, the same principles apply to all the grounds of discrimination where harassment is separately covered, such as homosexuality and disability.

The New South Wales Tribunal observed that "a person is sexually harassed if he or she is subjected to unsolicited and unwelcome sexual conduct by a person who stands in a position of power in relation to him or her": *O'Callaghan v Loder (No 2)* [1983] 3 NSWLR 89 at 92. This general concept has been developed into a statutory formula to set the parameters of the behaviour or actions of one person towards another which come within the definition of sexual harassment.

As the Federal Court has observed:

Unwelcome sexual conduct may be insensitive, even offensive, but it does not necessarily constitute sexual harassment. The word "harass" implies the instillation of fear or the infliction of damage, as is indicated by the definition of the term in the *Macquarie Dictionary*: 1. to trouble by repeated attacks, incursions, etc. as in war or hostilities; harry; raid; 2. to disturb persistently; torment, as with troubles, cares, etc. (*Hall v A & A Sheiban Pty Ltd* (1989) 85 ALR 503 at 531)

The legislative formula for sexual harassment has been described as:

> [O]nly striking at conduct that is an abuse of power or influence which an employer has over the career prospects or working conditions of an employee. The section does not make unlawful, per se, sexual advances made by an employer to an employee; nor does it seek to proscribe the acceptance of such advances by the employee. In other words the sub-section is not intending to change the tide of human affairs ... It is the demonstration of the preparedness to use the position of power and influence over the employee which is at the core of the conduct rendered unlawful. (*Spencer v Dowling* [1997] 2 VR 127 at 138)

Some acts of harassment could also be breaches of the criminal law as the harasser could be committing an act of assault or sexual assault. In many complaints, the victim will decide not to approach the police and will pursue a civil action for harassment instead. This means that the harasser is not subject to any penalty imposed as the outcome of the criminal proceedings. One advantage to the victim of pursuing the harasser under the auspices of the harassment law is that she directly obtains the benefit of any damages award instead of an amount being paid to the State as a fine. The onus of proof is lower in the discrimination area than with a criminal charge and this can be important where there are only two witnesses.

Discrimination and harassment

Many acts of sexual harassment can also be acts of direct sex discrimination: *O'Callaghan v Loder (No 2)* [1983] 3 NSWLR 89 at 92. When there is an employment relationship involved, then the act of sexual harassment may involve an act of sex discrimination in relation to a benefit of employment or a detriment (see Chapter 4).

As the Victorian Supreme Court has held:

> A benefit of employment is the entitlement to quiet enjoyment, that is, the freedom from physical intrusion, the freedom from being harassed, the freedom from being physically molested or approached in an unwelcome manner. (*R v Equal Opportunity Board; ex parte Burns* [1985] VR 317 at 323)

To establish sex discrimination, the behaviour or conduct would have to fall within the definition of direct sex discrimination and meet the requirements of less favourable treatment and establish the link between the conduct and the sex of the complainant as the ground for the behaviour or conduct:

It follows that not all unreasonable or offensive conduct by one person towards another, even a person of the opposite sex, constitutes sex discrimination. The first person may act unreasonably or offensively to all people, regardless of their sex. He or she may be actuated by some factor personal to the person, rather than the person's sex or by an actual or perceived characteristic of that person's sex. (*Hall v A & A Sheiban Pty Ltd* (1989) 20 FCR 217 at 233)

The other forms of harassment covered could also form the basis of a complaint of discrimination, such as on the ground of disability. Where there is no separate coverage of harassment, then acts of harassment could come within the wider provisions of direct discrimination on a specified ground, such as homosexuality. Certain actions may constitute acts of vilification in some States also.

Sexual harassment in employment

Sexual harassment continues to be a serious employment issue throughout Australia. It mainly involves acts of sexual harassment by men against women. There are few complaints by men of sexual harassment by women or men and no reported cases of any complaints by women against women.

When the *Sex Discrimination Act* was introduced in 1984 it contained a statutory proscription and a definition of the term "sexual harassment". These original provisions were extended and strengthened in 1992. All State discrimination laws have specific provisions making sexual harassment in employment unlawful.

Development of case law

Complaints of sexual harassment continue to be the largest percentage of complaints under the *Sex Discrimination Act*. This reflects a growing awareness among women, particularly young women, that certain actions of employers and co-workers no longer have to be tolerated and that they have some legal rights for prevention and redress.

Such complaints can be taken as only one indicator of the change which has occurred in the terms and conditions of employment of women. There has been a significant change in the attitude and responses of Australian employers, with most large and medium sized firms having some form of sexual harassment policies and some mechanisms for dealing with complaints in place, even if these are sometimes not adequate for an effective and immediate response.

The first sexual harassment cases brought under the *Sex Discrimination Act* and heard by the HR&EOC concerned young women in unskilled or semi-skilled jobs, where there was a high turnover in such positions and there were no or few other employees: for example, *Aldridge v Booth* (1986) EOC ¶92-177; *Bennett v Everitt* (1988) EOC ¶92-244. In New South Wales, the first case involving acts identified as "sexual harassment" under the *Anti-Discrimination Act* 1977 (NSW) was decided in 1983: *O'Callaghan v Loder (No 2)* [1983] 3 NSWLR 89.

In 1989, three Federal Court judges reviewed the United States and Australian case law and their decisions made an important contribution to the emerging jurisprudence in the area: *Hall v A & A Sheiban Pty Ltd* (1989) 20 FCR 217. These cases recognised and developed the concept of the "hostile work environment" as creating a detriment or a breach of the terms and conditions of work for a victim of sexual harassment. They reinforced the notion that women were entitled to work without being subjected to unwanted or unwelcome acts of a sexual nature.

Coverage of sexual harassment provisions

Section 28A(1) of the *Sex Discrimination Act* defines sexual harassment as a person sexually harassing another person if:

> (a) the person makes an unwelcome sexual advance, or an unwelcome request for sexual favours, to the person harassed; or
>
> (b) engages in other unwelcome conduct of a sexual nature in relation to the person harassed,
>
> in circumstances in which a reasonable person, having regard to all the circumstances, would have anticipated that the person harassed would be offended, humiliated or intimidated.

Section 28A(2) defines "conduct of a sexual nature" as including the making of a statement of a sexual nature to a person, or in the presence of a person, whether the statement is made orally or in writing.

The important elements of this definition include the making of the "unwelcome sexual advance" or "an unwelcome request for sexual favours". The concept then revolves around the meaning of the term "unwelcome". "By 'unwelcome' I take it that the advance, request or conduct was not solicited or invited by the employee, and the employee regarded the conduct as undesirable or offensive": *Aldridge v Booth* (1988) 80 ALR 1 at 5.

The definition of "conduct of a sexual nature" covers oral or written statements of "a sexual nature". This would include oral and written statements and images, physical gestures and contact and sexually explicit material in an e-mail or arranging for it to appear on a person's computer screen.

The test for whether a person has been sexually harassed is that a reasonable person would have anticipated that the person harassed would be offended, humiliated or intimidated. This is an objective test and there has been little judicial scrutiny on whether a reasonable person may or may not be offended, humiliated or intimidated when it is clear that the complainant responded in that way.

The State discrimination laws cover sexual harassment in a range of employment relationships: see Appendix A.

The *Sex Discrimination Act* covers a wide variety of relationships within the employment context. It is unlawful for a person to sexually harass:

- an employee of that person,
- a person seeking employment from that person,
- a fellow employee,
- a person seeking employment from the same employer,
- a commission agent or contract worker or a person seeking to become either,
- a fellow commission agent or contract worker,
- a partner or a person seeking to become a partner,
- another workplace participant at a place that is the workplace of both.

The *Sex Discrimination Act* also covers sexual harassment in relation to some other components to the employment relationship, including an authority or body with power in relation to an occupational qualification, registered organisations, including trade unions and employer organisations and employment agencies.

The Sex Discrimination Commissioner published *Sexual Harassment in the Workplace: A Code of Practice for Employers* which is a detailed analysis of the principles of sexual harassment law and the duties of employers to take both preventative and remedial measures and the issues of liability that can arise for employers, individual employees and trade unions. The Code sets a standard for employers and it is unlikely that an employer who fell below the level of actions set out in the Code would be able to avoid liability for the actions of an individual employee in harassing a co-worker, even if the employer considered there was some policy in operation.

An argument that sexual conversations and general sexual banter were part of the culture or atmosphere of a particular industry and hence not sexual harassment in the particular circumstances of the complaint has been rejected: *McLaren v Zucco* (1992) EOC ¶92-650; see also *Daniels v Hunter Water Board* (1994) EOC ¶92-626.

The area of unfair dismissal has also addressed the issue of sexual harassment, both in relation to constructive dismissal when an employee feels forced to leave their employment as they can no longer tolerate the acts of sexual harassment or the dismissal of the harasser by an employer (see Chapter 15).

Conduct constituting sexual harassment

There has been regular consideration of the various statutory formula of sexual harassment by courts and tribunals in recent years. Some of the conduct, actions and comments which have been found to be sexual harassment are:

- a woman was subjected to repeated requests for sexual favours and physical contact by a co-worker and she made her refusal and rejection clear; she was also exposed to a pornographic calendar and computer images. Later she was sexually assaulted by the same co-worker after a dinner with work colleagues after she passed out after drinking alcohol and she was later victimised by managers and other co-workers when she made a complaint of sexual harassment: *Lee v Smith* [2007] FMCA 59;

- during a weekend business trip to Sydney, the employer made sexually suggestive remarks, repeatedly suggested seeing a live sex show and then entered the applicant's bedroom uninvited, and in his underpants, with his pillow and only left when she made it clear that she would not sleep with him: *Cross v Hughes* (2006) 233 ALR 108;

- at a hotel on an island, a co-worker, who entered a colleague's bedroom at night on two occasions, made sexually suggestive remarks and requested that she engage in acts of sexual intercourse, was found to be within the employment relationship even though out of hours as the accommodation was provided by the employer and no visitors were permitted on the premises: *South Pacific Resort Hotels Pty Ltd v Trainor* (2005) 144 FCR 402;

- an assistant in a butcher's shop was subjected to sexual banter when she was asked repeatedly by a butcher: "how's you're love life" and subjected to other offensive sexist and racist comments including derogatory references to her boyfriend and his sexual prowess: *San v Dirluck Pty Ltd* (2005) 222 ALR 91.

Usually, the range of conduct and comments are not only inappropriate in the context of any type of relationship but are completely inappropriate in the relationship of an employer and an employee or between co-workers.

One form of sexual harassment which is the basis of an increasing number of complaints is sending unsuitable or inappropriate words or images, including pornographic material, through internal or external computer systems such as e-mail. With increased access to the internet, such images have become easily available and can be incorporated into a local computer network with minimal technical knowledge or skills and then the images manipulated.

These images are then sent to a number of people or to an individual, sometimes with alterations to the image or with words added to increase the impact of the message. This form of communication is referred to as "flame mail" and can constitute an act of sexual harassment. Organisations need to ensure that they have policies covering internet access and use of material as well as sexual harassment policies with links between the two policies clearly established. Breaches of such policies may properly form the ground for dismissal. Many organisations have filters on their internet system to prevent employees from having access to sexually explicit or otherwise inappropriate websites during work time or using their work computers.

Common law remedies

In some circumstances, a person sexually harassed at work may consider other options to obtain a remedy against their employer. One potential avenue for a remedy is a common law remedy for negligence or some other tortious action. This could be a preferred option where other legal liability for the act of discrimination, harassment or victimisation is not clear. Also, it may be that damages awarded, particularly by a jury where available, are significantly higher than those currently awarded in the discrimination arena.

In order to succeed in a claim of negligence, the plaintiff must establish three elements: that the defendant owed the plaintiff a duty of care, that the defendant breached that duty and that damage was caused by the breach and the damage was not too remote.

An employer owes an employee a duty of care at common law. Traditionally, the duty of care has been divided into three categories: to provide safe tools and equipment, a safe work place and a safe system of work: *Qualcast (Wolverhampton) Ltd v Haynes* [1959] AC 743 at 759, *Czatyrko v Edith Cowan University* (2005) 214 ALR 349. A further category has been added, that of the duty to select competent staff. These are not four different duties but are a combination of one duty.

The steps taken by an employer to provide a safe work environment can be important for establishing a breach of the duty to run a safe work place. There is no clear determination that the failure to take certain steps to reduce or eliminate the risk of injury in the general sense will be sufficient to establish causation. The High Court has held that "the question of whether a failure to take steps which would bring about a material reduction in the risk amounts to a material contribution to the injury" seems to be a problem that "awaits final resolution": *Bennett v Minister of Community Welfare* (1992) 176 CLR 408.

An employer was vicariously liable for the negligent acts and omissions of a supervisor who treated a staff-worker in such a poor manner that she suffered a mental breakdown and had to cease working. He failed to address workplace tensions and disputes, and victimised and harassed her, and so failed to provide a proper and safe work environment, despite recognising that the applicant had escalating health problems: *New South Wales v Mannall* [2005] NSWCA 367.

A police officer claimed that he had been victimised and harassed causing workplaces stress so that his employer was vicariously liable for acts of negligence by failing to provide him with a safe system of work by not preventing him from suffering a psychiatric injury: *Priest v New South Wales* [2006] NSWSC 12.

In 1993, a man complained about sexual harassment by a female co-worker and his transfer from the workplace as a consequence of their interactions. Later, he formed a strong view that the officials and his supervisors dealing with the complaint had not done so in a proper manner. In 1999, he was convicted on six counts of knowingly causing to be carried by post an article containing a totally prohibited substance (an explosive) and three counts of intentionally attempting to inflict grievous bodily harm on another person in late 1998, all being persons in some way connected with the handling or management of his complaint: *Dunstan v The Queen* [2001] FCA 147. He was subsequently imprisoned. Later, he brought proceedings against a range of people and organisations involved in handling his complaint, including some to whom he had previously sent letter bombs. His claims for administrative law review of certain decisions of the Human Rights and Equal Opportunity Commission, misfeasance in public office and defamation were all dismissed: *Dunstan v Human Rights and Equal Opportunity Commission (No 2)* [2005] FCA 1885. An appeal by the applicant was also dismissed: *Dunstan v Human Rights and Equal Opportunity Commission* [2007] FCA 191.

Sexual harassment in other areas

The other areas covered in the *Sex Discrimination Act* are set out specifically in relation to sexual harassment also. They make sexual harassment unlawful:

- between a member of staff of an educational institution and a student or a person seeking to become a student: *Obieta v New South Wales Department of Education and Training* [2007] FCA 86, *Gauci v Kennedy* [2007] FCA 1051;

- in the course of providing, or offering to provide, goods, services or facilities: *Evans v Lee* (1996) EOC ¶92-822;

- by a principal or agent to an applicant for accommodation or a tenant: *Macleod v B* (1996) EOC ¶92-812;

- by a principal or agent in disposing of or acquiring an interest in land;

- by a member of a club committee to an applicant or a member of the club;

- in the performance of any function or exercise of any power or carrying out any responsibility under a Commonwealth law or for the purposes of a Commonwealth program.

Some State laws cover some of these areas also: see Appendix B.

Disability harassment

The *Disability Discrimination Act* has extensive coverage of harassment against a person with a disability and their associate, with a similar formula and range as the sexual harassment provisions in the *Sex Discrimination Act*. These provisions recognise that people with a disability are harassed because of their disability and are subjected to unfair comments and actions based on their disability.

Homosexual harassment

There is no specific statutory formula or scheme which specifically refers to harassment on the ground of homosexuality in any Commonwealth law. The more general provisions of direct discrimination on the ground of homosexuality or sexuality can provide the basis for complaint in all States.

Derogatory comments with clear homosexual references such as "poofter" and "faggot" and references to particular forms of sexual intercourse between males can be harassment on the ground of homosexuality: *Tredinnick v Wentworth Area Health Service* [2000] NSWADT 172. Such statements if made publicly could also be in breach of the vilification or hatred laws: see Chapter 7.

7

VILIFICATION AND RACIAL HATRED

The discrimination laws extend to cover the general area of the written and spoken word as well as images and sounds by making certain acts unlawful.

This legislation includes the crucial components of the act occurring in a public place and so does not address private exchanges between individuals.

The issue of racial hatred or vilification has been seen as a matter warranting parliamentary intervention through the inclusion of special provisions in the discrimination laws or special laws. This reflects national concerns during the late 1980s and early 1990s that attacks on particular racial or ethnic groups were of sufficient strength to give rise to concerns about the general fabric of society. New South Wales passed the first racial vilification laws in 1989 and the other States followed. The Commonwealth Government amended the *Racial Discrimination Act* in 1995 by inserting a new Part addressing racial hatred.

These enactments have generated considerable public debate. Supporters of such legislation contend that it is essential to preserve the strength of a racially mixed society which is not riven by racial conflicts through drawing a line to demonstrate acceptable standards of behaviour and exchanges. The aim of the legislation is to address racism when it is manifests in a form of vilification or generates racial hatred.

Opponents are often advocates of free speech who view such legislation as poorly focused. They contend that permitting open debate of unpopular or marginal ideas strengthens society as it permits them to be demolished by counter argument and then rendered powerless as lacking in merit or any factual basis. They view such legislation as an unnecessary response to certain areas of debate and consider that it stifles genuine debate.

The conflict between these two approaches was recognised by the Keating Labor Government when the amendments were made. As the then Attorney-General, Michael Lavarch, said in his second reading speech:

> This bill has been mainly criticised on the grounds that it limits free expression and that to enact such legislation undermines one of the most fundamental principles of our democratic society. Yet few of these critics would argue that free expression should be absolute and unfettered. Throughout Australia, at all levels of government, free expression has had some limits placed on it when there is a counter-vailing public interest ...
>
> In this bill, free speech has been balanced against the rights of Australians to live free of fear and racial harassment. Surely the promotion of racial hatred and its inevitable link to violence is as damaging to our community as ... breaching the Trade Practices Act. (*Hansard (HR)*, 15 November 1994, at p 3337)

A comprehensive study of the history of the Australian legislation, the debate and the earlier cases is by Luke McNamara in *Regulating Racism: Racial Vilification Laws in Australia* (Sydney Institute of Criminology Monograph Series No 16, 2002).

There are no similar provisions in the *Sex Discrimination Act* or equivalent State Acts. Controversies over sexist images in advertising and similar community debates have not been seized by the legislature as warranting a legislative solution.

Similarly, there are no vilification provisions in the disability discrimination legislation. Fortunately, there are no similar forms of public debate in Australia about people with a disability as there are in terms of different racial groups and racist attacks on certain groups.

Federal racial hatred legislation

The *Racial Discrimination Act* prohibits offensive behaviour based on racial hatred, that is, because of a person's race, colour or national or ethnic origin. The heading to Part IIA is "Prohibition of Offensive Behaviour Based on Racial Hatred" and this heading must be taken into account when examining the context of the separate provisions in that Part: *Hagan v Trustees of Toowoomba Sports Ground Trust* [2000] FCA 1615 at [34].

Section 18C(1) of the *Racial Discrimination Act* provides that it is unlawful to do an act, otherwise than in private, if:

(a) the act is reasonably likely, in all the circumstances, to offend, insult, humiliate or intimidate another person or a group of people; and

(b) the act is because of the race, colour or national or ethnic origin of the other person or of some or all of the people in the group.

For an act not to be done in private, then there must be an element of public communication, being done in a public place or in the sight or hearing of people who are in a public place: s 18C(2), (3). The acts must be done in a "public place" which is defined as including "any place to which the public has access as of right or by invitation, whether express or implied or whether or not a charge is made for admission to the place". The act can be done for two or more reasons and the race of a person does not have to be the dominant or substantial reason: s 18B.

There is an exemption provision which reflects the compromise between the boundaries of inappropriate and unacceptable areas of public exchanges and the "right to free speech" as proclaimed by the opponents of the legislation. Section 18D provides:

> Section 18C does not render unlawful anything said or done reasonably and in good faith:
>
> (a) in the performance, exhibition or distribution of an artistic work; or
>
> (b) in the course of any statement, publication, discussion or debate made or held for any genuine academic, artistic or scientific purpose or any other genuine purpose in the public interest; or
>
> (c) in making or publishing:
>
> > (i) a fair and accurate report of any event or matter of public interest; or
> >
> > (ii) a fair comment on any event or matter of public interest if the comment is an expression of a genuine belief held by the person making the comment.

These exemptions are potentially extremely broad and at first blush may seem to limit the scope for a complaint to a significant degree. However, there are certain objective matters which need to be established before any one of them can operate to protect a respondent against a claim. These objective criteria include the concept of "reasonable" and "good faith" as well as the more subjective elements of "genuine purpose" or "genuine belief". A person may hold certain racist views firmly and considers that they are being honest in their views as they are formed on the basis of their own research or other endeavours. However, this will not necessarily mean that they can bring themselves within the exception as the views may not be said reasonably or in good faith as the evidence contrary to their views may be so overwhelming that the bona fides of the holder is open to serious challenge.

The concept of "public interest" is a further criteria in the two parts of the exception which relate to general publications. Notions of encouraging debate on contentious subjects must be put against the degree of offence or intimidation caused to others who are the victims of the racist views. Where the line falls varies depending on the nature of the racist views being propagated and the type of publication that contains the report. The capacity for wide dissemination through internet sites shows that rapidly changing technology will provide further avenues for the broad and uncontrolled dissemination of racism. Countering such forms of dissemination with reasoned debate and logic can be difficult as the readers of it are unknown and there is no definite method of providing those who have gained access to such material with countervailing views. As a consequence, the prohibition against material inciting race hatred can be a crucial mechanism to remove offensive material from such access.

The Federal Court has carefully scrutinised these provisions in several leading cases.

A cartoon depicting the return of Aboriginal remains from England published in a major newspaper was found to come within the exemption provisions and that good faith and the reasonableness requirements were to be established objectively: *Bropho v Human Rights and Equal Opportunity Commission* (2004) 135 FCR 105. An application for special leave to appeal to the High Court was rejected: [2005] HCATrans 9.

The Full Court examined the operation of the exemption and held:

> Section 18D places certain classes of acts outside the reach of s 18C. The broad class of acts covered is "anything said or done reasonably and in good faith" in the circumstances described in paras (a), (b) and (c) of that section. The immunities created by s 18D were described in the second reading speech and in the explanatory memorandum as "exemptions". It is important however to avoid using a simplistic taxonomy to read down s 18D. The proscription in s 18C itself creates an exception to the general principle that people should enjoy freedom of speech and expression. That general principle is reflected in the recognition of that freedom as fundamental in a number of international instruments and in national constitutions...
>
> Against that background s 18D may be seen as defining the limits of the proscription in s 18C and not as a free speech exception to it. It is appropriate therefore that s 18D be construed broadly rather than narrowly. The minister described the exemptions in his second reading speech as "broad". That was the approach to their construction taken by Commissioner Johnston in Bryl. It was the approach relied upon by the commissioner in the present case and approved by the learned

primary judge. His Honour observed, correctly in my respectful opinion (at [31]):

> There is consequently nothing in either the Explanatory Memorandum or second reading speech, reference to which is permissible under the provisions of s 15AB of the *Acts Interpretation Act 1901* (Cth) to suggest that the exemption provisions in s 18D should be read other than in a way which gives full force and effect to them. (at [72]-[73])

In scrutinising the ambit of the concept of "reasonableness" as it operates within the context of s 18D, the Full Court held:

> There are elements of rationality and proportionality in the relevant definitions of reasonably. A thing is done "reasonably" in one of the protected activities in paras (a), (b) and (c) of s 18D if it bears a rational relationship to that activity and is not disproportionate to what is necessary to carry it out. It imports an objective judgment. In this context that means a judgment independent of that which the actor thinks is reasonable. It does allow the possibility that there may be more than one way of doing things "reasonably". The judgment required in applying the section, is whether the thing done was done "reasonably" not whether it could have been done more reasonably or in a different way more acceptable to the court. The judgment will necessarily be informed by the normative elements of ss 18C and 18D and a recognition of the two competing values that are protected by those sections. (at [79])

In applying the "good faith" test, the Full Court held:

> In a statutory setting a requirement to act in good faith, absent any contrary intention express or implied, will require honest action and fidelity to whatever norm, or rule or obligation the statute prescribes as attracting the requirement of good faith observance. That fidelity may extend beyond compliance with the black letter of the law absent the good faith requirement. In ordinary parlance it may require adherence to the "spirit" of the law ... They are evaluative judgments which the courts are authorised and required by the legislature to make. A good faith provision offers a warning that game playing at the margins of a statutory proscription or obligation may attract a finding of liability. There is nothing in principle to prevent the legislature protecting a rule by attaching an uncertain risk of liability to conduct in the shadow of the rule.
>
> In my opinion, the balance struck in ss 18C and 18D between proscription and freedom requires more in the exercise of the protected freedom than honesty. Section 18D assumes that the conduct it covers would otherwise be unlawful under s 18C. The freedom it protects is broadly construed. But, given that its exercise is assumed to insult,

offend, humiliate or intimidate a person or group of persons on the grounds of race, colour or national or ethnic origin, there is no legislative policy which would support reading "good faith" more narrowly than its ordinary meaning. (at [93]-[94])

The Federal Court found that there must be appropriate evidence to establish the elements of s 18D, particularly reasonableness, public interest and good faith when a Holocaust denier published material on the internet that was in breach of s 18C in relation to Jewish people: *Jones v Bible Believers' Church* [2007] FCA 55.

A stand-up comedian who mimicked an Aboriginal person in performances in hotels and clubs and also sold videos of these performances and represented them in a poor manner was found not to have breached the provisions as the exemption relating to artistic work was made out and his performances were done reasonably and in good faith and not intended to offend or insult Aboriginal people: *Kelly-Country v Beers* (2004) 207 ALR 421.

A newspaper article which pictured the holiday camp of an Aboriginal family and the permanent home of a non-Aboriginal family in a way that could have conveyed that the Aboriginal family lived in substandard conditions when compared with the other family was found not to be in breach of the *Racial Discrimination Act* as there was not anything to suggest that race was a factor in the decision of the newspaper to publish the article and the photographs. Also, there must be a profound or serious effect and not just a mere slight in order to breach s 18C(1)(a): *Creek v Cairns Post Pty Ltd* (2001) 112 FCR 352 at 359.

A complaint by Ms Eliana Miller, a then member, against the retiring and the incoming President of the NSW Jewish Board of Deputies was summarily dismissed. She had complained that certain comments made by the retiring President vilified and intimidated Jewish people, that the incoming President failed to censure the speech and that it was likely to be offensive and insulting to members of the Orthodox Jewish Community who did not accept that the Board represented their interests and hence the interests of the Jewish people as a racial or ethnic group. The Full Federal Court found that the statements were about people "who adhered to the practices and beliefs of orthodox Judaism" and this was because of race: *Miller v Wertheim* [2002] FCAFC 156 at [13]. The High Court refused an application for special leave to appeal from that decision.

In *Hagan v Trustees of Toowoomba Sports Ground Trust* (2002) 105 FCR 56, the Full Federal Court upheld a decision of Drummond J that a sign on a stand at the Toowoomba oval reading "The E.S. 'Nigger' Brown Stand" was not a breach of the provisions. Applying an objective test, the court found that there was no basis to conclude that the Trust had offended indigenous Australians nor was the sign there because of the race of a group of people. Rather, this was the name by which Mr Brown was known and the Trustees had carefully considered whether there was any offence caused to the local Aboriginal community after Mr Hagan raised his concerns with them and concluded there was none, on the basis of race or any other basis. The important issue to be determined is that the reasons for the doing of the act must be considered through the operation of the phrase "because of" in s 18B: at 60. The High Court declined an application for special leave to appeal by Mr Hagan: (2002) 23(6) Leg Rep SL1.

A Western Australian politician was reported in the *Australia Financial Review* as making certain statements which were highly derogatory of Aboriginal people and their culture, including that "Aboriginal people in their native state were the most primitive on earth". The publication was found to be in breach of the racial hatred provisions: *McGlade v Lightfoot* (2002) 124 FCR 106.

The President of the Executive Council of Australian Jewry brought an action under the former HR&EOC mechanism against a woman who distributed "anti-Semitic literature in letter boxes in Launceston, Tasmania, and by selling or offering to sell such literature at a public market in Launceston": *Jones v Scully* (2002) 120 FCR 243. The court held that Jews in Australia comprised an "ethnic group" for the purposes of the *Racial Discrimination Act*. There were many indicators that the publications in question were published with race as a factor in that decision. The likely effect on the identified ethnic group is part of the focus of the provisions.

An internet site established by the appellant published various articles which professed scepticism about the number of Jewish people killed during the Holocaust and made certain other allegations against some Jewish people. Mr Toben is frequently referred to as a "Holocaust denier" and he refers to an international body of work to support his unpopular views. The Full Federal Court found that there was a breach of the provisions, including that the identification of a reason for the publication was to offend and insult Australian Jewish people who maintained that the Holocaust had occurred. The court found that the publications were intended to convey a negative and derogatory message about Jewish people and this could be an expression of racial prejudice: *Toben v Jones* (2003) 129 FCR 515. The court accepted that the exemption had not been made out as the material did not establish that it was done reasonably and in good faith for any genuine academic purpose or any other purpose. On the contrary, the material was designed to be deliberately provocative and inflammatory. The orders of Branson J in the court below required Mr Toben to remove the offending material, and any other material the content of which was substantially similar to the offending material, from all World Wide Web sites controlled by him or the Adelaide Institute and not to publish or republish such material: [2002] FCA 1150 at [113].

A visitor abused a correctional officer at the prison gatehouse when he refused her permission to visit her de facto spouse. The visitor was an Aboriginal woman and the officer was Caucasian. She called him various derogatory epithets which included references to "white" and some common swear words. The Federal Magistrates Court held that "white" was used when the visitor was expressing her frustration and a reasonable prison officer would have found the words offensive but not on the grounds of race. Further, the conversation did not meet the test of being "otherwise than in private": *McLeod v Power* (2003) 173 FLR 31. A previous decision had found that abusive remarks from an Aboriginal prisoner to a Caucasian correctional officer within a prison did not have the characteristic of "otherwise than in private" as it arose during a conversation between two people, one of whom had power and control over the maker of the comments: *Gibbs v Wanganeen* (2001) 162 FLR 333. In both cases, the court expressed strong reluctance to make any order if they had found a breach of the racial hatred provisions as other internal mechanisms had been invoked in each case.

The Federal Magistrates Court found that some abusive comments from a neighbour to children and their father when a ball was hit over the fence, including the term "black bastard" was a breach of the provisions. The words could be heard on the street and there were people on the street: *McMahon v Bowman* [2000] FMCA 3. Words exchanged over a back fence between neighbours in dispute which included racial references by one neighbour to another could be within the provisions as they may have been overheard from a public place although not occurring in one: *Chambers v Darley* [2002] FMCA 3.

The courts have shown some disinclination to entertain disputes where the person bringing the complaint has some form of power or control over the person saying the offensive words and where there is some other form of penalty capable of being imposed, such as within the prison context for visitors or prisoners. This reluctance demonstrates an understanding of the intention of the legislation and the international position on which it is substantially based.

The use of the legislation against "Holocaust deniers" still stirs some controversy from opponents of the legislation who contend that this is exactly the type of debate which should be permitted to be aired as, while it may be unpopular and out of step with mainstream views, this of itself is not sufficient to stop its publication. The courts have consistently held that the fabric of any such views must have a clearly identifiable link with "race" before it can be shown to be in breach of the *Racial Discrimination Act*. More generalised abusive comments or derogatory remarks will not breach the legislation if they do not have that essential flavour about them. Generous interpretations have not been propounded, and careful identification of the actual element of race and the offensive behaviour based on that racial element have been essential to the successful pursuit of establishing a breach.

State legislation

There are various different provisions in the State legislation covering vilification or inciting hatred towards a nominated person or group of persons. The common components are that the proscribed acts must be in public or observable by the public and the communications covered are broadly defined to encompass all forms, not just the written or oral word but also images and sounds. The proscribed unlawful act is for the inciting of hatred towards, serious contempt for or severe ridicule of a person or a member of a group on the specified ground. Some States also make the more serious matters a criminal offence.

All include exceptions to the main coverage similar to the Federal approach with the basis being that the conduct was engaged in reasonably and in good faith. Some include further provisions relating to academic, artistic, religious or scientific purposes and which are conducted in the public interest.

Racial vilification

All States have similar legislation addressing "racial vilification".

In New South Wales, Queensland, Tasmania and the Australian Capital Territory, the general discrimination law includes specific provisions making it an unlawful act or a criminal act for the incitement to racial hatred and some include the further provision of inciting serious contempt or severe ridicule of a person or a member of a group on the ground of their race. There is separate legislation in Victoria, Western Australia and South Australia which covers racial hatred. There is a variety of coverage between States, with some making serious racial vilification a criminal offence. The general principles are common across the States and they reflect the federal approach.

In New South Wales, the crucial word "incite" has been held to have its ordinary natural meaning which is to "urge, spur on, ... stir up, animate; stimulate to do something" or "urge on; stimulate or prompt to action": *Western Aboriginal Legal Service v Jones* [2000] NSWADT 102.

Where a major newspaper publisher canvassed one opinion on the Palestinian issue and then within a week published a different opinion and a variety of views expressed in a letter, then this was found to be within the context of a reasonable action and done in good faith for promoting public debate and not inciting racial hatred: *John Fairfax Publications Pty Ltd v Kazak* [2002] NSWADTAP 35.

Police officers who caught up with an Aboriginal driver of a stolen vehicle following a lengthy night time car chase through rural New South Wales and abused him with derogatory references to his being "black" were found to have racially vilified him. While it was 3 am and in an isolated spot, it was on a public road and the occupants of a nearby house gave evidence of the statements made by some police officers: *Russell v Commissioner of Police, New South Wales Police Service* [2001] NSWADT 32.

A candidate for the 2001 Federal election published certain views about Muslims which demonstrated a degree of illogicality. No breach of the incitement to racial hatred provisions was found to exist, however, as the Queensland Tribunal considered it was important that voters knew of the views of their candidates. The tribunal also considered that an order to prevent further publication of the views was not consistent with the overall objectives of the legislation: *Deen v Lamb* [2001] QADT 20.

The President of the New South Wales Anti-Discrimination Board unsuccessfully endeavoured to use the existence of the racial hatred provisions in support of an application to the Federal Court to review a decision of the Australian Broadcasting Tribunal to decline to bar a radio personality from broadcasting after he made certain racist slurs: *Mark v Australian Broadcasting Tribunal* (1991) 32 FCR 476.

There has been limited use of joint complaints of both discrimination and incitement to racial hatred and this may be because many of the racial discrimination cases arise in workplaces which do not meet the public place criteria, being closed working environments not readily accessible to members of the public. Also, the existence of two separate complaints for the same set of facts does not usually increase the damages awarded by the State tribunals and so it may be that time is wasted establishing an interesting legal concept which does not provide any real remedy to the applicants.

Sexual orientation and HIV/AIDS vilification

In the New South Wales Act, there are provisions making vilification on both the ground of homosexuality and HIV/AIDS unlawful. Both were introduced in 1994. The Tasmanian law covers sexual orientation or lawful sexual activity and Queensland covers sexuality.

The NSW Appeal Panel found that certain statements on a website constituted homosexual vilification. The statements included opposition to gay marriage and adoption by gay couples and some offensive statements such as "Faggots are all wicked evil people" and "God will burn Sydney to the Ground because of the evilness of these fags". The Appeal Panel concluded that the test for incitement "requires an objective assessment of the capacity of the public act to incite the requisite impact": *Sunol v Collier* (EOD) [2006] NSWADTAP 51. Orders included that the material be removed from various websites and that an apology be added to those websites.

In *Attorney-General (NSW) v 2UE Sydney Pty Ltd* [2006] NSWCA 349, the NSW Court of Appeal found that the NSW Administrative Decisions Tribunal did not have the jurisdiction to hear and determine an attempted challenge to these laws on the basis that they contravened the implied constitutional immunity for political speech.

Disability vilification

In Tasmania, the provisions cover an unlawful act for inciting hatred towards, serious contempt for or severe ridicule of a person or a member of a group on the ground of the disability of any person or any member of the group.

Transgender vilification

The New South Wales Act covers vilification on the ground that the person is a transgender person and creates the criminal offence of serious transgender vilification. The Queensland law covers gender identity.

Religious belief vilification

In Victoria, the *Racial and Religious Tolerance Act* 2001 (Vic) makes inciting hatred against, serious contempt for, or revulsion or severe ridicule of a person or class of persons on the ground of religious belief or activity unlawful. It is a criminal offence to commit an act of "serious vilification", including physical harm.

Statements at a public meeting, a newsletter and an internet article which made derogatory and inflammatory comments about Muslims breached the Victorian legislation: *Catch the Fire Ministries Inc v Islamic Council of Victoria Inc* (2006) 206 FLR 56. The Court of Appeal summarised the main components needed to be established as:

- The phrase "on the grounds of religious belief" does not refer to the ground which caused the alleged inciter to act, but to the ground on which people exposed to the alleged inciter's words or conduct were incited to hatred, or other relevant emotion against another person or group.
- It is not necessary to show that the audience was actually incited to hatred, serious contempt for, or revulsion or severe ridicule of, a person or class of persons on the grounds of their religious belief. A breach of s 8 occurs if the words or conduct has the tendency to incite that response.
- In considering whether s 8 has been breached, it is necessary to take account of the effect of the words or conduct on an ordinary member of the audience to which they were directed.

Further, the Court rejected the argument that the legislation breached the freedom of political communication implied in the Commonwealth Constitution.

In Tasmania, the provisions cover the person's religious belief or affiliation or religious activity of any person or any member of the group and the Queensland law specifies religion as one ground.

8

OTHER AREAS OF DISCRIMINATION

There are a range of other areas of public life which are covered by the various discrimination laws and these are discussed in this chapter.

The specific provisions in relation to each area in the different discrimination laws are set out below. See Appendix B for specific reference to the sections in State and Federal legislation. See Chapter 2 for a discussion of the different grounds of unlawful discrimination and the coverage of the various Acts. See Chapter 3 for a discussion of the definitions of direct and indirect discrimination. "Ground" is used throughout the chapter for clarity and incorporates the same concept as the term "attribute" or "on the basis of", which is used in some State legislation.

Goods, services and facilities

Section 22 of the *Sex Discrimination Act* 1984 (Cth) makes it unlawful in the provision of goods or services and the provisions of facilities to discriminate on a specified ground:

(a) by refusing to provide the other person with those goods or services or make those facilities available to the other person;

(b) in the terms or conditions on which the first-mentioned person provides the other person with the goods or services or makes those facilities available to the other person; or

(c) in the manner in which the first-mentioned person provides the other person with those goods or services or makes those facilities available to the other person.

All other discrimination laws follow a similar formula. The *Racial Discrimination Act* 1975 (Cth) and the New South Wales, Victoria,

Queensland and South Australia laws do not use the term "facilities" and cover only goods and services.

Some of the State laws have an extra criterion that the goods or services must be available to the public or sections of the public. It is then necessary for a complainant to establish that element as well as the other components to maintain a successful action.

Definition of "services"

The term "services" is defined in the *Sex Discrimination Act* as including:

    (a)   services relating to banking, insurance and the provision of grants, loans, credit or finance;

    (b)   services relating to entertainment, recreation or refreshment;

    (c)   services relating to transport or travel;

    (d)   services of the kind provided by the members of any profession or trade; and

    (e)   services of the kind provided by a government, a government authority or a local government body.

Similar definitions are included in all other discrimination laws except the *Racial Discrimination Act*. That Act has a more limited definition which provides that the term "services" includes "services consisting of the provision of facilities by way of banking or insurance or of facilities for grants, loans, credit or finance". The wider coverage of the other definition would still be open to a complainant under the *Racial Discrimination Act* as the definition is inclusive and not restrictive.

The term "services" was subject to High Court scrutiny in 1997 of a disability complaint from a representative of a group called People Living With AIDS who were refused planning approval by the City of Perth Council. The complainant was a member of the group and was HIV infected. The Council refused a planning development for a day-time drop-in centre for people who were HIV infected. A majority of the High Court dismissed the appeal in *IW v City of Perth* (1997) 191 CLR 1, essentially on the point that a refusal to grant planning approval was not a refusal to provide a service within the terms of the then Western Australian Act. The Council had a duty to consider the application and a statutory discretion on whether to grant it and any conditions to apply. To provide the service required only that the Council consider the application. It had not refused to do so as it had considered and rejected the application.

Two judges dissented from this view. Kirby J held that a narrow construction of the word "services" would frustrate the intended operation of the Act.

Brennan CJ and McHugh J held:

> Although a provision of the Act must be given a liberal and beneficial construction, a court or tribunal is not at liberty to give it a construction that is unreasonable or unnatural. But subject to that proviso, if the term "service", read in the context of the Act and its object, is capable of applying to an activity, a court or tribunal, exercising jurisdiction under the Act, should hold that that activity is a "service" for the purpose of the Act. (at 12)

Dawson and Gaudron JJ held:

> Although [the definition section] of the Act purports to define "services", it does so by use of the word apparently defined. It does so by indicating what is included in the definition, not what is excluded. As the matters included in the definition are all matters which fall within the ordinary notion of "services", the definition is to be taken as signifying everything which falls within that notion. And as neither the terms of [the goods and services section] nor its context provides any contrary indication, "services" should be read in that subsection as having its ordinary and broad meaning. (at 23)

A wide variety of government services have been the subject of discrimination complaints. Authorities demonstrate that the word "services" is of a general application to a range of "things" delivered by government and there is no necessity for a positive or benevolent factor to be involved. The identification of the services is a question of fact: *Waters v Public Transport Corporation* (1991) 173 CLR 349 at 361.

Recent cases have been based on a wide range of services including:

- the Full Federal Court found that the alteration of a person's sex on their birth registration comes within the meaning of the term "service", the majority found that there was no breach of the *Sex Discrimination Act* when the Victorian legislation restricted the capacity to have a birth certificate altered for a post-operative transsexual to an "unmarried person" when the applicant at the time was a married person: *AB v Registrar of Births, Deaths and Marriages* [2007] FCAFC 140;

- the provision of adoption services such as receiving and assessing applications from foster carers is a service provided by the relevant State government department: *Director-General, Department of Community Services v MM* [2003] NSWSC 1241;

- a Muslim prisoner was denied access to Halal food by the State corrective services department when he was imprisoned for over two years and this was unlawful discrimination on the ground of religious belief: *Queensland v Mahommed* [2007] QSC 018;

- an unsuccessful claim where the Federal Court found that the transporting of prisoners from the prison to the court and then holding them in cells did not constitute a "service": *Rainsford v Victoria* (2007) 96 ALD 90;

- the performance of duties by executors under a will to give full effect to the terms of the will was not the provision of services: *R v Anti-Discrimination Commissioner* (2000) 9 Tas R 332.

Merely because the act constituting the discrimination appears to be sanctioned by State legislation does not result in the discriminator avoiding liability where Federal legislation covers the same field. Therefore it was held that the Royal Women's Hospital could not escape liability for discrimination in the provision of services on the grounds of marital status under the *Sex Discrimination Act* when they refused a single woman access to their donor insemination program on the basis that they were not permitted to do so under the *Victorian Infertility (Medical Procedures) Act* 1984: *W & D & Royal Women's Hospital* (2000) EOC ¶93-045. A similar conclusion was reached by the Federal Court when it held that where the *Victorian Infertility Treatment Act* 1995 denied access by single women to infertility treatment, then it was inconsistent with the provisions of the Federal *Sex Discrimination Act* which rendered discrimination on the basis of martial status unlawful. Hence, the former legislation was invalid pursuant to s 109 of the Australian Constitution: *McBain v Victoria* (2000) 99 FCR 116, see also *Re McBain; ex parte Australian Catholic Bishops Conference* (2002) 209 CLR 372. A similar conclusion was reached in relation to South Australian legislation: *Pearce v South Australian Health Commission* (unreported, SASC, 10 September 1996).

There has been a significant increase in the number of complaints based on the goods and services provisions on the ground of disability including:

- two health care facilities refused access to a man with a disability and his assistance dog on the basis that the dog had not been formally assessed and was not a trained guide dog and also as they had concerns about high levels of hygiene and infection control. They discriminated on the ground of disability against the applicant and his assistance animal: *Forest v Queensland Health* (2007) 161 FCR 152;

- a disability community group failed to sustain a challenge to public transport infrastructure as they did not demonstrate that they were or could be "aggrieved": *Access For All Alliance (Hervey Bay) Inc v Hervey Bay City Council* [2007] FCA 615;

- the applicant failed to establish a breach of services provision when a hospital declined to provide certain services at home rather than at the hospital premises as there were no services of that type available and being provided at the time the request was made: *Wood v Calvary Health Care ACT Ltd* (2006) 155 FCR 489;

- a taxi provider's failure to give priority to wheelchair users of its services, despite licensing requirements, was not disability discrimination in the provision of transport but a poor administration system: *Ball v Silver Top Taxi Service Ltd* [2004] FMCA 967;

- a cinema which discriminated against a wheelchair bound complainant by not providing wheelchair access in its cinemas where the cinema chain was financially able to make such provision: *Hall-Bentick v Greater Union Organisation Pty Ltd* (2000) EOC ¶93-107.

Exceptions

Section 24(2) of the *Disability Discrimination Act* 1992 (Cth) contains an exception where the provision of the goods or services or the making of the facilities available would impose "unjustifiable hardship" on the person providing or making it (see Chapter 10). All State laws have similar coverage and a similar exception. It was held in New South Wales that a large bus company had a valid reason for not installing access facilities that would enable a wheelchair user to use their buses because the cost of doing so would have resulted in an unjustifiable hardship on the company: *Moxon v Westbus Pty Ltd* (2002) EOC ¶93-180; *Moxon v Westbus Pty Ltd (No 2)* (2002) EOC ¶93-248.

Accommodation

Few complaints are made in the area of accommodation and they arise in relation to residential premises. This is a reflection of the nature of the relationship between an applicant for accommodation and an estate agent or a property owner. While seeking accommodation, a person has a particular focus and following up on an individual refusal to offer premises may not be a fruitful exercise. Given the usual delays in the complaint handling processes, a complaint may not do anything to assist the person in securing accommodation, their first priority. The dynamics of the relationship are different to those that arise in other relationships such as employment or with a financial institution where there is long-term on-going contact.

The provisions cover principals and agents. An estate agent who endeavoured to argue that they were only carrying out the instructions of their client, the property owner, when they refused to rent a house to an Aboriginal person would not be able to avoid their own liability for their actions. An estate agent in those circumstances is required to decline to carry out the property owner's instructions otherwise they will be exposed to a complaint of unlawful discrimination and any remedy awarded may be against both parties. As they are the contact point with the prospective tenant, it is more usual that they are the respondent to any complaint. To establish liability of an agent, that person must be authorised by the property owner to act on their behalf in relation to the property. If the agent acts without the owner's authorisation or not on their request, then the agent may be solely liable.

The provisions of the *Disability Discrimination Act* have been held to be valid as access to housing for people with a disability compared with people without a disability is a matter of international concern: *O'Connor v Ross (No 1)* [2002] FMCA 210.

Definition of "accommodation"

The *Sex Discrimination Act* defines "accommodation" as including residential and business accommodation. There is a similar definition in the other laws except the *Racial Discrimination Act*.

The State Government housing authorities are covered by the legislation. The methods they adopt to prioritise applications for housing and the decisions made on allocations of houses to particular applicants could be open to scrutiny under the discrimination laws. The eligibility criteria can be applied and a failure to grant housing that has particular regard to a person's disability may not be disability discrimination: *New South Wales Department of Housing v Moskalev* (2007) 158 FCR 206.

Applicants for accommodation

Section 23(1) of the *Sex Discrimination Act* makes it unlawful for a principal or agent to discriminate on a specified ground:

> (a) by refusing the other person's application for accommodation;
> (b) in the terms or conditions on which the accommodation is offered to the other person; or

(c) by deferring the other person's application for accommodation or according to the other person a lower order of precedence in any list of applicants for that accommodation.

The Victorian, Queensland, Western Australia, Tasmania, Australian Capital Territory and Northern Territory Acts prohibit discrimination on the ground of the status of the person as a parent or carer or on the ground of family responsibilities. This could have particular potential in the area of accommodation as having children has been used as a basis for the refusal to rent properties.

Access to rental accommodation for some people continues to be a matter of complaint. Some young people find it difficult to rent a home due to stereotyped assumptions about the way young people behave including irresponsible treatment of other people's property. This could also amount to unlawful discrimination on the ground of age.

Single women with children may also confront difficulties based on assumptions about their capacity to meet their financial obligations due to the absence of a male partner. This may amount to unlawful discrimination on the ground of sex or marital status.

A common theme of other complaints of racial discrimination is where a telephone inquiry is positive about the availability of accommodation and, when the Aboriginal person arrives at the premises or the agents, the potential property becomes unavailable.

Tenants

Section 23(2) of the *Sex Discrimination Act* makes it unlawful for a principal or an agent to discriminate on a specified ground:

(a) by denying the tenant access, or limiting the tenant's access, to any benefit associated with accommodation occupied by the tenant;

(b) by evicting the tenant from accommodation occupied by the tenant; or

(c) by subjecting the tenant to any other detriment in relation to accommodation occupied by the tenant.

Eviction from premises can be devastating for the former tenant, especially if they have previously had difficulty finding accommodation and then have further difficulty in finding other accommodation.

The *Disability Discrimination Act* contains a further provision in recognition that, in some circumstances, for a person with a disability to be able to live in premises, certain physical changes need to be made to permit access to the premises, parts of the premises or to ensure that the person can utilise all the facilities, such as the equipment and benches in the kitchen and all the bathroom facilities. To provide for this situation, the Act makes it unlawful to refuse to permit a tenant to make reasonable alterations to accommodation occupied by the tenant if:

(a) the tenant has undertaken to restore the accommodation to its condition before alteration on leaving the accommodation; and

(b) in all the circumstances, it is likely that the person will perform the undertaking; and

(c) in all the circumstances, the action required to restore the accommodation to its condition before alteration is reasonably practical; and

(d) the alteration does not involve alteration of the premises of any other occupier; and

(e) the alteration is at the tenant's expense.

Other States have similar provisions.

Instances of discrimination in the provision of rental accommodation include:

- the refusal of a landlord to formally lease premises to an Aboriginal woman because she was Aboriginal, where the woman had been living in them for six months with a friend and wanted to take over the lease when her friend moved out: *Sheather v Daley* (2003) ¶93-278;

- where a landlord terminated the tenancy of a woman after she rebuffed his sexual advances, it was held that he had sexually harassed her in the course of providing accommodation: *Ross v Heinz Loock* (2000) EOC ¶93-078.

Exceptions

There are a range of exceptions in all the laws. Section 23(3) of the *Sex Discrimination Act* contains several exceptions covering when the person or a relative resides on the premises, where there are no more than three people living on the premises, the accommodation is provided by a religious body or by a charitable or non-profit body solely for persons of one sex or a particular marital status. There are similar exceptions in all other laws.

Section 25(3)(c) of the *Disability Discrimination Act* excepts a person providing or proposing to provide accommodation where the person with a disability requires special services or facilities and it would be "unjustifiable hardship" on that person to provide them. There are similar exceptions in State laws with disability or impairment as a ground of discrimination.

State laws have an exception on the ground of age which permits the building, selling and leasing of age-specific premises such as retirement villages or premises only available to people over age 55.

Some of the State laws have specific and detailed exceptions and reference to the relevant legislation should be made where necessary.

Access to premises

Section 23(1) of the *Disability Discrimination Act* makes it unlawful for a person to discriminate on the ground of disability or the disability of any of the person's associates:

    (a)   by refusing to allow the other person access to, or use of, any premises that the public or a section of the public is entitled or allowed to enter or use (whether for payment or not); or

    (b)   in the terms or conditions on which the person is prepared to allow the other person access to, or use of, any such premises; or

    (c)   in relation to the provision of means of access to such premises; or

    (d)   by refusing to allow the other person the use of any facilities in such premises that the public or a section of the public is entitled or allowed to use (whether for payment or not): or

    (e)   in the terms or conditions on which the person is prepared to allow the other person the use of any such facilities; or

    (f)   by requiring the other person to leave the premises or cease to use such facilities.

The *Racial Discrimination Act* contains a similar provision while the *Sex Discrimination Act* does not. None of the State laws makes specific provision for access to premises and such complaints would usually come within the goods and services provision.

The premises in question must be available to the public or sections of the public. A complainant would need to establish that element as well as the other components to maintain a successful action.

Access to premises is an important issue for some people with a disability who find their capacity to engage fully in all aspects of community life are curtailed by the lack of wheelchair and related access to public places. The *Disability Discrimination Act* has been used to require cinemas to install provide access to people with mobility difficulties: *Hall-Bentick v Greater Union Organisation Pty Ltd* (2000) EOC ¶93-107.

Access issues have been the subject of on-going controversy in the disability field and have led to other complaints about lack of access to certain public buildings, including planned shopping malls and related facilities (*Woods v Wollongong City Council* (1993) EOC ¶92-486) and planned large public buildings: *Cocks v Queensland* (1994) EOC ¶92-612.

Action plans pursuant to ss 59-65 of the *Disability Discrimination Act* are a mechanism for an organisation to plan to make their premises accessible by reviewing the access and then setting goals and targets to meet the principles behind the legislation as well as the legislation itself. An action plan can cover not only physical access issues but also methods and mechanisms of service delivery.

Exceptions

Section 23(2) of the *Disability Discrimination Act* contains a provision which excepts a person providing access to premises where the premises are so designed and constructed as to be inaccessible to a person with a disability and any alteration would impose unjustifiable hardship on the person providing the access.

Clubs

The inclusion of clubs was controversial when first introduced into sex discrimination laws. Most clubs throughout Australia had various categories of membership. It was common for only men to be able to gain full membership and with it the related rights to vote for the management committee and run for election to that committee. Women members were usually associate members with no such rights. By requiring that clubs alter their membership criteria and remove the blatant sex discrimination, the laws challenged some long held traditions of many clubs. There was an initial spate of challenges by women who were denied access to full membership despite the legislative changes: *Umina Beach Bowling Club Ltd v Ryan* (1984) EOC ¶92-110; *Corry v Keperra Country Golf Club* (1986) EOC ¶92-150.

Definition of "club"

A "club" is defined in the *Sex Discrimination Act* as meaning an incorporated or unincorporated association of not less than 30 members associated for social, literary, cultural, political, sporting, athletic or other lawful purpose that:

    (a)   provides and maintains its facilities, in whole or in part, from the funds of the association; and

    (b)   sells or supplies liquor for consumption on its premises.

There is no specific provision covering clubs in the *Racial Discrimination Act*, although the access to premises provision could be used as the basis of a complaint if access to a club or part of a club gave rise to a complaint. There are similar provisions in all other laws.

As the Federal Court has noted:

> The ambit of s 27 [DDA] is extensive. It is clear from the definition of a "club" in s 4(1) and the wide area of activity of incorporated associations that such bodies will extend across the whole spectrum of social, literary, cultural, political, sporting, athletic and other lawful creative or recreational activities in the Australian community. (*Soulitopoulos v La Trobe University Liberal Club* (2002) 120 FCR 584)

Admission of members

Section 25(1) of the *Sex Discrimination Act* makes it unlawful for a club, a club's committee or a member of a committee to discriminate on the specified grounds in relation to the admission of membership of a club:

(a) by refusing or failing to accept the person's application for membership; or

(b) in the terms or conditions on which the club is prepared to admit the person to membership.

There are similar provisions in all other laws except the *Racial Discrimination Act*.

The requirement for membership including swearing an oath of loyalty was a statement relating to political activity for a person opposed to the monarchy and so came within the Tasmanian legislation on that basis: *Lindisfarne R&SLA Sub-Branch and Citizen's Club Inc v Buchanan* (2004) 80 ALD 122.

Membership of clubs

Section 25(2) of the *Sex Discrimination Act* makes it unlawful for a club, a club's committee or a member of a committee to discriminate on the specified grounds in relation to a member of a club:

(a) in the terms or conditions of membership that are afforded to the member;

(b) by refusing or failing to accept the member's application for a particular class or type of membership;

(c) by denying the member access, or limiting the member's access, to any benefit provided by the club;

(d) by depriving the member of any membership or varying the terms of membership; or

(e) by subjecting the member to any other detriment.

There are similar provisions in all other laws except the *Racial Discrimination Act*.

The initial impact of the legislation was to require clubs to alter their requirements for entry into a particular class of membership which were usually specifically gender based. The other change was the access to certain facilities within the club. Male only bars and other facilities such as saunas and pools were common in many larger clubs. These facilities had to alter to admit women once they became full members. Entry into such facilities can be controlled by the category of membership but not by the gender of the person seeking entry or access. Consequently, there can be an area of the club for full members only, where associate members or guests of a member are not admitted: *Judge v South Hurstville RSL Club Ltd* (1984) EOC ¶92-113.

For the discrimination to be unlawful the club must, however, be aware of the attribute said to constitute the discrimination. So, for example, if a club is not aware of the psychological condition of one of its members which caused the member's bad behaviour resulting in his expulsion from the club, then this cannot be said to constitute unlawful discrimination: *Tate v Rafin* (2001) EOC ¶93-125.

Exceptions

The on-going controversy about single-sex clubs, particularly elite male only clubs, and access to certain facilities for one gender at a time, particularly for men, has resulted in some exceptions to the discrimination laws which on the face of them appear to be entirely contradictory to the general proposition in asserting that discrimination is unlawful. This reflects one of the compromises made to ensure the passage of the legislation overall with some give and take on some of the provisions which were viewed as less central to the main objects of the legislation.

Section 25(3) of the *Sex Discrimination Act* preserves single-sex clubs and there are similar provisions in all State legislation.

Section 25(4) and (5) of the *Sex Discrimination Act* contain convoluted provisions which are designed to ensure that facilities can be used by men or women only where it is not practicable for them to be enjoyed simultaneously or to the same extent. The test is based on notions of fair and reasonable use and proportionality of and opportunities for use.

Section 27(3) of the *Disability Discrimination Act* contains a provision which exempts a club where a person with a disability requires a benefit to be provided in a special manner and the benefit cannot be provided without imposing an unjustifiable hardship on the club.

Section 27(3) of the *Disability Discrimination Act* contains a provision which exempts a club or an unincorporated association where its membership is for persons with a particular disability and the person does not have that disability.

Sport

Section 28(1) and (2) of the *Disability Discrimination Act* make it unlawful for a person to discriminate against a person with a disability or their associate by excluding the person from a sporting activity, including an administrative or coaching activity. There is no specific coverage of sport as an area of unlawful discrimination in the *Sex Discrimination Act* or the *Racial Discrimination Act*. At a State level coverage varies as between the various jurisdictions; for example, the Victorian Act covers sport on all prescribed grounds whereas the Western Australian Act covers sport on the ground of impairment and age only.

Exceptions

Most Acts contain broad exceptions in the area of sport, which are discussed in Chapter 11.

Section 28(3) of the *Disability Discrimination Act* contains a specific exception from the coverage of sport as an area. It is not unlawful to discriminate against a person:

    (a) if the person is not reasonably capable of performing the actions reasonably required in relation to the sporting activity; or

    (b) if the persons who participate or are to participate in the sporting activities are selected by a method which is reasonable on the basis of their skills and abilities relevant to the sporting activity and relative to each other; or

    (c) if a sporting activity is conducted only for persons who have a particular disability and the person does not have that disability.

With male sporting competitions and prizes still attracting considerably higher levels of corporate sponsorship, it can be anticipated that there will be some complaints by women in the same sport who claim discrimination by the sports administrators. The outcome will depend on a variety of factors, including the availability of a valid comparison with male competitors and identifying any difference as arising from their sex.

Administration of Commonwealth laws and programs

In an attempt to widen the impact of the *Sex Discrimination Act*, a head of unlawful discrimination was incorporated which covered the administration of Commonwealth laws and programs.

Section 26(1) of the *Sex Discrimination Act* provides that "it is unlawful for a person who performs any function or exercises any power under a Commonwealth law or for the purposes of a Commonwealth program, or has any responsibility for the administration of a Commonwealth law or the conduct of a Commonwealth program" to discriminate on any of the specified grounds.

In turn, "Commonwealth program" is defined as meaning "a program conducted by or on behalf of the Commonwealth Government".

Section 26(2) specifies that the section binds the Crown in the right of the State. This is designed to ensure that any of the constitutional difficulties which may arise with other sections is not in doubt in relation to the coverage of State Governments in this particular section. Section 29 of the *Disability Discrimination Act* is in similar terms. The Queensland Act includes a similar provision.

The various terms have received some judicial consideration. The term "program" has been examined several times by the Federal Court. Spender J in *Hough v Council of the Shire of Caboolture* (1992) 39 FCR 514 did not consider it appropriate to circumscribe the term and held that the Council was performing a function for the purposes of the Commonwealth Employment Program, established under a Federal law to create employment for long-term unemployed or for unemployed people in special disadvantaged categories.

Morling J saw no reason to confine the term "program" within narrow limits in *Harris v Bryce* (1993) 30 ALD 833 at 835. He found that Commonwealth participation in providing education in Pitjantjatjara schools in co-operation with other governments was a Commonwealth program "notwithstanding that it is a program in which other governments participate".

In *MW v Royal Women's Hospital* (1997) EOC ¶92-886, several women complained about the denial of their access to fertility treatment on the basis that they were not married. They used s 26 as part of their complaint on the basis that the hospitals were in receipt of Commonwealth funds from Medicare. This part of the complaint was dismissed as it was found that there was no direct contractual relationship between Medicare, a Commonwealth program, and one hospital. The relationship was between the doctor and the patient. The patient was responsible for paying the account to the doctor which in turn may give rise to a subsequent entitlement for a refund from Medicare. In *Dranichnikov v Department of Immigration and Multicultural Affairs* [2002] FCA 1463, s 26 of the *Sex Discrimination Act* was used to found a complaint, which was ultimately dismissed, that the applicant had been discriminated against on the grounds of sex and marital status in the manner in which her application for refugee status had been determined.

Requests for information

The provision of information, including on application forms, is included, as in some circumstances the main employment, education or other provisions may not apply where there is not a sufficient degree of any relationship between the parties to bring the act alleged to be discriminatory within the parameters of the discrimination laws.

Section 27(1) of the *Sex Discrimination Act* makes it unlawful for a person to request or require another person to provide different information from any other person on any ground covered by the Act. This section specifically binds the Crown in the right of the State. Section 30 of the *Disability Discrimination Act* contains a similar provision as do some of the State laws.

Exceptions

Section 27(2) of the *Sex Discrimination Act* exempts information relating to a person's medical history as it relates to sex-specific medical conditions and medical information on a woman's pregnancy.

Insurance

The *Sex Discrimination Act* (see s 41), the *Disability Discrimination Act* (see s 46) and the *Age Discrimination Act* (see s 37) make discrimination in the provision of insurance lawful where it is based on reasonably reliable actuarial or statistical data. Section 46 of the *Disability Discrimination Act* states:

> (1) This Part does not render it unlawful for a person to discriminate against another person, on the ground of the other person's disability, by refusing to offer the other person:
>
> (a)   an annuity; or
> (b)   a life insurance policy; or
> (c)   a policy of insurance against accident or any other policy of insurance; or
> (d)   membership of a superannuation or provident fund; or
> (e)   membership of a superannuation or provident scheme;
> if:
> (f)   the discrimination:

       (i)   is based upon actuarial or statistical data on which it is reasonable for the first-mentioned person to rely; and

      (ii)   is reasonable having regard to the matter of the data and other relevant factors; or

   (g)   in a case where no such actuarial or statistical data is available and cannot reasonably be obtained—the discrimination is reasonable having regard to any other relevant factors.

The State and Territory legislation is similar to its Federal counterparts although the grounds upon which an insurer may discriminate are usually limited to matters such as sex, disability or age.

Where there was no actual actuarial data on which to fix premiums and offer insurance to persons over the age of 70 in a barristers' sickness and accident fund but there was actuarial advice, which in turn was based on an analysis of the available statistical data, which showed that to offer insurance to such members could jeopardise the financial viability of the fund, the NSW Administrative Decisions Tribunal held that the fund's decision was not unlawfully discriminatory because the decision was nevertheless reasonable having regard to the advice upon which it was based: *Leslie v Barrister's Sickness & Accident Fund Pty Limited* [2003] NSWADT 216.

Likewise, where a life insurance applicant was required to complete a questionnaire directed at HIV infection, the questionnaire having been compiled with respect to statistical data which confirmed that certain classes of individuals, namely, homosexual men, intravenous drug users and persons with multiple sexual partners, had a greater risk of contracting HIV, it was not held to be discriminatory: *Lombardo v Tower Life Insurance* (2000) EOC ¶93-088; *Xiros v Fortis Life Assurance* (2001) 162 FLR 433.

By contrast, in the landmark case of *QBE Travel Insurance v Bassanelli* (2004) 137 FCR 88the, the Federal Court upheld a decision of the Federal Magistrates Court that the refusal by an insurance company to offer travel insurance to a woman who was suffering from metastatic breast cancer was discriminatory under the *Disability Discrimination Act*. The applicant had not sought insurance for any cancer-related claim but only for potential losses in the course of travel which were not related to her pre-existing condition such as theft, lost luggage and other accidental injury. The issue was one of the reasonableness of the refusal to provide cover. No statistical data was provided by the respondent insurance company and so the court below had taken into account all relevant circumstances.

In examining the operation of s 46(1)(f) of the *Disability Discrimination Act*, Mansfield J held:

Section 46(1)(f) requires that:

(1) the discrimination is based upon actuarial or statistical data and is information which it is reasonable for the discriminator to rely on, and

(2) the discrimination is reasonable having regard to the data and "to other relevant factors".

The first of those elements focuses upon the decision-making of the discriminator. The use of the expression "is based" and the reference to reliance must mean that the discriminator actually based its decision upon certain actuarial or statistical data. Then the inquiry directs attention to the reasonableness of the discriminator in having relied upon the data. It involves an objective judgment about the nature and quality of the actuarial or statistical data relied on. The actuary or statistician (or the data itself) may indicate that for whatever reason it would not be reasonable to rely upon it. It may be qualified, or be an insufficient sample for reliable use, or not be directly applicable to the particular decision. There may be other reasons why, on its face, it would not be reasonable to rely upon it. There may be actuarial or statistical data upon which it may be unreasonable to rely for other reasons external to the data being relied upon. The data may be incomplete, or out-of-date, or discredited, and the decision-maker ought, in the circumstances, to have known that.

Once the haven of s 46(1)(f)(i) is reached, to be eligible for protection under s 46(1)(f), it is also necessary for the discrimination to have been reasonable having regard to the data and to other relevant factors. That clearly also involves an objective judgment. It is a judgment to be made objectively with the knowledge and in the circumstances of the discriminator, but including factors of which the discriminator ought to have been aware. Section 46(1)(f)(ii) refers to the reasonableness of the discrimination whereas s 46(1)(f)(i) refers to the discrimination being based upon data having a certain quality. (at [29]-[31])

In examining the operation of s 46(1)(g) of the *Disability Discrimination Act*, Mansfield J held:

I consider that, on its proper construction, the exemption for which s 46(1)(g) provides is only available if there is no actuarial or statistical data available to, or reasonably obtainable by, the discriminator upon which the discriminator may reasonably form a judgment about whether to engage in the discriminatory conduct. If such data is available, then the exemption provided by s 46(1)(g) cannot be availed of. The decision made upon the basis of such data must run the gauntlet of s 46(1)(f)(ii), that is the discriminatory decision must be reasonable having regard to the matter of the data and other relevant factors. If the data (and other relevant factors) do not expose the discriminatory decision as reasonable, then there is no room for the insurer to move to s 46(1)(g) and thereby to ignore such data. If such data were not available to the insurer but were reasonably obtainable, so that its discriminatory decision might have been measured through the prism of s 46(1)(f), again there would be no room for the insurer to invoke the exemption under s 46(1)(g). (at [33])

Superannuation

Until recently, the focus of superannuation law and practice was on providing men who participated in full time employment for their working lives with a comfortable standard of living on retirement. Many women were denied access to superannuation or were required to leave funds when they married or had a child. When they returned to work after an absence, they were denied entry to a superannuation fund in any way which recognised their previous years' work. So, for many women, superannuation was not a benefit associated with employment. The participation of women as part-time workers, and with breaks in their employment patterns, meant that many women were outside the protective net of the superannuation system.

When the *Sex Discrimination Act* was passed there was an exemption for superannuation which was based on the "actuarial or statistical data" which was reasonable to rely on. There were on-going complaints from women about their exclusion from superannuation funds or the continued denial of access to equal benefits with male contributors.

In 1990, the Commonwealth Attorney-General conducted an inquiry into the superannuation and insurance exemptions under *the Sex Discrimination Act* and called for public submissions. The report recommended the removal of the exemptions by various amendments. In 1991, an amendment Bill to the *Sex Discrimination Act* was passed and the amendments came into operation in 1994. A planned commencement date in mid-1993 was deferred for 12 months.

Section 14(4) of the *Sex Discrimination Act* was inserted in 1991 and commenced operation on 25 June 1993. It provides:

> Where a person exercises a discretion in relation to the payment of a superannuation benefit to or in respect of a member of a superannuation fund, it is unlawful for the person to discriminate, in the exercise of the discretion, against the member or another person on the ground, in either case, of the sex or marital status of the member or that other person.

A "member" is defined to include a person who has been a member at any time.

Section 14(4) does not apply if the exemption in s 41B applies. Sections 41A and 41B of the *Sex Discrimination Act* render sex discrimination in new and existing superannuation funds unlawful in certain circumstances only, and an exception applies in other circumstances. These are complex provisions which need to be examined closely before any complaint in the area of superannuation is pursued.

However, what is clear is that it remains lawful to discriminate in the area of death and disability payments on the grounds of sexuality. Accordingly, upon the death of a partner in a same-sex relationship payment of benefits to the surviving partner, irrespective of the length of the relationship, can be refused by the fund. In *Nolan v Repatriation Commission* (2003) EOC ¶93-258, it was held that a refusal of a pension for the same sex partner of a war veteran did not amount to unlawful discrimination notwithstanding that the couple had been together for a considerable period of time. The NSW Administrative Decisions Tribunal held that, although the relevant provisions of the *Veterans Entitlement Act* 1986 (Cth) were discriminatory, they did not fall foul of the *Anti-Discrimination Act* and that the discrimination was therefore not unlawful.

The Federal Court has held that superannuation is the provision of a service within the goods and services provision of the *Sex Discrimination Act*: *Australian Education Union v HR&EOC* (1997) 77 IR 1. This means that the State Government employment exception in relation to s 14 employment provisions does not apply so a complaint of unlawful discrimination concerning the terms of a superannuation scheme for State Government employees, including teachers, is not automatically exempt from the terms of the Act, and an inquiry can properly be held into the terms themselves.

9

VICTIMISATION AND OTHER UNLAWFUL ACTS AND OFFENCES

Victimisation

All discrimination laws make it unlawful, but not an offence, to victimise a person who lodges a complaint or takes certain, related actions.

The intention of such protective measures is to ensure that a person who wants to use or does use their statutory rights to protect themselves against discrimination or harassment, is not further disadvantaged by other detriments being imposed on them. Victimisation had been held to require an element of unfairness: *Von Stalheim v Anti Discrimination Tribunal and Attorney General (Tas)* [2007] TASSC 9 at [15].

Laws against victimisation are meant to be a deterrent to employer respondents particularly, and to require them to act in good faith when they are informed about a person's intention to lodge a complaint or that a complaint has been lodged and is being pursued. Few cases of harassment are brought by a person still working in the same position. Some discrimination cases are brought by people still in their jobs, but they are often public sector employees or employees of larger corporations where they are able to continue to work without necessarily coming into contact with the people who are alleged to have committed the act of discrimination or harassment.

An ultimate failure to sustain a discrimination complaint does not dissolve any liability for a victimisation complaint. It may be that, in the final analysis, the discrimination claim fails on its facts but that during the course of the complaint handling processes, an act or acts of victimisation did occur. Such an act may have been based on a mistaken view by the respondent that the complaint would be sustained, on concerns about public exposure of the respondent or for a myriad of other reasons.

On some occasions, it is necessary for a person to lodge a second, separate complaint of victimisation, as the acts alleged to constitute that complaint arise after the lodging of the discrimination complaint. If facts are not alleged in the complaint, they cannot later be deemed to be included in the original complaint. This exclusion can occur at the conciliation stage or, more importantly, at the hearing and decision stage. Consequently, it is important for a complainant who considers they have been subjected to an act of victimisation to lodge a second or subsequent complaint covering the factual basis for the allegation and asserting that there has been an act of victimisation. It is usual practice that, once the matters come to a hearing, the complaints are joined and heard together.

The *Sex Discrimination Act* has a complicated statutory scheme which makes victimisation both an unlawful act and an offence. Section 94 makes it an offence and s 47A makes any act that is an offence pursuant to s 94 an act that is unlawful also. Section 47A was inserted in 1992 after the offence provisions were found to be unworkable as they required the Director of Public Prosecutions to launch the action and there was no capacity for a complainant to pursue their own rights and remedies or to link it with a discrimination complaint. The coverage of the victimisation provisions is similar in this Act to all State Acts.

Section 94(2) provides that an act of victimisation occurs where a person subjects or threatens to subject another person to any detriment on the ground that the person:

(a) has made, or proposes to make, a complaint under the Act;

(b) has brought, or proposes to bring, proceedings under the Act against any person;

(c) has furnished, or proposes to furnish, any information, or has produced, or proposes to produce, any documents to any person exercising or performing any power or function under the Act;

(d) has attended, or proposes to attend, a compulsory conference;

(e) has appeared, or proposes to appear, as a witness in a hearing;

(f) has reasonably asserted, or proposes to assert, any rights of the person or the rights of any other person under the Act; or

(g) has made an allegation that a person has done an act that is unlawful under the Act.

The unlawful discrimination provisions of the *Sex Discrimination Act* are covered by s 8, which applies when there are two or more reasons for carrying out an act, and discrimination does not have to be the dominant or substantial reason (see Chapter 3). This section does not apply to the victimisation provisions.

Therefore, the phrase "on the ground of" may have a different interpretation when applied to victimisation than discrimination. In victimisation complaints, the test is that the ground must be the "substantial and operative factor": *Morrison-Liddy v Director, Department of TAFE* (1995) EOC ¶92-744 at 77,362-3.

Components of victimisation

There are three separate components to the victimisation provisions and each must be met by appropriate evidence for a victimisation claim to be sustained.

The first component is that the person must be "subjected to" or threatened to be subjected to a detriment. The second is establishing a detriment and the third is demonstrating the causal nexus between any detriment and one of the matters listed in the legislation, such as lodging a complaint.

The term "subjected to" has been considered by the New South Wales Tribunal in the context of victimisation claims. It has held:

> [T]he word "subjected" carries with it a requirement that the respondent intended to cause detrimental consequences to flow to the complainant. (*Bhattacharya v Department of Public Works* (1984) EOC ¶92-117 at 76,133)

This may not be the correct test. The issue of intention or motivation has not been finally determined in relation to victimisation. Therefore while it is necessary that detriment be established, it is not clear whether or not it is additionally necessary to establish that the detriment was intended: *Waters v Public Transport Commission* (1991) 173 CLR 349 at 359. In some instances, the evidence of intention may form an integral part of the victimisation claim as there may be oral or written statements which indicate the link.

The second component is identifying and establishing the "detriment". In relation to "detriment", the NSW Tribunal has held that:

> [A]ll that is required to constitute "detriment" in a victimisation complaint is that the complainant has been placed under a disadvantage as to a matter of substance as distinct from a trivial matter. (*Bogie v University of Western Sydney* (1990) EOC ¶92-313 at 78,146)

The HR&EOC considered the various elements of the statutory provisions of victimisation at some length and stated:

> Victimisation occurs where the complainant suffers a material difference in treatment based on the fact that she made a complaint or an

allegation within the terms [of the victimisation] section. (*Bailey v Australian National University* (1995) EOC ¶92-744 at 78,553)

The New South Wales Tribunal has rejected this interpretation of the word "detriment" as being too narrow, when a broad interpretation was to be preferred. That tribunal considered the word meant "loss, damage or injury": *Shaikh v Commissioner, NSW Fire Brigade* (1996) EOC ¶92-808 at 78,986. Equally, in the decision of *Hautlieu Pty Ltd t/as Russell Pathology v McIntosh* [2000] WASCA 146 at [164]-[167], the Supreme Court of Western Australia defined "detriment" broadly to include loss, damage or injury, the latter of which meant "harm of any kind done or sustained or a wrong or injustice suffered" and was not limited to physical harm but included psychological harm. However, the court went on to hold that, amongst other things, the restriction of an applicant's access to certain computer programs did not amount to a detriment .

The crucial issue which emerges in many cases is establishing the causal nexus between the detriment perceived by the complainant and the lodging of the complaint or other actions taken by them to assert their rights.

Many victimisation complaints fail as that link cannot be demonstrated. This is often because the link is not there, rather than there being any lack of credible evidence to demonstrate it. It is an unfortunate part of the whole discrimination complaint process that some complainants may come to perceive themselves as a "whistle blower" within an organisation. They view any action taken by the organisation as an act of retribution or retaliation for the complaint, especially after it has been lodged with an outside agency. Doubtless, that does occur in some situations and those are the very ones the legislative proscription is directed towards.

However, it is also correct that in some circumstances some complainants view all subsequent events from the position of "victim" and seek to draw interconnecting links when there is none available.

This difficulty can arise particularly for an employer or any respondent where there is an ongoing relationship or connection with a complainant. Given the sometimes lengthy delays in investigating and conciliating a complaint, there may be a period of 12 months or even longer in which the relationship continues. This can mean that anything that occurs to a complainant which is not to their own liking or request can form the basis of a complaint of victimisation, even when there is no link at all. For example, where a person lodges a complaint and it is unresolved and they unsuccessfully apply for a promotion, this can form part of their perception of victimisation. In fact, their inability to be promoted on that occasion may only be related to a decision on the merit of the competing candidates.

This is not to underestimate the difficulty for a complainant in establishing the causal nexus. It is trite to say that just because the complainant perceives an act of victimisation does not mean that no such act has occurred.

The further difficulty is the balance which a respondent is required to strike between the interests of the complainant in a particular circumstance and the interests of others, including other employees. To act deliberately to ensure that there is no perception of victimisation may result in a complainant in some circumstances being treated more favourably than if they had not lodged a complaint.

A flow of events is not automatically an act of victimisation just because one event follows another event. Mere knowledge that a person is asserting or has asserted their rights is not sufficient to meet the test for an act of victimisation to be established. The link must be able to be demonstrated.

If there is no evidence on the face of the act complained of, apart from the subjective view of the complainant that one leads to the other, then there is no basis for a complaint of victimisation to be sustained.

An employer can be held to be vicariously liable of the victimisation by an employee of an individual (see Chapter 10). The basis for this liability has been explained as:

> I am satisfied that in the circumstances of the findings ... that the acts of victimisation related to conduct by the Second and Third Respondents who held supervisory or management positions in respect of the Applicant and conduct by other employees with whom she had contact. Further, it is clear that the Second and Third Respondents had ostensible authority to behave in the manner outlined in the evidence and under general common law agency principles, they had authority to bind their principal, the Fourth Respondent. I am satisfied ... that the Fourth Respondent is vicariously liable for the acts of victimisation either on the basis of ordinary common law concepts relating to vicarious liability for the acts of an employee arising in the course of their employment or on the basis of primary responsibility of a principal for the conduct of an agent giving ostensible authority to bind the principal. (*Lee v Smith* [2007] FMCA 59 at [213])

Conduct constituting victimisation

There has been consideration of the various statutory formulae of victimisation by tribunals and courts in recent years. Some of the conduct which has been found to be victimisation includes:

- following repeated acts of sexual harassment and one act of serious sexual assault, the complainant was subjected to repeated acts of bullying and intimidation by the perpetrator and others in the workplace and wide publication within the workplace of her complaints and poor handling of that complaint, with many acts of derogatory conduct and comments: *Lee v Smith* [2007] FMCA 59;

- a refusal to employ a contractor with a long history with the company after an unsuccessful complaint of disability discrimination and a threat to make a further complaint: *Drury v Andreco-Hurll Refractory Services Pty Ltd (No 4)* (2005) 225 ALR 339;

- the sending of an email to a complainant's work colleagues to attend a union meeting to discuss the complaint in circumstances where it was clear that, without naming him in the email, he was the complainant and the summary dismissal of the man notwithstanding that the primary age bias claim failed: *Kennedy v Department of Industrial Relations* [2002] NSWADT 186.

However, a very significant proportion of victimisation claims fail, usually because no causal link can be demonstrated by the applicant. Some examples are:

- an allegation that certain actions including correspondence and a draft deed of release provided to a complainant in an ultimately unsuccessful endeavour to settle the proceedings was a standard approach to such negotiations and not victimisation: *Penhall-Jones v New South Wales* [2007] FCA 925;

- a refusal to discuss disability complaints by a school principal, shouting over the telephone and a failure to return calls could not amount to victimisation as the complaints were trivial and not particularised: *Damiano v Wilkinson* [2004] FMCA 891;

- an allegation of race discrimination was dismissed on the basis that the reason that the employment of an Aboriginal woman was terminated was her failure to attain the enrolments necessary to secure the funds upon which her employment contract was conditional. As the decision to terminate her was based on the failure to secure funding and not her intention to complain, the allegation of victimisation was also dismissed: *Riley v Western College of Adult Education* (2003) EOC ¶93-253;

- an allegation by an applicant that he had been victimised in the refusal of the Commissioner for Housing to provide him with housing assistance was dismissed, the refusal a result of the applicant's arrears in respect of previous tenancies: *Harrison v Commissioner for Housing* [2003] ACTSC 22;

- a complaint of victimisation due to an employer's failure to pay an employee a bonus after a complaint of sexual harassment had been made was dismissed on the basis that the refusal to pay the bonus was because of the complainant's failure to complete a training course: *Font v Paspaley Pearls* [2002] FMCA 142.

The absence of policies and dispute resolution mechanisms may have an impact on liability (see Chapter 10) but not necessarily a finding of victimisation: *Aleksovski v AAA Pty Ltd* [2002] FMCA 81.

Defence

There are exceptions in all the discrimination laws to the act of victimisation, but these are limited in scope. As an exception, the respondent carries the onus of proof to establish the counter claim involved in the defence. Consequently, if the complainant establishes all the necessary components of a victimisation complaint, the complaint will stand unless the respondent can affirmatively establish the necessary matters to give rise to the defence: *AMP Society v Goulden* (1986) 160 CLR 330 at 339.

Section 94(3) of the *Sex Discrimination Act* provides that it is a defence where the person has made an allegation and the allegation was false and not made in good faith.

Such an exception means that it is only available in relation to the person making the allegation itself. Therefore, if any other person involved in the complaint process is subjected to any victimisation, the respondent cannot avail themselves of this defence.

The allegation must also be both false and not in good faith so both components must be established. Where, therefore, a complainant made allegations of sexual harassment and was then victimised, it was irrelevant to the claim of victimisation that she was found to have given untruthful evidence during the hearing. While the allegation of sexual harassment may have been false it was nevertheless made in good faith and consequently the victimisation claim was upheld notwithstanding that the complaint of sexual harassment failed: *Kistler v RE Laing Trading* (2000) EOC ¶93-064. Further, simply establishing that a complaint was eventually not made out does not make it "false". There must be an element of deception or lack of genuineness at the time it was made to meet the descriptor. There can be many reasons for a complaint being found to be unsubstantiated and these may be completely unrelated to either the views of the complainant at the time the complaint was lodged or their intentions towards the respondent.

Other unlawful acts and offences

There are some other acts which are unlawful but which are not specifically tied to a ground of discrimination. Liability and aiding and permitting provisions are discussed in Chapter 10.

The other unlawful acts are advertisements, incitement and a range of other offences and these are discussed below. The coverage of such acts varies between the various statutes.

Acts of unlawful discrimination, harassment and victimisation are not offences and they form the basis of a civil remedy only.

Some of the legislation creates a series of offences in which the Director of Public Prosecutions or the equivalent State body is required to intervene and conduct a prosecution in the criminal courts. This means that a complainant has no direct control over the conduct of such proceedings and the discretion to proceed is not a decision in which the complainant necessarily has any input. Any remedy of a financial penalty is paid to the coffers of the government involved and is of no direct pecuniary benefit to the complainant.

Advertisements

Sexist or racist advertisements for commercial products, especially on television or radio, are not covered by the provisions in the discrimination law as they are more general in nature. Any person who may be offended by stereotypes such as women in the kitchen or the laundry achieving personal happiness and achievement through the use of margarine or washing powder does not have the direct personal interest needed to base a discrimination claim. Consequently, anyone offended or insulted by such an advertisement can take it up with the manufacturer and the venue for its exposure, such as the television station. Consumer resistance to certain advertisements has achieved withdrawal of some of the more contentious, although usually after more media exposure to the advertisement itself.

Section 86(1) of the *Sex Discrimination Act* 1984 makes it an offence to publish or display or cause or permit to be published or displayed an advertisement or notice that indicates or could reasonably be understood as indicating an intention to do an act that is an act of unlawful discrimination.

"Advertisement" is defined in s 86(2) in an extremely wide manner and covers all forms and manner of advertising and all forums of transmission or display.

The *Disability Discrimination Act,* the *Age Discrimination Act* and the *Anti-Discrimination Act* 1977 (NSW) also make advertisements an offence. All the other States and Territories have similar provisions in their Acts.

Incitement

Section 43 of the *Disability Discrimination Act* creates the offence to incite the doing of an act of unlawful discrimination or harassment, to incite the doing of an act that is an offence or to assist or promote whether by financial assistance or otherwise the doing of such an act. There have been no prosecutions under this provision.

Incitement is also included in the *Racial Discrimination Act* 1975, and in most other State enactments.

These provisions differ from the provisions covering aiding and permitting others to do an act, which are discussed in Chapter 10.

Other offences

There are a range of other offences created which vary considerably between the various statutes.

For example, the *Sex Discrimination Act* contains the following offences:

- failing to provide actuarial or statistical data, especially applicable in the area of insurance and superannuation;
- divulging or communicating the contents of any complaint except for staff and Commissioners performing their duties unless there is an inquiry proceeding;
- providing false or misleading information;
- insulting, hindering, obstructing, molesting or interfering with a person exercising a power or performing a function under the Act.

The *Racial Discrimination Act*, the *Disability Discrimination Act* and the *Age Discrimination Act* contain similar offence provisions.

10

LIABILITY, VICARIOUS LIABILITY AND DEFENCES

While the complainant in any conciliation or inquiry process carries the onus of proof, the respondent has a role which varies depending on the nature of the complaint and the remedies sought by the complainant.

Many organisations, particularly employers, are surprised when they are notified by a discrimination agency that a complaint has been received from a person making certain allegations of which they may be unaware. An immediate reaction can be to disregard the correspondence as the organisation does not perceive that any issue of liability may arise for the organisation itself. This reaction is based on a failure to appreciate the impact of the principles of vicarious liability and the nature of the employment relationship which underpins that liability. This chapter discusses these issues.

A person may be liable if they aid or permit another person to breach any part of the discrimination legislation and this issue is considered in this chapter.

During any proceedings, if a respondent wants to base part or all of their response to a complaint on a defence available under the legislation, then the onus rests on the respondent to run it. The conduct of a defence is examined in this chapter.

Vicarious liability

An employer can be liable for the acts of an employee or agent through the wording of the statute which sets out the areas covered, and also through the vicarious liability provisions. This part of the chapter looks at the latter proposition.

An employer is liable for the authorised acts of an employee. An employee is subject to the authority of the employer to control the work of the employee as a development of the classic master and servant relationship. The way that vicarious liability arises is two-fold: an employer's duty of care to the complainant and an employer's responsibility for the acts of any other employee. In employment complaints liability may arise in relation to an employee-complainant, and in other cases such as providing goods and services, the basis of responsibility arises solely in relation to the complainant.

The basis for the employer liability demonstrates the fundamental relationship between an employer and an employee. Three crucial elements to this relationship have been identified by the High Court:

> It will be seen that three elements are involved: first, the relationship must entail, on the part of the servant, obedience to orders; secondly, the obedience to orders that is required is obedience to orders in doing work; and thirdly, the doing of the work must be for the benefit of the master, that is, it must relate to his own affairs. (*Attorney-General (NSW) v Perpetual Trustee Co Ltd* (1952) 85 CLR 237 at 299-300)

At common law, an employer owes a duty of care to each employee. A breach of this duty may give rise to an action for negligence. An employer is also liable for the negligence of a worker, whether towards another worker or in some external way (see Chapter 4).

In relation to the breach of any duty of care owed, the complainant must show that it was reasonably foreseeable as a possible outcome that the defendant's carelessness might cause damage of some kind to the complainant. This means that a way or mechanism for removing or eliminating the possibility of damage was available to the employer and a reasonable person in the employer's position would have adopted such a course of action. This is the basis for the statutory exception to a claim for vicarious liability: *Sex Discrimination Act* 1984 (Cth) s 106(2).

These elements arise in common law and have been adapted to the statutory responsibility of an employer towards a complainant, whether the employer is aware of either the statutory responsibility or the acts that gave rise to a claim coming forward.

There has been considerable judicial consideration of the "control test" within the context of determining whether an employer-employee relationship exists or whether a contract for services exists. The distinction in terms of the vicarious liability provisions of discrimination law is irrelevant as the statutory formula covers the acts of employees and of agents.

Section 106(1) of the *Sex Discrimination Act* provides that, subject to the exception where an employee or agent of a person does, in connection with the employment of the employee or with the duties of the agent as an agent, an act that would, if it were done by the person, be unlawful discrimination or harassment, then this Act applies in relation to that person as if that person had also done the act.

The critical words are "in connection with" and these have been construed broadly. In *South Pacific Resort Hotels Pty Ltd v Trainor* (2005) 144 FCR 402 at [42], the Full Federal Court stated:

> We add that the expression chosen by parliament to impose vicarious liability for sexual harassment would seem, on its face, to be somewhat wider than the familiar expression 'in the course of' used with reference to employment in cases about vicarious liability at common law or in the distinctive context of worker's compensation statutes.

A body must be incorporated and have some form of legal status before an order can be made against it: *Jones v Bible Believers' Church* [2007] FCA 55 at [65].

All discrimination laws have a similar provision.

The State discrimination laws cover the Commonwealth and its agents in relation to any acts of discrimination or harassment performed by them in breach of that State law: *Commonwealth v Wood* (2006) 148 FCR 276.

Development of case law

A number of cases have looked at this important issue, often within the context of an employment complaint. Obviously, if an employer wants some consideration of any points about the avoidance of vicarious liability, then the employer must raise them during the proceedings. A failure to do so will give rise to a rebuttable presumption that the employer is liable.

Usually it is in the complainant's interests to pursue their complaint against the employer instead of, or as well as, an individual employee as the employer is more likely to have funds available to meet any damages award made. It is not necessary to have the individual employee joined as a party to establish liability against an employer. Once a prima facie case is established against an employee, then the employer is deemed to be liable for those acts of the employee: *Ingram-Nader v Brinks Australia Pty Ltd* (2006) 151 FCR 524.

It is necessary to establish the element of employer-employee or principal-agent in the relationship before consideration of any other issue needs to occur. Thus it has been found that a police officer is an "employee" of the Commissioner of Police for the purposes of establishing vicarious liability under the New South Wales *Anti-Discrimination Act*: *Commissioner of Police v Estate of Russell* (2002) 55 NSWLR 232. Likewise, the Commonwealth has been held to be the employer of

Australian Federal Police members and can therefore be vicariously liable for victimisation claims: *Taylor v Morrison* [2003] FMCA 79.

Also, the employer may be subject to other orders such as not repeating or continuing the act of discrimination or putting in place some measures which respond to the issues in the complaint. The responsibility for employers when their employees act contrary to specific directions and policies will be determined on the facts of the policies themselves, and the efforts made by employers to fully and properly inform their employees of the policies and the ramifications of them on their terms and conditions of employment.

The mere existence of policies is insufficient to avoid liability. A failure by an employer to make sure that the policies are communicated in an effective manner to employees may mean that they are liable for acts of discrimination and harassment by their employees against a co-worker. Employers also have a responsibility if there were no women in a particular workplace to set in place certain training and staff development before the first women started working. Failure to do so, accompanied by acts of unlawful discrimination or harassment by any employees, may mean that the employer is liable for any damage suffered by a complainant.

Failure to take a complaint seriously and cause it to be properly investigated may be the basis for a finding of liability against the employer: *NSW Breeding and Racing Stables Pty Ltd v V and X* [2005] NSWCA 114 at [33] (application for special leave refused).

The duties performed by the employee and the actions forming the basis of the complaint may be matters which need to be examined in evidence. The treasurer and a director of a company is acting with implied, usual and ostensible authority if he speaks to the company administrator about financial matters and attends company meetings. When acts of sexual harassment occurred while he was performing his duties as a treasurer, then he was acting as an agent of the company and the company will be liable for the sexual harassment also: *Brown v Moore* (1996) 68 IR 176. Therefore, where a director and major shareholder of a company to whom the complainant had complained of an employee's conduct towards her did nothing pursuant to the complaint, the director was found to be vicariously liable for the sexual harassment of the complainant.

Two situations commonly arise in employment complaints. One is where the employer has a small number of employees and the person alleged to have committed the act of discrimination or harassment is the main director or plays a significant role in the management of the company. These complaints often arise in a workplace only attended by the complainant and the respondent or, on some occasions, by the respondent's wife or other family member. This means that not only are there no policies which could protect the employee from the behaviour but also there are no witnesses for either side to call upon as all the transactions the subject of complaint have only the protagonists as witnesses.

The company may be incorporated but for all legal and factual purposes may be run by one person only, as their "alter ago", and hence it should properly be liable for the acts of sexual harassment of that person: *Cross v Hughes* (2006) 233 ALR 108 at 112 [26].

The second scenario arises with large government or private sector employers, where there are policies and significant efforts to promote them and inform all employees of their operation. The allegations of sexual harassment may differ in response to those of sex discrimination as the former are acts of aberrant individual behaviour which need to be resolved appropriately at an institutional level, while the latter may constitute a broader attack on general employment practices within the organisation.

Acts done by an employee out of business hours can give rise to vicarious liability for an employer when they are sufficiently connected to the employment relationship, such as being on a continuum of sexual harassment commenced within the workplace and where the invitation to the social event arose entirely within the context of the workplace and work colleagues: *Lee v Smith* [2007] FMCA 59 at [203].

Drinks at lunchtime with a work colleague can give rise to liability for an employer where there is a potential for the response to any act of sexual harassment to adversely flow back into the workplace: *Smith v Christchurch Press Company Ltd* [2001] 1 NZLR 407.

Obviously, the issues of vicarious liability and the method of establishing it from the complainant's perspective and the avoidance of it from the respondent's position, will require different approaches, but the same issues need to be presented in evidence. The presence or absence of a policy, the methods of communicating it, the knowledge of relevant individuals and the status and focus within the organisation, will all be essential factors to be taken into account by the decision-maker.

The applicability of federal legislation to State entities varies between the Acts themselves and the areas of discrimination or harassment. In some instances, reliance on the vicarious liability provisions will not be available to a complainant and then the individual respondents will need to be identified and joined as individual parties to obviate the difficulty of not being able to proceed. In such circumstances, the option of proceeding under State laws themselves should be actively considered by a potential complainant.

It is doubtful that as a general principle the lack of knowledge about the legal and corporate structure of a respondent would of itself be sufficient to defeat a claim of vicarious liability. Such knowledge would often be beyond the capacity of the complainant before lodging her complaint and could not reasonably be interpreted as being fatal to a claim. Courts and tribunals have shown a flexible approach to the joining of other persons or organisations as respondents when the complainant nominates insufficient or incorrect persons.

There may be some occasions where it is appropriate to lift the corporate veil and ascertain the "real" employer of a complainant or for some other reason. On other occasions, liability may be found against an individual respondent and establishing liability against the corporation may not be necessary, particularly if it is solely owned and conducted by the individuals who are found to have committed the acts of discrimination or harassment.

Exception – reasonable steps

There is a general exception in all discrimination laws that provides a way to avoid liability for employers who have taken reasonable steps to ensure that the discrimination or harassment does not occur.

Section 106 of the *Sex Discrimination Act* provides that the liability does not apply if it is established that the person took all reasonable steps to prevent the employee or agent from doing acts of discrimination or harassment.

Under s 106(1) the complainant bears the onus of proof in establishing that there is a relationship of employment or agency. However, once the complainant has satisfied s 106(1) on the balance of probabilities, the onus then shifts to the employer or principal to establish that it took all reasonable steps to prevent the alleged acts taking place pursuant to s 106(2).

A person claiming the advantage of this exception would need to lead evidence to demonstrate that these steps were taken and that they were reasonable. This may involve identifying the appropriate standard applicable and any peculiarities of the industry or the occupation involved. For example, if an employer had followed the Sex Discrimination Commissioner's publication, *Sexual Harassment in the Workplace: A Code of Practice for Employers* (HR&EOC, 2004), particularly the preventative and remedial measures, then it could be anticipated that absent any blatant defects in their approach, they would have a reasonable chance of convincing a court or tribunal that they had successfully discharged their duty towards the complainant.

There are no precise guidelines which offer any solace or a certain avenue to an employer seeking to avoid liability through the operation of this exception.

The defence has been rejected where there was no evidence led about any steps taken to prevent a sexual harasser acting in the way he did: *Brown v Moore* (1996) 68 IR 176. There was no published sexual harassment policy and no communication of any policy to employees to establish a basis for the defence.

The defence will also not be available merely when the employer has no knowledge that any unlawful behaviour has occurred or is threatened.

While s 106 of the *Sex Discrimination Act* does not distinguish between large and small employers, there is nevertheless a relationship between the size of the employer and the defence under s 106. It has been held that the size of an employer is relevant to the question of whether the steps taken by the employer to prevent the acts in question were reasonable. Thus, as was stated in *Johanson v Blackledge Meats* [2001] FMCA 6 at [101], "large corporations will be expected to do more than small businesses in order to be held to have acted reasonably". This view is consistent with earlier authority (*Evans v Lee & Commonwealth Bank* (1996) EOC ¶92-822) and was endorsed in *McAlister v SEQ Aboriginal Corporation & Lamb* [2002] FMCA 109 at [10].

What is reasonable with respect to a particular employer will of course be different according to the circumstances of each employer and many factors will be examined by a court or tribunal in determining whether or not all reasonable steps were taken by the employer.

Aiding or permitting

Another person can be liable for an act of unlawful discrimination if they insert themselves in the process in any way.

Section 105 of the *Sex Discrimination Act* provides that any person who causes, instructs, induces, aids or permits another person to do an unlawful act of discrimination shall be taken to have done the act. Curiously, the section does not cover sexual harassment.

There is a similar general provision in all other discrimination laws except the *Racial Discrimination Act* 1975.

The impact of this provision arises when the acts of identified individuals are behind or shadow the act of discrimination found against the employer. The words themselves may present difficulties to a complainant in those circumstances. Where other employees are responsible for the various acts, the mechanism of the aiding and permitting section may not be of any significant advantage to the complainant.

Issues have arisen as to the meaning of the word "permit", that is, does it require knowledge on the part of the permitter. In *Cooper v*

HR&EOC (1999) 93 FCR 481, Madgwick J considered the equivalent provision in the *Disability Discrimination Act* and held that it was not essential to the concept of permission that the permitter needed to know or believe that there was no unjustifiable hardship in order to establish liability.

In *Elliott v Nanda* (2001) 111 FCR 240, the issue was whether the Commonwealth Employment Service has permitted acts of discrimination on the grounds of sex involving sexual harassment. The complainant obtained employment as a receptionist with a doctor through the CES. There was evidence that the CES knew that some young women placed with the doctor had complained of behaviour amounting to sexual harassment. Moore J stated that *Cooper* had held that the notion of "permit" should not be narrowly interpreted and that a person can "permit" for the purpose of s 105 of the *Sex Discrimination Act* if, before the unlawful act occurs, the permitter knowingly places the victim of the conduct in a position where (at 293) "there is a real, and something more than a remote, possibility that the unlawful conduct will occur". His Honour went on to state that "this is certainly so in circumstances where the permitter can require the person to put in place measures designed to influence, if not control, the person's conduct or the conduct of the person's employees". It was held that CES had permitted the discrimination to take place. The fact that the particular caseworker who facilitated the employment in the particular case of the complainant was unaware of the problem, did not matter. The collective knowledge of the officers of the CES was sufficient to found liability on the part of the organisation.

Overall, limited use has been made of this provision by itself and this may be because of the potential difficulties in establishing a positive causal link between the person doing the act and the person to whom the responsibility is directed through the aiding and permitting provision. The broader coverage of the vicarious liability provisions make that an easier route to follow for a complainant seeking to extend the range of persons or organisations against whom they seek recovery.

Finding sufficient evidence to support an assertion that another person actually instructed or induced a person to act in a discriminatory manner may be difficult. If there are written memos or directives by a senior employee to a more junior employee sending them down a path that may later be demonstrated to be discriminatory, a complainant may well prefer just to pursue a remedy against the employer rather than the individuals who made or implemented the decisions which form the basis of the discriminatory act.

Acts done on behalf of others

Responsibility for the acts of others arises where a person may be required to take over the liability for those acts as well. This can lead to some dispute about the level of authority and the degree of independence and effect of this on the arrangements between them.

Earlier disputes on this basis have resulted in specific statutory provisions which remove any basis for technical disputes. For example, s 107 of the *Sex Discrimination Act* provides that where it is necessary to establish that a body corporate did an act, it is sufficient to establish that a person who acted on behalf of the body corporate in the matter so acted on that ground.

Provisions such as this are unremarkable and are in line with the usual rules of implied and ostensible authority which operate in corporations law.

Government employers

There have been attempts to avoid liability by the raising of technical defences by government departments on the naming of the proper respondent. This has led to disputes about the identification and hence titling of the correct respondent to take responsibility for the proper conduct of the matter. In some cases, this has led to the organisation making the decision being challenged, also raising the competence of the case brought against them, on this technical ground.

Section 108 of the *Sex Discrimination Act* circumvents this potential problem by deeming the Commonwealth Government to be the employer of all Commonwealth employees.

Defences

Respondents are provided with certain specific defences which they can plead to a complaint of unlawful discrimination. A respondent who wants to pursue a certain line of defence carries the onus of proof to establish the factual and legal basis of the defence and to demonstrate that the conduct is, in fact, exempt from the legislation.

A specific statutory defence is of a different complexion to responding to a complaint by denying the events alleged occurred at all or occurred in the context in which the complainant alleges. While strictly not required to respond at all, as the complainant bears the onus of proof, a respondent usually defends the decisions or actions which are the subject of the challenge.

A further step in this process can be invoking one of the available defences, such as establishing the operation of one of the exemptions such as unjustifiable hardship in a disability complaint (see Chapter 11).

Statutory defences

The reliance on exemptions and exceptions is based on the provisions of the statutory scheme which recognise that, in certain situations, a balancing of competing rights and interests may need to occur, and the outcome of an act of discrimination may be avoided through this mechanism.

Both Federal and State laws have various formula which more directly place the onus of proving exemptions or exceptions on the respondent who claims it. However, there is no effect in real terms of such provisions as the respondent carries in any event the responsibility to put before the court or tribunal any evidence which they consider will assist them to avoid liability.

Technical defences

In a practical sense, when preparing and conducting proceedings, a respondent which has denied the alleged acts needs to adduce any evidence in support of this position. To merely wait for a complainant to fail to meet their onus of proof can be a tricky and unreliable process as some merit in the complainant's arguments, not immediately apparent to the respondent, may be identified by the court or tribunal.

Technical defences can be mounted to demonstrate that the respondent was not the employer at the relevant time or that the person alleged to have committed the discriminatory act had no legal relationship with the respondent.

Jurisdictional defences

On some occasions, when examining a complaint, it may be apparent that even if the complaint was made out, there would be no breach of the discrimination legislation as the act is not covered. The ground of discrimination as alleged may not exist, for example, with a disability complaint or the act may not fall within the area set out (see Chapter 2). This can occur as the legislation is aimed at areas of public life only. Some of the definitions of terms such as "club" or "services" may mean that a respondent seeks to challenge the potential coverage of the legislation.

In most jurisdictions, where there is a jurisdictional point or a technical point which if resolved in the manner put forward by the respondent would end the litigation, this is heard and determined initially: *Neate v Totally and Permanently Incapacitated Veterans' Association of New South Wales* [2007] FMCA 488. This will only occur where there appears to be some validity to the point being taken and it is not perceived merely as a ruse to avoid the process. If the respondent is successful, this is the end of the matter and there can be significant time and cost benefits to both sides and the body hearing the case. If the respondent is unsuccessful, then the matter can proceed to a full hearing on all the facts.

Evidence

For a respondent to successfully conduct a defence, they need to adduce all the necessary evidence in support of the contention they seek to advance (see Chapter 13).

In an unjustifiable hardship defence relying on a costs argument, it would be necessary to provide detailed financial and related material for objective assessment by the court or tribunal of fact. If the evidence is commercial in confidence, the respondent can seek a suppression order on the evidence so it is not available for scrutiny during the proceedings, in media reports or in the final decision: *Scott v Telstra Corporation Ltd* (1995) EOC ¶92-717, *Moxon (No 2) v Westbus Pty Ltd* (2002) EOC ¶93-248.

When developing a cost-benefit analysis before a court or tribunal, no steps should be assumed to be understood, especially if they involve some peculiarity arising from the nature of the business or the occupation involved. Some relevant factors which may arise for one type of work and workforce may not be relevant for another. General assumptions and assertions should be avoided and reliance on evidence in the usual legal sense is the preferred path to pursue to successfully mount a defence.

11

GENERAL EXEMPTIONS

There are two categories of exemptions. One is positive and is designed to assist in the promotion and protection of equal opportunity and affirmative action measures. The second category is to provide some limited avenues to avoid the impact of discrimination laws. These latter exemptions have provided little comfort to those who seek to avoid the legislation, with only minor anomalies arising.

As the use of a general exemption would be done by a respondent in the form of a defence, all laws require that the respondent carries the onus of proof in order to come within the terms: *Nadjovska v Australian Iron and Steel Pty Ltd* (1985) EOC ¶92-140 (see Chapter 10).

The exemptions which operate at a Federal level and the main ones operating at a State level are discussed in this chapter. All the State laws have particular exemptions, often arising out of special issues of concern in that State, and having no general application so they are not discussed in this chapter.

Where there is an overlap between two exemptions, or a general exemption and an exception applying in one area only, it has been held that one exemption should not be read down as a method of construction to bring it in line with an apparently narrower exemption: *Commonwealth v HR&EOC (X's case)* (1998) 76 FCR 513 (affirmed by the High Court in *X v Commonwealth* (1999) 200 CLR 177). Burchett J quoted with approval Lord Herschell in *Inland Revenue Commissioners v Scott* [1892] 2 QB 152 at 156: "[L]ittle weight is to be attached to the mere fact that specific exemptions are found which could be covered by the wider general word". After referring with approval to other authorities, he held that "arguments from redundancy and tautology provided 'rather slight grounds' for departing from the construction a legislative provision would otherwise have received".

Therefore, each exception or exemption should be construed on their own basis only and no referential or inferential points should be read in just because another exception or exemption in the same legislation would appear to assist in leading to a certain conclusion.

This chapter is divided into four parts: positive measures, the main exemptions, the minor exemptions and procedural exemptions.

Positive measures

Protecting "special measures"

In the first category of exemptions are those which are designed to cover "special measures": *Racial Discrimination Act* 1975 s 8(1). This term is based on the international conventions which form the constitutional basis for the Commonwealth discrimination laws.

After considering the terms of the *International Convention on the Elimination of All Forms of Racial Discrimination*, Brennan J set out the criteria for a "special measure":

> The occasion for taking a special measure is that the circumstances warrant the taking of the measure to guarantee that the members of the benefited class shall have "the full and equal enjoyment of human rights and fundamental freedoms". A special measure (1) confers a benefit on some or all members of a class, (2) the membership of which is based on race, colour, descent, or national or ethnic origin, (3) for the sole purpose of securing adequate advancement of the beneficiaries in order that they may enjoy and exercise equally with others human rights and fundamental freedoms, (4) in circumstances where the protection given to the beneficiaries by the special measure is necessary in order that they may enjoy and exercise equally with others human rights and fundamental freedoms. (*Gerhardy v Brown* (1985) 159 CLR 70 at 133)

It appears that his Honour's second proposition is a statement embracing a wider exception than that actually covered in the Act. There is no apparent basis for the extension of that part of the exemption to more general areas. Section 8(1) specifically refers to Article 1.4 of the *International Convention on the Elimination of All Forms of Racial Discrimination*. In turn, Article 1.4 applies only to "racial or ethnic groups". The distinction between the various terms is clear on the face of Article 1.1, where the definition of "racial discrimination" covers the different descriptors and the term "national origin" is a separate criteria from either "race" or "ethnic origin".

The taking of special measures is not an unlawful act of discrimination. This exception is designed to promote actions to further implement the spirit and intention of discrimination legislation by preventing a person who is not in the minority group for whom the program or policy is designed, from complaining they have no access to a program or policy and that this is unlawful discrimination. Therefore, in *Bruch v Commonwealth* [2002] FMCA 29, it was held that the Commonwealth had not discriminated against a non-Indigenous Australian student by refusing to award him ABSTUDY because the ABSTUDY scheme constituted a "special measure" for the benefit of Indigenous people within the meaning of s 8(1) of the *Racial Discrimination Act*.

Section 7D of the *Sex Discrimination Act* 1984 provides that a person may take special measures for the purpose of achieving substantial equality between:

(a)   men and women; and

(b)   people of different marital status; or

(c)   women who are pregnant and people who are not pregnant; or

(d)   women who are potentially pregnant and people who are not potentially pregnant.

This section was inserted in 1995 and replaced an earlier, narrower version with the same intention.

The Federal Court found that the rule of a trade union that reserved a certain number of spaces on the union's board of management was a "special measure" under s 7D:

> The phrase "special measures", and the provision that a "special measure" is not discriminatory (s 7D(2)), cannot be understood without recognising that the SDA is implementing the express wording of the convention in this regard or without recognising the context, object and purpose of the convention. "Special measure", as a phrase construed according to its plain or ordinary meaning means a measure which is exceptional, out of the ordinary or unusual. Where the word "special" qualifies laws, as in the races power, s 51(xxvi) of the Constitution, it denotes laws which are special to, or for, a particular group, or special because they address special needs: *Koowarta* at CLR 210 ... per Stephen J. Equally, laws may be special because they operate differentially: see *Western Australia v Commonwealth* at CLR 461. per Mason CJ and Brennan, Deane, Toohey, Gaudron and McHugh JJ:
>
>> A special quality appears when the law confers a right or benefit or imposes an obligation or disadvantage especially on the people of a particular race. The law may be special even when it confers a benefit generally, provided the benefit is of particular significance or importance to the people of a particular race ...

A "special measure" as referred to in s 7D, and as construed by reference not only to the ordinary meaning of words repeated from the convention, but also by reference to the context, object and purpose of the convention is one which has as at least one of its purposes, achieving genuine equality between men and women. The phrase "special measure" is wide enough to include, what is known as, affirmative action. A special measure may on the face of it be discriminatory but to the extent that it has, as one of its purposes, overcoming discrimination, it is to be characterised as non-discriminatory. Without reference to the legislative history and the convention, it would not necessarily be easy to appreciate the characterisation of a "special measure" as non-discriminatory when s 19 contains explicit prohibitions against discrimination in the workplace. (*Jacomb v Australian Municipal Administrative Clerical and Services Union* (2004) 140 FCR 149 at [42]-[44])

Section 45 of the *Disability Discrimination Act* contains a more detailed exception provision when it provides that it is not unlawful discrimination or harassment to do an act that is reasonably intended to:

(a)　ensure that persons who have a disability have equal opportunities with other persons in circumstances provided for by the Act; or

(b)　afford persons who have a disability or a particular disability, goods or access to facilities, services or opportunities to meet their special needs in relation to:

(i)　employment, education, accommodation, clubs or sport; or

(ii)　the provision of goods, services, facilities or land; or

(iii)　the making available of facilities; or

(iv)　the administration of Commonwealth laws and programs; or

(v)　their capacity to live independently; or

(c)　afford persons who have a disability or a particular disability, grants, benefits or programs, whether direct or indirect, to meet their special needs in relation to:

(i)　employment, education, accommodation, clubs or sport; or

(ii)　the provision of goods, services, facilities or land; or

(iii)　the making available of facilities; or

(iv)　the administration of Commonwealth laws and programs; or

(v)　their capacity to live independently.

This style of extensive exemption recognises the particular issues which arise in relation to people with a disability and this is consolidated in the form of the last, general exemption relating to a capacity of the person to live independently. The test of "reasonableness" is an objective one to assess whether any of the objectives are reached: *Catholic Education Office v Clarke* (2004) 138 FCR 121 at [129]-[132].

Where special housing for disabled persons is provided by the government housing agency, then it may be exempt through the operation of s 45:

> The respondent submits that Richardson's case supports the respondent's submission that if the respondent intended to provide services to the applicant to achieve as far as possible equality for him, and if the respondent's conduct was capable of meeting his special needs, then s 45 of the Disability Discrimination Act exempts that conduct from what may or may not have been unlawful discrimination (there being a denial that in any event the respondent has discriminated against the applicant and I finding that the respondent has not). I accept that submission and rely upon the affidavit of Mary Reid and the exhibits thereto which establish that the intention of the respondent in providing services to the applicant was to meet his social needs and the respondent's conduct was both capable of meeting those needs and in fact did meet those needs.
>
> The applicant complains that the services provided by the respondent do not meet his needs and expectations. That is not the point when considering s 45. The course of conduct by the respondent as evidenced by the affidavit of Mary Reid is consistent only with a non-colourable intention by the respondent to afford the applicant access to facilities and services to meet his special needs in relation to accommodation, the provision of goods, services, facilities and land and to enhance his capacity to live independently ... [I]f a genuine and non-colourable intention can be discerned from the actions of the service provider in the position of the respondent, then it is not the point that the services so provided do not meet the expectations of the person to whom those services are provided, or are in fact, discriminatory and otherwise unlawful under the Act. (*Soreng v Victorian State Director of Public Housing* [2002] FMCA 124 at [25]-[26])

The State laws have similar exemptions: see, generally, *Colyer v Victoria* [1998] 3 VR 759. The Full Federal Court has observed in relation to the *Discrimination Act 1991* (ACT):

> To determine whether discriminatory conduct is rendered lawful by the application of s 27 [of the ACT Act] the act of discrimination must be for a permitted purpose. That is, the conduct which s 27 protects is not discrimination that has the effect of achieving equality, but discrimination which is intended to have that effect. The word "purpose" refers to the actual intention of the decision-maker or actor. The decision-

maker's intention is a matter to be established by reference to the facts, including reference to the circumstances from which inferences may be drawn as to the state of mind of the decision-maker ... To determine whether the decision-maker holds the requisite state of mind, it will be permissible to enquire whether the conduct in question was capable of achieving equal opportunity (s 27(a)) or meeting special needs (s 27(b)). That enquiry may be necessary for the purpose of establishing that the claimed intention is one that is likely to have been held by the decision-maker. It is not, however, to substitute for an enquiry into the subjective state of mind of the decision-maker an objective criterion. It is merely one of the means by which a claimed subjective intention can be established, in cases where there may be doubt. (*Richardson v ACT Health & Community Care Service* (2000) 100 FCR 1 at 5)

Pregnancy or childbirth

The exemption for pregnancy and childbirth in s 31 of the *Sex Discrimination Act* is a narrow exemption relating to the immediate period connected with the birth and is intended to provide an exemption for maternity leave and any related matters "in connection with" pregnancy or childbirth. There are similar exemptions in the State laws.

Services for members of one sex

In s 32 of the *Sex Discrimination Act,* where services are provided to one sex and are of such a nature that they cannot be provided to members of the other sex, then there is no act of unlawful discrimination on the ground of sex. In *Proudfoot v ACT Board of Health* (1992) EOC ¶92-417, a women's health centre was found to come within this exemption.

Main exceptions

Unjustifiable hardship

There is a broad exemption in the *Disability Discrimination Act* for "unjustifiable hardship". This exemption applies to many of the areas of unlawful disability discrimination covered by the Act but not to all parts of the process. For example, in the area of education, the unjustifiable hardship defence can arise when assessing the admission of a person with a disability as a student to an education institution. Once the person is admitted as a student, the exemption does not apply.

Section 11 of the *Disability Discrimination Act* provides that, in determining what constitutes unjustifiable hardship, all relevant circumstances of the particular case are to be taken into account including:

    (a)   the nature of the benefit or detriment likely to accrue or be suffered by any persons concerned; and

    (b)   the effect of the disability on a person concerned; and

    (c)   the financial circumstances and the estimated amount of expenditure required to be made by the person claiming unjustifiable hardship; and

    (d)   in the case of the provision of services, or the making available of facilities – an action plan given to the Commission under s 64.

The section provides the framework for a balancing act of potentially competing interests to be undertaken. Structured essentially on a cost-benefit analysis, an assessment of the potential coverage of the section and the area of unlawful discrimination needs to be able to isolate the various factors that will form the basis of the vying interests. Often, these factors will vary depending on the area within which the complaint arises.

There has been some examination of the exemption, commonly within the context of complaints about denial of goods and services. In a leading case on the use of the exemption, Telstra unsuccessfully submitted that providing a certain handset to all people with profound hearing loss would be an unjustifiable hardship: *Scott v Telstra Corporation Ltd* (1995) EOC ¶92-717.

The general approach of the service provider and their actions in complying with the *Disability Discrimination Act* were factors taken into account as well as their lack of attention to details which may have assisted in formulating a policy, but which appeared to have received no attention from Telstra.

In an employment complaint, the assessment will vary depending on the size and financial resources of the employer as the agency claiming recourse to the unjustifiable hardship exemption. For example, a national employer such as a bank or a store would be assessed from a different basis than an employer with three staff and one rented work site.

The requirements for a person with a disability will vary depending on the disability and the effect the disability has on the person. A visually impaired person may require extra equipment such as a magnifier or tape and computer equipment to assist them to perform their job duties and these may cost between $5000 and $10,000. A person using a wheelchair may require access to the premises or a part of the premises to be altered and these could cost many thousands of dollars. One factor could be that altering the access to premises could affect many people, not only wheelchair users but also others with mobility restrictions, people with prams and anyone who finds stairs difficult to use.

The current interpretation of s 11 was summarised by the Federal Court as:

> A number of general principles have developed in relation to the concept of "unjustifiable hardship" within the terms of the DD Act. These principles include the following:
> - the issue whether the alleged discriminator is potentially subject to unjustifiable hardship arises only once the applicant establishes that the alleged discriminator has engaged in unlawful conduct: *Cooper* at FCR 491-2, *Sluggett* at FCR 568, *Daghlian* at [113]-[114];
> - the respondent bears the onus of showing unjustifiable hardship within the meaning of s 24(2): *Cooper* at FCR 492, *Sluggett* at FCR 568;
> - the concept of "unjustifiable" hardship suggests that some hardship is justifiable, and requires a consideration of whether the hardship is of such a nature or degree as to be unjustifiable following a weighing of relevant factors: *Hills Grammar School v Human Rights and Equal Opportunity Commission* (2000) 100 FCR 306 at [48]. (*Forest v Queensland Health* (2007) 161 FCR 152 at [157])

The possibility of any disability complaint arising in relation to the provision of transport services continues while there are any inaccessible services or facilities. However, the availability of a defence of unjustifiable hardship may be open to the service provider, depending on the facts. Factors such as the cost to the service provider of making the requested alterations and alternate means of travel will be factors to be considered under the general principle of "fairness" and striking the balance between the competing interests. Given the significant costs of altering existing structures, planning ahead and incorporating accessible facilities wherever possible will mean that eventually the public transport systems will become accessible to all travellers with mobility difficulties. The 20-year phase-in period permitted under the terms of the *Disability Standards for Accessible Public Transport 2002* will have a major impact on the assessment of the defence of unjustifiable hardship for those organisations covered by the extensive obligations imposed.

In the provision of education to students with a disability, issues such as the costs and level of resources needed for integration, the effect on other students of disruptive behaviour and demands on the classroom teacher arising from the student's behavioural problems may be relevant (see Chapter 5). The operation of the *Disability Standards in Education 2005* will be relevant also (see below).

There are some substantive sections of the *Disability Discrimination Act* which do not contain the unjustifiable hardship defence making it not available. A broad reading of the goods and services provisions, where the defence is available, has been held not to be open when the subject of the complaint is a club covered specifically by the clubs and associations provisions and which has no equivalent exception: *Rana v HR&EOC and Nepal Friendship Association* (1997) 74 FCR 451.

If a respondent to a complaint can demonstrate that they have instituted an action plan, then they will be able to show that they have planned to incorporate the principles of the disability discrimination legislation into their overall operation. Such evidence will assist them in meeting the requirements of the unjustifiable hardship defence.

Actions plans are made pursuant to the terms of s 61 of the *Disability Discrimination Act* and are given to HR&EOC. They can cover a wide range of plans, including long-term plans to make buildings or parts of building accessible to changing the nature of service delivery to ensure it meets the needs of people with a disability.

A number of different action plans have been lodged with the Commission from tertiary education institutions, State, Federal and local government agencies and businesses. Copies of these action plans can be purchased from the Commission.

The future use of the defence of unjustifiable hardship is difficult to predict with any precision but it can be anticipated that the evidence adduced by a respondent will become more detailed and extensive, depending on the nature of the complaint and the defence, than it has been so far.

Acts done under statutory authority

There are two types of exemptions in relation to other legislation. The main one is where an act which would otherwise be unlawful is exempt as it is done in direct compliance or in compliance with other legislation. The second exemption is for decisions of other courts and tribunals.

Direct compliance with other legislation

All discrimination laws recognise the general principle that there is some legislation which may conflict with the content of the discrimination laws and which cannot be amended, as other problems will arise and they will not be able to be readily overcome.

Current coverage

Section 40(2) of the *Sex Discrimination Act* exempts certain marital relationships and their connection to the payment of pensions and benefits to certain categories of people. It also exempts marital status preference in income tax arrangements and sales tax and gift duty benefits. The exemption is for anything done in "direct compliance" with the other law.

The *Disability Discrimination Act* has taken a slightly different approach and provided in s 47 an exemption for anything done in direct compliance with another Federal, State or Territory law for three years, that is, until 1 March 1996. After that, any exemption must be by a pre-scribed law. Regulation 2A of the *Disability Discrimination Regulations* 1996 was amended in 1999 to prescribe some sections from three laws from NSW and five from South Australia.

Section 39 of the *Age Discrimination Act* provides a scheme for exemptions and Schedules 1 and 2 set out the detailed provisions of Federal and State legislation which are excluded from the operation of that Act.

The South Australian Act does not contain any general exemption for Acts and regulations. All others Acts have broad exemptions.

The New South Wales Act has a broad exemption for all statutory instruments and anything done by a person "if it was necessary for the person to do it in order to comply with a requirement" of the Act or regu-lation. The Victorian Act has a similar exemption and also exempts any discrimination if it "is authorised" by the legislation: *Waters v Public Transport Commission* (1991) 173 CLR 349. The Queensland Act contains a broad exemption for an act that is "necessary to comply with, or is specifically authorised by an existing provision of another Act", that is, one in existence as at 30 June 1992. The Tasmanian and the Australian Capital Territory Acts use a similar formula for the opening words but have no date limitation for the State or Territory and Federal laws they exempt.

The Western Australian Act exempts Acts and most instruments ex-cept a limited number relating to financial institutions which were in force on 8 July 1985 and where "it was necessary for the person to do in order to comply with a requirement of" it. The Northern Territory Act uses in its opening words "for the purpose of complying with" a law of the Territory.

Development of case law

There has been some significant judicial and tribunal consideration of the impact of this exemption and the most significant cases are referred to below.

The High Court in *Waters v Public Transport Commission* (1991) 173 CLR 349 considered the operation of the exemption in the Victorian Act and gave it a narrow interpretation. The Minister for Transport made a direction under the *Transport Act* 1983 (Vic) but as there was a discretion in the making of the direction, it was held that it did not come within the exemption as it was not done to comply with the other Act. The other Act did not require the Corporation to do any specific thing. Mason CJ and Gaudron J, with Deane J in agreement, held in relation to the phrase "in order to comply with" the legislative "provision":

> If the relevant words fell to be construed in isolation, we would favour the wide construction of them. When [the phrase] is construed in its context in the Act, however, it appears to us that the narrow construction is the preferable one ... More importantly, wide construction seems to us to be inconsistent with the general scheme of the [discrimination] Act. It is one thing to provide that the Act should give way to an express direction contained in an actual provision of another Act or in a statutory instrument. It is a quite different thing to provide, in effect, that the Act shall give way to any subordinate direction, no matter how informal, to which a provision of any other Act requires obedience. (at 368-9)

This line of reasoning accords with an earlier decision of the then Human Rights Commission which found that a notice prohibiting women kick boxers from performing publicly gazetted pursuant to a New South Wales Act was not exempt under the then s 40 of the *Sex Discrimination Act*. The Attorney-General was not required to gazette the notice excluding women and there was no specific legislative direction with which he needed to comply. There was therefore an act of sex discrimination against women kick boxers: *Gulliver v Council of City of Sydney* (1987) EOC ¶92-185; see also *Clinch v Commissioner of Police* (1984) EOC ¶92-115.

HR&EOC has held that the term "direct compliance":

> [I]s to be distinguished from, for example, mere "compliance", but it is a term which is less strong than say "strict compliance". If, for example, the term "strict compliance" had been used, then that may well have meant that only clauses which were mandatory in their expression and prescribed specific steps or actions would be covered. But "direct" compliance would appear to go to a broader class of provisions and would, in my view, cover action made necessary by reasonably-specific clauses as distinct possibly from ones that were very generally expressed. (*Gibbs v Commonwealth Bank of Australia* (1997) EOC ¶92-977 at 77,140)

The Federal Magistrates Court rejected an attempt by an employer to rely on the terms of an industrial agreement to justify its treatment of a pregnant flight attendant. This claim failed as the industrial agreement only dictated when a pregnant flight attendant should stop flying and not the way that Qantas dealt with her once she was no longer flying. The employer's conduct was not in "direct compliance" with the agreement: *Howe v Qantas Airways Ltd* (2004) 188 FLR 1.

The exemption in the *Sex Discrimination Act* applies to all the provisions in the *Social Security Act* 1947 (Cth) and so a complaint made about the terms of eligibility for rent assistance payable under that Act falls outside the ambit of complaints that may be investigated by the HR&EOC: *Keller v Tay* [2004] FMCA 182.

The cases under State legislation concerning the intersection of the disability provisions and the occupational health and safety laws do not arise under the Federal legislation as there is no exception for the latter legislation.

Orders of courts and tribunals

In order to ensure that there is no confusion or overlap within or through different jurisdictions, there is a general exemption in all discrimination laws except South Australia for the orders of courts and tribunals. These commonly include industrial relations commissions and courts.

Industrial awards

There is an exemption in some of the laws for industrial awards or related instruments.

The *Sex Discrimination Act*, the *Disability Discrimination Act* and the *Age Discrimination Act* exempt certified agreements made pursuant to the *Workplace Relations Act* 1996 (Cth). The *Disability Discrimination Act* also exempts particular Australian workplace agreements which make specific provision for people with a disability in receipt of wages or salaries, where the rate set is determined by the capacity of the person. This exemption permits the continuation of productivity based wages for a small proportion of people with a disability who have been through specially established processes and receive a proportionate wage based on their capacity to perform the job duties.

In *Mackie v Tay* (2001) 116 FCR 209, the Federal Court dismissed an application from a complainant who alleged unlawful discrimination by a psychologist who was appointed by the Family Court to prepare a family assessment report. The court held that s 40(1) of the *Sex Discrimination Act* had the effect that anything done by a person in direct compliance with a court order was not unlawful and because the psychologist was acting in direct compliance with an order from the Family Court, in interviewing the applicant and expressing his opinion in the report, his conduct did not amount to unlawful discrimination.

For a discussion of the broader relationship and the connections between discrimination laws and industrial relations laws, see Chapter 15.

Superannuation

The coverage of superannuation is discussed in Chapter 8.

There is a complex exemption for superannuation from the *Sex Discrimination Act*, the *Disability Discrimination Act* and the *Age Discrimination Act*. The exemption applies in different terms to new and existing superannuation fund conditions. Essentially, existing funds can continue to discriminate on the grounds of sex and marital status while new funds have to meet more rigorous requirements. The *Age Discrimination Act* has a further specific exemption for superannuation legislation: s 38.

The primary exemptions rely on the proof of the basis for the term to be on "actuarial or statistical data" on which it was "reasonable" for the fund to rely. These refer to the tables prepared by insurance companies covering such issues as morbidity and mortality analysed by gender, age, occupational status, disability and related issues. The second criterion is that the discrimination is reasonable having regard to the matter of the data and any other relevant factors.

Where there is no actuarial or statistical data on which the respondent can rely, then the exemption only operates where the discrimination is reasonable having regard to any other relevant factors.

The extent of the potential for the operation of these exemptions is only just starting to be tested. The capacity of insurance companies and others to establish their data base is reasonable and any other factors relied on are reasonable to base a discriminatory policy remains undetermined.

The arrangements made to offer new non-discriminatory policies and the transfer options are issues that will be taken into account where determining whether the exemption provisions operate to counteract the unlawful discrimination: *Wylie v WA Government Employees Superannuation Board* (1997) EOC ¶92-873, see also *Martin v Queensland Electricity Transmission Corp Ltd* [2003] QSC 309.

Insurance

Some employers provide benefits to an employee as part of a salary package. These can include employer-provided insurance policies or policies to which the employer and the employee contribute. In some instances, there are different terms of an insurance policy between women and men. Absent any specific exemption, such insurance policies would come within the employment provisions.

Sections 41 and 41A of the *Sex Discrimination Act* provides an exemption in the area of insurance. "Insurance policy" is defined as including an annuity, a life assurance policy, an accident insurance policy and an illness insurance policy. The exemption in the *Sex Discrimination Act* permits discrimination on the ground of sex where the discrimination is in the terms of the policy and there is actuarial or statistical data which forms the basis of the discrimination and it is reasonable for the insurer to rely on the data and the data is provided to the client on the basis of a written request.

The *Disability Discrimination Act* exemption in s 46 does not contain the same requirements for the provision of information, but it does use the same concept of the exemption being based on actuarial and statistical data and where it is reasonable to have regard to that data. This is the same exemption as covers superannuation (see above). The *Age Discrimination Act* in s 37 is in similar terms.

A similar model for exemptions based on actuarial and statistical data is provided under State laws.

In dismissing a claim for the exemption in the *Disability Discrimination Act*, the Federal Court observed:

> For the reasons given, I consider the appellant applied a decision-making process which was too formulaic or which tended to stereotype the respondent by reference to her disability. Such grouping of individuals, whether by race or disability, without proper regard to an individual's circumstances or to the characteristics that they possess, may cause distress or hurt. This case provides an illustration. Legislation such as the DD Act is aimed to reduce or prevent such harm. Section 46 of the DD Act recognises that there are circumstances in which discrimination by reason of disability may be justified (or, at least, not be unlawful). It requires that the particular circumstances of an individual who is discriminated against be addressed, but not in a formulaic way. Even if the exemption pathway provided by s 46(1)(f) is utilised, the reference to "any other relevant factors" confirms that legislative intention. (*QBE Travel Insurance v Bassanelli* (2004) 137 FCR 88 at [85])

There have been complaints under the *Disability Discrimination Act* by people who are HIV positive and who have claimed on insurance when they have stopped working due to their disability or made claims under loan contract insurance. These complaints indicate that the exemption, while applicable in some circumstances, do not provide blanket exemption for all insurance policies. As a consequence, some insurance companies have rewritten their HIV exclusion clauses to ensure they meet the requirements of the Federal and State discrimination laws and this has resulted in a narrowing of the application of the exemption and hence increased access to the capacity to make claims under insurance policies.

The disability exemption was successfully used by an insurance company to justify relying on an HIV/AIDS exclusion clause as the basis for declining to pay a claim on a mortgage protection insurance policy when the applicant ceased working due to illness related to his HIV status: *Xiros v Fortis Life Assurance Ltd* (2001) 162 FLR 433.

The exemptions are limited in relation to the grounds or attributes of discrimination to which they apply and the main focus is on sex and disability discrimination. The ground of homosexuality was successfully used in New South Wales to challenge the refusal by a health insurance company to provide concessional family rates for two homosexual men and the child living with them that would have been available for a heterosexual couple and a child: *NIB Health Funds Ltd v Hope* (unreported, NSWSC, McInerney J, 15 November 1996).

Minor exemptions

Certain accommodation

There are a series of limited exemptions relating to the provision of accommodation in certain circumstances for employees and students and in relation to the residential care of children under some laws.

Charities

Bequests to charities in deeds, wills or other documents and acts done to give effect to such a conferral of charitable benefits are exempt: *Kay v South Eastern Sydney Area Health Service* [2003] NSWSC 292.

Voluntary bodies

The acts of voluntary bodies in relation to the admission of members and the provision of benefits, facilities or services to members are exempt. Voluntary bodies are usually defined as non-profit making bodies. The exemption does not cover clubs or trade unions.

Religious bodies

Religious practices are exempt from the sex and age discrimination laws in recognition of the sensitivities of those members of the community who practise religions which contain tenets which are essentially or fundamentally discriminatory towards women.

Section 37 of the *Sex Discrimination Act* includes an exemption for the on-going exclusion by some religions of the training, selection and appointment of women as priests, ministers of religion or members of religious orders or acts or practices established for religious purposes. Section 38 exempts the selection of staff to work in educational institutions where such training is provided and the provision of education or training in such institutions. There are similar exemptions in State laws and in s 35 of the *Age Discrimination Act*.

In *Hazan v Victorian Jewish Board of Deputies* (1990) EOC ¶92-298, the exemption was held to apply when the complainant was expelled from a Jewish War Memorial Centre as the expulsion was necessary to avoid the religious susceptibilities of the adherents to the Jewish religion.

Sport

There are exemptions relating to participating in some roles in competitive sporting activities on the ground of sex where the strength, stamina or physique of competitors is relevant: s 42 of the *Sex Discrimination Act*. Therefore, in *Ferneley v Boxing Authority of New South Wales* (2001) 115 FCR 306, the Federal Court held that the Boxing Authority had not breached the *Sex Discrimination Act* by refusing to consider the application of a female boxer where registration was limited to males only. See also *South v Royal Victorian Bowls Association* [2001] VCAT 207.

Combat duties

Combat duties are covered by an exemption in s 43 of the *Sex Discrimination Act* and ss 54 and 55 of the *Disability Discrimination Act*. The combat duties covered are set out in reg 3 of the *Sex Discrimination Regulations* 1984 and reg 4 of the *Disability Discrimination Regulations* 1996.

Public health and infectious diseases

Under the disability discrimination laws, there are some exemptions where a person carries an infectious disease and the discrimination is reasonably necessary to protect public health: see, for example, s 48 of the *Disability Discrimination Act*.

In considering the dismissal of an HIV-infected soldier by the Australian Defence Forces, the High Court rejected an argument that in the case of disability by way of an infectious disease in an employment context, it was not enough to justify the discrimination by reference to s 48 but that in "determining whether the employee poses a risk to the health or safety of others because of his or her disability, the risk must be specifically referable to those persons or things affected by the particular employment": *X v Commonwealth* (1999) 200 CLR 177 at [42], [104]. This means that it is not permissible in determining whether or not the discrimination was lawful to have regard to the exception in s 48 and nothing further. The case concerned a recruit who failed a blood test which tested for, amongst other things, HIV. The matter was remitted back to the Commission for redetermination. It was not contested that an HIV infection was an infectious disease within the terms of the exemption.

The segregation of HIV-infected prisoners from other prisoners and the denial of access to work and other opportunities within the prison system were found not to be necessary to protect public health. This was rejected and it was found that the rule which supported the segregated system was contrary to public health interests and should be removed: *X v Western Australia* (1997) EOC ¶92-878.

Health programs

Section 42 of the *Age Discrimination Act* has a specific exemption for exempted health programs and for individual decisions on the provision of health care or medical goods and services where the basis of the decision was the person's age. Hence, special health programs provided only to older persons or immunisation programs for young children would be exempt.

Migration law

Discrimination on the ground of disability in relation to the administration of the migration program is not unlawful pursuant to s 52 of the *Disability Discrimination Act*. This is included as the criteria for persons to be accepted into the migration program blatantly discriminate on the ground of disability by imposing strict health requirements. This has resulted in several rejections of families for migration as they have a child with a disability and an assessment by the government of the potential health, education and other costs provides the basis for rejecting the family.

Discrimination on the ground of age in relation to the administration of the migration program, the grant of citizenship or eligibility to attend certain federally funded language education programs is not unlawful pursuant to s 43 of the *Age Discrimination Act.*

Procedural exemptions

Limited term exemptions

All the discrimination laws have procedures for a specified statutory body to grant an exemption from the operation of the discrimination law itself. These are basically designed to deal with unusual and short-term events which may breach the law without an exemption, but which will not provide the basis for an on-going, long-term breach of the Act.

There has been some use of the exemptions albeit infrequent. They have been used to enable some short-term special measures to be implemented in order to produce an equal outcome in areas such as the employment of Aboriginal teachers or women teachers into certain, nominated positions.

A person must apply and, in essence, make out their case to the agency involved in the decision-making. Any exemption granted must be publicised and can only last for a limited period.

The HR&EOC has issued guidelines for applying for exemptions in the areas of sex, disability and age discrimination. Some limited exemptions have been granted. The guidelines and the previous and existing exemptions are on their website: <www.hreoc.gov.au/legal/exemptions>.

In sex discrimination, two recent exemptions have been for programs for a male-only health program at a country health centre and for male counsellors to be trained and employed in a crisis support service. Other exemptions have previously been granted but are now expired.

In disability discrimination, a limited term exemption has been granted to clarify issues arising from taking assistance animals onto trains and light rail directed at ensuring an appropriate level of training for such dogs to cover their behaviour in public and the observance of appropriate health standards. A five-year exemption from June 2004 was granted to cover the roll out of captioning on television programs and for television stations to meet certain percentages of broadcast time over that period. A range of other limited term exemptions to cover special programs have also been granted.

In age discrimination, a two-year exemption was granted for the Federal Department of Health and Ageing for a continence aids assistance scheme, and declined for a specialist employment agency providing services to job seekers over age 40 on the basis that it was covered by the special measures exemption and did not need a temporary exemption.

The relationship between national occupational health and safety standards for the lead industry and the *Sex Discrimination Act* caused some litigation during the early 1990s which partly addressed the issue of the role of the Act itself on Commonwealth agencies and employees in their roles exercising discretionary powers to develop national standards. The exemption power could be exercised to exempt a standard which would or may otherwise be in breach of the Act: *HR&EOC v Mt Isa Mines Ltd* (1993) 118 ALR 80. In some instances, it would be necessary for an individual employer that was implementing a national standard to apply for an exemption.

Previously, exemptions had been granted to individual lead smelting companies to exclude women from working in areas where they would be exposed to high lead levels. This occurred because of concerns about dangers to female fertility and to the developmental health of a foetus: *BHP Associated Smelters Pty Ltd v HR&EOC* (1988) EOC ¶92-235; (1990) EOC ¶92-302, *In the matter of an application for exemptions by Pasminco Metals – BHAS Ltd* (1987) EOC ¶92-210, (1991) EOC ¶92-384.

Disability standards

Sections 31 to 34 of the *Disability Discrimination Act* make provision for the implementation of disability standards which could be a complete defence to the raising of a discrimination complaint where the person has acted in accordance with a disability standard.

The proposal for standards has a potential to extend the operation of the Act and design and implement practical mechanisms to overcome long-standing disability discrimination issues such as access to public buildings and public transport. Although the Act was passed in 1992, only one set of disability standards have come into operation.

The *Disability Standards for Accessible Public Transport* commenced operation on 23 October 2002 and impose rigorous requirements on the providers of certain public transport such as buses, trains and trams as well as at the access points such as stations and stops. The public transport provider is required to meet a certain percentage of accessible transport by 2007 and then every five years until 2022. The *Disability Standards for Accessible Public Transport Guidelines 2004 (No 3)* provide further details on the areas covered and also on the rights and responsibilities being "assumed" in the *Transport Standards*.

Most large public transport providers will meet the initial targets relatively easily and it will be the later periods which will give rise to the necessity for often substantial expenditure to comply. Providers with old infrastructure such as train stations may have enormous difficulties in altering older, heritage-listed premises to bring them within the new requirements. It is too early to assess the impact of this as yet.

The *Disability Standards for Education* commenced operation on 18 August 2005. They impose obligations on education providers, including schools, universities and bodies preparing curriculum. They cover enrolment, participation, curriculum development, accreditation and delivery, student support services and elimination of harassment and victimisation. They set out the obligations that are imposed and then provide some measures that will be taken as evidence of compliance with the Standards. *Guidance Notes* have been issued that are designed to provide further information on the ways to comply with the Standards but their contents are not enforceable. The *Education Standards* have adopted a different approach to the *Transport Standards*, probably due to the different activities and the way to measure compliance.

There are some complex legal issues about the attempted ambit and coverage of both of the Standards. It is arguable that they try and extend beyond the coverage of the *Disability Discrimination Act* and so are not valid. In some parts, they seek to impose a range of positive obligations on the transport provider or the education provider. As the High Court made clear in *Purvis v New South Wales (Department of Education and Training)* (2003) 217 CLR 92, in obiter comments, s 5(2) of the Act does not require different accommodation or different services to be provided to a person with a disability to meet a direct discrimination claim based on s 5(1). Close judicial scrutiny of the Standards may eventually determine that they go beyond their enabling statute where they seek to impose positive obligations.

There have been draft education and employment standards which, at this stage, have not proceeded to implementation.

12

COMPLAINT-HANDLING PROCESSES

There is no general or common law in respect of acts of unlawful discrimination. The various laws create statutory rights which are only able to be activated through the mechanism established by the legislation.

The system applies nationally, with some minor local variations. To commence the process, it is necessary to lodge a written complaint with the appropriate government agency set up under the relevant legislation and this will trigger a series of investigations and attempts at conciliation. For example, under the Federal legislation it is the Human Rights and Equal Opportunity Commission whereas in New South Wales it is the Anti-Discrimination Board. These steps are discussed in this chapter. In some circumstances, complaints are referred to a court or specialist tribunal for a public hearing. The processes connected to Federal proceedings are discussed in Chapter 13.

The term "agency" is used in this chapter to describe the statutory body, and the staff working for that body, created especially to handle conciliation of complaints. The formal name varies from "President" to "Commissioner" or "Commission" to "Board". The term "tribunal" or "court" is used to describe the body set up specifically to hear and determine discrimination complaints through a process of public inquiry and decisions.

The term "complainant" is used to describe the person who initiates the process by lodging a complaint. The term "respondent" is used to describe the person or organisation who is the subject of the complaint; for example, in an employment complaint the respondent would usually be the employer. A second respondent may be an individual co-worker responsible for the acts of discrimination or harassment.

Approaches to conciliation of complaints

The focus of all Australian discrimination legislation is on conciliation, that is, an attempt to bring the parties together with an agreed outcome which fully and effectively resolves the dispute between them. There are specific statutory powers to assist the conciliation process and these are discussed in this chapter.

Generally, the process starts with a complaint. This may follow some informal contact between the person and the agency before the complaint is lodged, and the person may obtain information about their rights and preliminary views on whether they may have some basis for a complaint to be lodged.

Sometimes, having been given some preliminary information, a person is able to approach the other party and resolve it without resort to the formal mechanisms. In other circumstances, the community education material and general awareness of the law means that people are able to rely on the existence of such material to resolve difficulties without going through the formal processes. Newspaper and television reports of individual cases often increase the number of telephone inquiries about the issue, particularly when sexual harassment is given media prominence.

Any person who considers that they have been subjected to an act of unlawful discrimination or harassment can make a complaint. In all jurisdictions, this complaint must be in writing. There are special requirements for a person with a disability to have a complaint written by another person.

The approaches to complaints handling vary slightly between the agencies, but essentially all adopt the same general approach.

Complaints vary enormously in their depth and complexity. The agencies take a "hands on" approach to the complaint and often seek out more information from a complainant before they inform the respondent that a complaint has been made. This approach can sometimes delay the progress of the complaint considerably, but can be important when the complainant has not obtained any legal or other advice before lodging the complaint and the complaint itself does not contain sufficient details.

The legislation requires a focus on a two-part process: the investigation of a complaint and the conciliation. There is a division between these two processes, although sometimes the distinction is blurred and the complaint may move back and forth between the two stages.

The agency then approaches the respondent, usually in writing, informing them of the contents of the complaint and sometimes asking a series of questions to elucidate the issues. This may be the first time that the respondent is aware that a complaint has been lodged. Once the respondent has replied, then the contents of the reply or some part of it are supplied to the complainant and they are usually given an opportunity to reply.

If there are urgent issues, then more immediate methods of communication may be used and, on some occasions, an interim order to preserve a person's rights may be obtained from the court or tribunal. This can arise when a dismissal is threatened or about to be put into place, for example, after a woman has told her employer that she is pregnant.

The agency may call a compulsory conciliation conference, requiring all parties to appear. The mechanisms of the approach to a conciliation conference are varied and may involve a face-to-face meeting between all parties with an agency conciliator present. This is a common approach. On other occasions, depending on the sensitivity of the issues, the parties may be on the premises at the same time, but in different locations, with the conciliator moving between the two groups, conveying information and offers and counter-offers.

The essence and foundation of conciliation is to resolve issues where both parties genuinely seek out an answer that does not involve litigation, and where there is some commitment and goodwill to sorting out the problems. Many complaints are conciliated with the parties remaining a long way apart in their view of the events giving rise to the complaint. There can still be a successful conciliation as the parties are able to make some accommodation while starting from completely different perspectives.

One variant is where the process is conducted only by letter or telephone contact of each party with the agency as opposed to a face-to-face conciliation meeting. A basis for those different approaches is the circumstances of the complaint. Geographical location may be a factor in determining whether an actual meeting occurs. In some cases, after some initial assistance from the agency, the parties may be able to resolve the matter between themselves or through their legal representatives.

If, at any point, a complaint is resolved, then the parties usually enter into a deed or terms of settlement which sets out the agreement between them. While the enforceability of these deeds has never been extensively tested, they are usually a method of properly disposing of a complaint once the issues between the parties have been resolved, or an agreement reached to side-step the issues and just resolve the complaint itself. They are enforceable within the usual court system but not within the discrimination arena.

If a complaint is not able to be resolved, then the complainant can apply to a court or tribunal for the complaint to be heard (see Chapter 13).

The dynamics of conciliation vary enormously. A conciliation meeting can be productive for a complainant as they are given an opportunity to explain their perception of the issues and their response to them and also their views on an outcome which would be acceptable.

Delay can be deleterious to achieving a prompt settlement. Often, when initially lodging a complaint, a person has a more flexible approach to the desired outcome. A need for the respondent to know and understand their concerns and not repeat their action, either to the complainant or to any other person, can be an important factor. A recalcitrant respondent who approaches conciliation from a hostile or completely negative perspective will not usually come away with an outcome acceptable to themselves as well as the complainant.

There is no doubt that some people lodge complaints which are misdirected or which misunderstand the legislation or the intersection of their own circumstances with the legislation. Once explained to them, they may withdraw or amend their complaint. In some circumstances, this outcome cannot be achieved and they insist on pursuing their rights or their perception of their rights. The number of complaints dismissed by the courts and tribunals indicates that not all complaints made are valid. This does not mean that the person making them has acted other than in good faith based on their understanding of the circumstances at the time.

A conciliation process based on a misperception by a complainant and strongly opposed by a respondent is bound to fail. Similarly, a valid complaint which meets a hostile response is not able to be conciliated.

Some respondents make a business decision early in the conciliation process and even though they do not agree with or accept the complainant's understanding of events, as a commercial decision they decide to pay some financial compensation to end the matter. This decision can be based on the weighing up of the management time to be spent on the complaint, and potential legal costs, compared to the immediate termination of the complaint processes and the end of any contact or relationship with the complainant.

Some complainants make unrealistically high demands for financial compensation. If the economic loss component is low or nil, then the amounts involved are likely to be relatively small, as the compensation awarded by the various tribunals and courts is usually relatively minor. See Chapter 14 for a discussion of the factors affecting the range.

A "complaint"

The steps set out in the various Acts for making a complaint and the investigation and conciliation processes are set out below.

The discrimination agencies are not usually able to act formally without a complaint. The complaint is a crucial document as it is on the basis of the complaint itself that the rest of the system flows. Without a complaint, there is no jurisdiction to proceed.

The complaint does not need to be technical or lengthy, but it must contain sufficient details to demonstrate discrimination or harassment within the meaning of the legislation. The complaint must specify all the factual material to be relied on by setting out all the conduct said to be the complaint: *Queensland (through the Queensland Police Service) v Walters* [2007] QSC 012. Vague or general assertions will be insufficient and may have a detrimental impact on the conduct of a later hearing unless amendments are permitted.

If the allegations made are incapable of amounting to discrimination or harassment as set out, then it may be that it is not a "complaint" as required by the legislation: *Nestle Aust Ltd v Equal Opportunity Board* [1990] VR 805. While agreeing that there should be a liberal rather than a narrow or unduly restrictive approach when interpreting the Victorian Act, Vincent J held:

> Nevertheless, despite these provisions it is clear that the written complaint, although it is not to be treated as a formal document of pleading, must on its face raise a question of possible discrimination of a kind which will bring the matter within the Board's jurisdiction. (at 813)

This narrower approach has been rejected as inapplicable for the Federal legislation, which does not have the requirement that the Victorian Act has for "setting out the details".

Consequently, in the Federal Acts and the other State Acts, all that is required is a statement that makes an allegation that a person has done an unlawful act by reference to the alleged acts of discrimination. The complaint is not to be treated in the same way as a pleading drafted by a lawyer would be: *Travers v New South Wales* [2000] FCA 1565 at [8]. Furthermore, the complaint need not necessarily be limited to the letter of complaint to the relevant agency. Other material provided by the complainant at a later stage may be included also.

If the agency rejects the matter as not demonstrating any valid ground of discrimination or for any other technical reason, then administrative law proceedings may be the only avenue for review under State legislation: *Dixon v Anti-Discrimination Commissioner of Queensland* [2005] 1 Qd R 33.

The "complainant"

Some of the State laws define the term "complainant" as essentially being the person who lodges a complaint.

"Aggrieved person"

A complaint may only be lodged by one or more person(s) "aggrieved" by the alleged unlawful discrimination either by that person or on behalf of that person: *HR&EOC Act* ss 46P and 46PF.

As Mason J said in *Koowarta v Bjelke-Petersen* (1982) 153 CLR 168 at 236:

> [A] reference in a statute to a "person" includes a reference to a body corporate, unless a contrary intention appears ... the object of the Convention being to eliminate all forms of racial discrimination and the purpose of s 12 [of the *Racial Discrimination Act*] being to prohibit acts involving racial discrimination, there is a strong reason for giving the words its statutory sense so that the section applies to discrimination against a corporation by reason of the race, colour or national or ethnic origin of any associate of that corporation.

The majority of the High Court in *IW v City of Perth* (1997) 191 CLR 1 found that the complainant was not an "aggrieved person". Even though he was a member of the organisation which had made the application for planning permission, he was held not to have met the statutory requirements.

> It is clear from the structure of the Act generally ... that an "aggrieved person" is a person who is discriminated against in a manner which the Act renders unlawful. And when regard is had to the precise terms of the [goods and services section], it is clear that the person discriminated against is the person who is refused services on terms or conditions or in a manner that is discriminatory ... there was no refusal of services in this case. And if anyone was the recipient of treatment which might constitute discrimination, it was PLWA, not the appellant. Accordingly, the appellant was not an "aggrieved person" within the meaning of that expression ... And that being so, he is in no position to assert that the City of Perth engaged in unlawful discrimination in the exercise of its discretion to grant or withhold planning approval for PWLA's drop-in centre. (at 25)

The difficulty with this narrow view of the standing provisions is that it seems to run counter to the actual words of the legislation which require "a person" to make the complaint. The implication of the High Court's decision is that an organisation can meet that description. This appears to be creating a false distinction as the only method for an organisation to establish that it was "aggrieved" within the terms of the definition would be for it to demonstrate that its constituent members as a whole or in some substantial part were aggrieved or had some negative view of the decision. On the basis of this decision, an unincorporated association may face some difficulties in meeting the test.

The question of whether a person is a "person aggrieved" is a mixed question of law and fact and must be determined objectively, a mere feeling of being aggrieved will not be sufficient: *Cameron v HR&EOC* (1993) 119 ALR 279.

> This result should not, however, be taken as establishing a principle that only persons directly affected by unlawful conduct may seek redress in respect of it as persons aggrieved ... It is at least arguable that derivative or relational interests will support the claim of a person to be "aggrieved" for the purposes of the section. A close connection between two people which has personal or economic dimensions, or a mix of both, may suffice. The spouse or other relative of a victim of discrimination or a dependent of such a person may be a person aggrieved for the purposes of the section. It is conceivable that circumstances could arise in which a person in a close professional relationship with another might find that relationship affected by discriminatory conduct and have the necessary standing to lay a complaint. (at 289)

An organisation comprised mainly of members with a disability was found not to be a "person aggrieved" and so did not have standing to commence or pursue Federal Court disability discrimination proceedings. The court held:

> Notwithstanding its intellectual and emotional concern in the subject matter of the proceedings, the interest of the applicant is no more than that of an ordinary member of the public; the applicant is not affected to an extent greater than an ordinary member of the public, nor would the applicant gain an advantage if successful nor suffer a disadvantage if unsuccessful. To adopt the language of Lockhart J in *Right to Life* 56 FCR at 68:
>
>> Wide and liberal though the laws of standing should be, the courts of this country have drawn the line of demarcation between an open system and the requirement of some form of interest in the subject matter of the proceeding other than a mere emotional attachment or intellectual pursuit or satisfaction.
>
> (*Access For All Alliance (Hervey Bay) Inc v Hervey Bay City Council* [2007] FCA 615 at [67])

Death of complainant

Apart from New South Wales, none of the discrimination laws specifically addresses the issue of the death of the complainant. The Full Federal Court has held that where a complaint was lodged and the complainant died before the matter was finalised, including through a hearing, the complaint survives.

> Whilst the death of a complainant may create practical difficulties, especially if she or he has not yet given evidence, these difficulties will be no greater than those which courts routinely face when death removes a party or important witness. The absence of a party or witness does not derogate from the substance of the complaint. (*Stephenson, as Executrix of the Late Alyschia Dibble v HR&EOC* (1996) 139 ALR 678 at 687)

In essence, this means that a finding of unlawful discrimination can be made based on facts of the complaint: *Abbott Australia Pty Ltd v HR&EOC* (1999) 88 FCR 132.

Where the act of discrimination has occurred but the person dies before the complaint is lodged, then an authorised representative of the deceased may lodge a complaint and pursue the complaint processes on their behalf: *Commonwealth v Wood* (2006) 148 FCR 276 at [40]. In *Wood's case*, the suicide of the 15-year-old complainant was directly related to the subject matter of the complaint made by her mother on her behalf and on her own behalf.

Different issues arise if a person dies before the act of unlawful discrimination occurred. Then there is no basis to lodge a complaint: *CUNA Mutual Group Ltd v Bryant* (2000) 102 FCR 270.

Representative actions

The Federal discrimination laws and some of the State laws have provision for representative actions, where one person is nominated as the representative of the group. Little use has been made of these provisions and their potential impact still remains largely unexplored.

Unlike an individual complaint, the complaint itself must meet the following criteria set out in ss 46PB and 46PC of the *HR&EOC Act* for it to constitute a representative complaint and do the following:

- the class members have complaints against the same person;
- all the complaints are in respect of or arise out of the same similar or related circumstances;
- all the complaints give rise to a substantially common issue of law or fact;

- describe or otherwise identify the class members;
- specify the nature of the complaints made on behalf of the class members; and
- specify the nature of the relief sought.

It is not necessary to have the consent of all the members of the class when the complaint is lodged. However, a person who is a class member in a representative complaint is precluded from lodging a separate individual complaint in respect of the same subject-matter. There are complex rules relating to the conduct of a representative complaint during an inquiry and some of these are discussed in Chapter 13.

An associate

The *Disability Discrimination Act* and some State Acts cover discrimination against a person's "associate". "Associate" is defined in s 4(1) of that Act as:

(a) a spouse of the person; and
(b) another person who is living with the person on a genuine domestic basis
(c) a relative of the person; and
(d) a carer of the person; and
(e) another person who is in a business, sporting or recreational relationship with the person

This potentially extends the jurisdiction of the legislation and provides some protection to those closely related to or associated with a person with a disability. In some circumstances, the link between the act of discrimination and any less favourable treatment of the associate may be difficult to establish. That nexus remains a crucial part of establishing a discrimination claim and is not rendered irrelevant just by the introduction of the associate concept.

Trade unions

Section 46P of the *HR&EOC Act* provides that a complaint may be lodged by a person or a trade union on behalf of one or more other persons having the same complaint.

There have been some complaints lodged by trade unions on behalf of their members, with the trade union conducting the proceedings. The Finance Sector Union conducted a lengthy and complex Commission hearing and an unsuccessful Federal Court appeal against the Commonwealth Bank on behalf of its members arising from a restructure of the bank's staff: *Commonwealth Bank v HR&EOC* (1997) 80 FCR 78.

Time factors

Time limit to complain

All the Acts have a time limit within which a person can complain. Usually it is within 6-12 months after the alleged act of discrimination occurs. There is typically a discretion to accept a complaint out of time: see, for example, *HR&EOC Act* s 46PH(1)(b).

Where there has been an ongoing pattern of conduct, it is necessary for the complainant to identify discriminatory conduct within the 12-month period: *Commissioner of Fire Brigades (New South Wales) v Lavery* [2005] NSWSC 268 at [62].

A decision to accept a complaint out of time can only be made on the facts explaining the delay in lodging the complaint. The merits of the actual complaint cannot be reviewed or used as any basis for the out-of-time decision: *McAuliffe v Puplick* (1996) EOC ¶92-800. This is in contrast to the exercise of a discretion by a court or tribunal to extend the time for making an application to a court or tribunal, where the merits of the application are to be taken into account, together with a range of other factors. For a fuller discussion of these principles, see Chapter 13.

If a decision is made not to accept the complaint because it is out of time, the complainant can have that decision reviewed by the relevant court or tribunal and the grounds for the decision can be judicially scrutinised: *GCE v Anti-Discrimination Commissioner* [2006] QSC 058, see also *Buderim Ginger Ltd v Booth* [2003] 1 Qd R 147.

When considering whether to accept a complaint out of time, the agency often asks the respondent for their views as to possible prejudice or disadvantage if the complaint was accepted. The agency needs to provide an opportunity for the complainant to review and address any issues raised by the respondent or a breach of procedural fairness may occur: *Stokes v President of the Anti-Discrimination Board of NSW* [2006] NSWSC 351.

Care should be taken to make the application to the court or tribunal within the time prescribed under the legislation. There is a period of 28 days from the date of the termination of the complaint by the HR&EOC to file an application in either the Federal Court or the Federal Magistrates Court.

Date of complaint

The date of the complaint can be a crucial element to a complaint. Any events which occur after the date on which the complaint is lodged cannot be the basis for any finding of unlawful discrimination as they cannot be included in the complaint itself. The only exception will arise if the complaint itself is about some future event such as the construction of a building or the holding of an event. A complaint may be amended after it is lodged with the Human Rights and Equal Opportunity Commission, with the leave of the President: HR&EOC Act s 46PA.

Later events cannot be included in any decision and so any remedy such as financial compensation cannot take them into account: *Charles v Fuji Xerox Australia Pty Ltd* (2000) 105 FCR 573; *Travers v New South Wales* [2000] FCA 1565 and *Miller v Wertheim* [2001] FMCA 103. Sometimes, it is necessary for a complainant to lodge a second or even a third complaint covering events arising after the date on which the first complaint was lodged. This is often required if there are allegations of victimisation said to arise specifically from the lodging of the initial complaint.

However, while all the Acts have a statutory time limit of six or 12 months in which to lodge a complaint, there is a discretion to accept a complaint out of time. This discretion is sometimes not properly exercised when the complaint covers a period of several years and a pattern of conduct during that period forms the complaint. It is arguable whether any events before the cut off of the time period can form part of the complaint without a specific exercise of the statutory discretion to accept an out-of-time complaint. The approach to this issue varies between jurisdictions.

It can be a crucial matter for a respondent when assessing the case to be met and whether conciliation is feasible, as a review of comparable damages awards needs to be based on such fundamental information.

Some State tribunals have side-stepped the time question by admitting into evidence material covering earlier dates under the nebulous heading of "background". This may be completely inappropriate and not a proper exercise of the discretion to admit evidence during proceedings, as the only relevant issue is the allegation of an unlawful act. Even if it is demonstrated that there was similar conduct on a prior occasion, this will not generally assist any factual dispute on whether it occurred at the time in question.

Confidentiality

One of the key elements of the conciliation process as it works around Australia is that the lodging of a complaint and the investigation and conciliation processes are confidential. The confidentiality falls into two categories.

The first category is the confidentiality that applies during the conciliation process itself. This is agreed to between the parties at the commencement of any conciliation meeting. The correspondence to and from the agency with either party is not usually confidential at the inquiry stage unless it contains details of "without prejudice" settlement negotiations, including any offers and responses.

This practice has been a long established tradition of discrimination conciliation as it is considered to be an important component of the whole process. It is based on the view that parties will take a more flexible approach if no-one is locked into any form of public position. More candid and straight-forward propositions and responses will be able to be given in such an environment. Often matters will be traversed which are not within the terms of the formal complaint and could not be raised during any inquiry. It is in all parties' interests that such matters and any offers made to settle the complaint remain confidential.

Except in one limited area, there are no powers to keep matters confidential by a party. If one party decides to go public by advising the media or other persons, then there is no recourse for the opposing party except moral outrage and a termination of conciliation endeavours. Defamation proceedings have been threatened after the contents of complaints have been made publicly available. Often, they are threatened by alleged harassers as an immediate response and an attempt to intimidate or silence a complainant into abandoning their complaint. This response may reflect the power imbalance in the relationship during the period of discrimination or harassment. If the complaint is under Federal legislation, then the protection against civil action provisions would protect the complainant: *Sex Discrimination Act* s 111. The conduct may also give rise to an additional complaint of victimisation (see above Chapter 9).

The one limitation on the parties is that evidence of anything "said or done in the course of conciliation proceedings", including a compulsory conciliation conference, is inadmissible in any subsequent hearing: *Bender v Bovis Lend Lease Pty Ltd* [2003] FMCA 277, *HR&EOC Act* s 46PS(2). In that case, the court held that an affidavit which traversed some of the events at a conciliation conference could not be admitted into evidence at the hearing. There is some dispute about the extent of this protection and it has been interpreted broadly to cover any matters arising during oral or written negotiations, particularly covering admissions made for the purpose of progressing a settlement, and the amounts of any damages or the types of other remedies offered.

The Federal legislation has a further statutory restriction which imposes a duty on any Commissioner and any staff not to disclose any information obtained about complaints to any other person or to any court: *Sex Discrimination Act* s 112.

Termination of complaint

When a document is initially received by an agency, a view has to be formed on whether it is a "complaint" and whether it should be processed as one.

Even though a matter has all the hallmarks of a complaint, it can be terminated or rejected at any stage of the complaint-handling process. In common with all the discrimination laws, s 46PH of the *HR&EOC Act* provides the basis for the President to decide not to inquire, or to further inquire into a complaint, initially on receipt or at any later time because:

- the President is satisfied that the act is not unlawful;
- the President is of the opinion that the complainant does not want to continue;
- it is more than 12 months since the act complained of was done;
- the President is of the view that the complaint is frivolous, vexatious, misconceived or lacking in substance;
- there is some other more appropriate remedy which has already been sought by the complainant or ought to be sought by the complainant;
- the subject-matter of the complaint has already been dealt with by an appropriate statutory authority or ought to be dealt with by a more appropriate statutory authority;
- the President is satisfied that the subject-matter of the complaint involves an issue of public importance that should be considered by the Federal Court or the Federal Magistrates Court; or
- the President is satisfied that there is no reasonable prospect of the matter being settled by conciliation.

The President is required to notify the complainant of the decision and the complainant then has the right under s 46PO of that Act to make an application to the Federal Magistrates Court or the Federal Court.

Under State legislation, the system is that for most grounds of rejection of the complaint, the complainant can require that it be referred to the tribunal for hearing. Interestingly, few complaints referred to the tribunal after rejection by the agency are ultimately successful. For the few that are eventually upheld, further vital information not available at the conciliation phase often comes to light during the hearing. This sometimes occurs when a lawyer becomes involved and refines the evidence and the legal points to be raised. However, more commonly, the complainant who has failed to establish a viable complaint before the agency, fails to obtain a successful outcome from the tribunal also, often after having presented lengthy and detailed evidence.

There has been some discussion about limiting the automatic access to the court or tribunal in these circumstances as it is often a waste of significant time and resources of the respondent and the court or tribunal on a matter that was without substance or merit from the beginning. No States have taken any action to so restrict the access. Arguably, the fact that some are upheld is a justification for continuing the safety valve of review through a full hearing and the increasingly real threat of a costs order made against a complainant who persists with a complaint that is frivolous, vexatious or misconceived is arguably sufficient to deter most matters falling into this description.

For the approach taken to the summary dismissal of complaints, see Chapter 13.

Once a complaint has been terminated by the HR&EOC, then the Commission no longer has jurisdiction over that complaint. This is so even in circumstances where the complaint is terminated in error; for example, where the wrong parties have been named in the termination notice.

Powers during conciliation

Under the Federal laws, there is a more extensive statutory scheme of powers during the conciliation phase than in most State laws. There does not appear to be any significant difference in outcomes through the use of the powers. If a respondent decides to ignore the agency's communications and not respond in any way, then while the powers may be useful in finally convincing them to participate, such complaints usually end up being referred for an inquiry, or dropped by the complainant as being too difficult to pursue any further.

The powers of the Commission's President include issuing written notices for the production of information or documents as specified in the notice: *HR&EOC Act* s 46PI.

Compulsory conference

There is a power to call a compulsory conference and require attendance from nominated persons: *HR&EOC Act* s 46PJ.

Three different categories of persons can be directed to attend a compulsory conference: the complainant, the respondent and any person the President considers can provide information, or whose presence will be conducive to settlement: s 46PJ(4).

The conference is held in private: s 46PK(2). It is usually presided over by a member of the President's staff. On rare occasions, depending on the nature of the complaint and the potential importance of the complaint on a number of different bases, the President may preside.

At a compulsory conference, neither side is entitled to legal representation except with the consent of the person presiding. While there are no formal guidelines, one approach which is commonly adopted is that if the complainant is unrepresented, then any request by a respondent for representation will be refused without some particularly outstanding reason for their attendance. This may not solve any perceptions of power imbalance between the parties as any large or medium organisation can send any staff member, including an in-house lawyer, to attend. It is common for the complainant to be accompanied by a support person such as a family member or friend who sits in during the conference.

Compulsory conferences may have to be called when the respondent refuses to attend on a voluntary basis. Most conciliation conferences are organised without resorting to the use of the formal power and, essentially, both types are conducted in the same manner and form (see above).

Expedition

All systems have a capacity and a practice to deal with complaints on an urgent basis. This may be an internal bureaucratic arrangement, such as in the Federal or New South Wales system, or a formal statutory regime, such as in the Victorian Act.

This means that a complaint is given priority and is able to "skip" the usual queue so contact with the respondent can be immediately after the complaint is lodged. This usually occurs where a person is about to be dismissed from their job or there is some immediate flow-on effect from the denial of a particular service.

Interim orders

The legislation has an avenue for the complainant, Commission or agency to apply to the relevant court or tribunal for an interim order, that is, to prevent any actions being taken to preserve the status quo or the rights of the parties: *HR&EOC Act* s 46PP. Significantly, and unlike other instances where injunctions are sought, no undertaking as to damages need necessarily be given by an applicant for an injunction. At a Federal level a court is precluded from requiring a person to give any such undertaking:

HR&EOC Act ss 46PO(8), 46PP(5). This is no doubt a reflection of the fact that many of the applicants seeking injunctions would simply not be in a position to give such an undertaking and this interim remedy would not be pursued. An injunction cannot be granted after the complaint has been withdrawn as there would be no basis for issuing one, the subject-matter the basis of the injunction no longer being in existence.

For a discussion of the tests to be applied for an interim order, see Interim orders in Chapter 13.

Outcome of conciliation

If conciliation is unsuccessful, then the complainant may apply to the relevant court or tribunal for a hearing (see Chapter 13).

A complaint may be successfully resolved between the parties, although often this involves both parties engaging in a process of abandoning their starting positions and genuinely endeavouring to find a common meeting ground. Sometimes it is only achieved after a form of "Dutch auction" is conducted, and a series of high offers and lower, often significantly lower, counter offers are put until a point is reached at which both parties can agree to walk away.

Settlement

There may be other parts to a settlement as well as the payment of compensation. Some complainants are not interested in any financial payments and are pursuing the matter for some other relief or to reflect their deep personal sense of grievance.

Often in settlements, the matters agreed to are not ones which any court or tribunal could make formal orders about as they would be beyond their powers. Examples include an agreement that the employer will dismiss or discipline an employee or implement a sexual harassment awareness program amongst a designated group of employees. These are matters which a complainant may request even knowing that if there were a hearing, such final orders may not be possible.

The boundaries of a settlement are only limited by the imagination of the parties and the willingness of the respondent to meet the demands of the complainant.

Settlements in employment matters have contained, apart from financial compensation, agreements to:

- provide a reference with details of job duties and skill level – this can be useful as it can assist a complainant to obtain a new position without having to request that a potential employer telephone the former employer for a reference when the relationship may have completely broken down through the events giving rise to the complaint or the complaint processes themselves;

- issue a private apology – from an individual or from an organisation, though these are often in terms of "we didn't mean to, but if you were offended by X, then we apologise";
- issue a public statement within the organisation that the company is committed to a workplace free of any discrimination or harassment and the possible outcomes if any person breaches the policy;
- issue a public statement that the complaint has been settled and neither party will be making any further comment, or a short comment to be included from one or both parties;
- that all the workforce, or certain identified parts of it, will undergo some relevant training, such as a course on preventing and eliminating sexual harassment for management or racial harassment for the staff;
- leave which was taken as a direct result of the unlawful act will be re-credited – this can be useful for both parties when the employment relationship continues, as it is a payment of compensation to an employee in an indirect form as the leave is simply available to be retaken, and it can be managed within the usual employer commitments;
- provide special paid leave – to assist a complainant to recuperate where there is evidence of psychological damage arising from the unlawful acts;
- transfer of the complainant to a new workplace or a new position,
- dismiss or impose disciplinary measures or transfer an employee identified as playing an active role in the discrimination or harassment;
- amend personnel files to remove any discriminatory matter or material that reflects a particular, possibly unfounded, view of the complainant and her actions;
- repeat the conduct of a staff appraisal or review by a different, independent person and destruction of a previous negative one;
- for the complainant to resign and an immediate payment of full statutory rights such as long service leave and holiday pay;
- return all property of the respondent, such as a car, laptop computer or other equipment.

In other areas of unlawful discrimination, settlement options have covered:

- removal of a discriminatory policy or practice;
- implementation of a new policy to ensure no further similar acts of discrimination;
- dismissal, disciplinary measures or a transfer for any employee identified as playing an active role in the discrimination or harassment;
- publication in a newspaper of an apology when the statements etc were initially made publicly;
- issuing a policy to all staff to ensure that the delivery of the service or access to the goods is non-discriminatory, such as the conditions for entry into a hotel will be without reference to the race of the client;
- providing access to the service on non-discriminatory terms and conditions, such as a loan.

Terms of settlement

It is a common, and preferred, practice for the contents of any settlement agreement to be reduced to writing and signed by both parties. This is one reason for a corporation sending a person of sufficient authority to the conciliation conference, as often these documents are produced immediately and are signed before anyone leaves the conference.

All terms of settlement should include some form of release for the respondent from the complainant. If it is an employment matter, the employee's worker's compensation rights cannot be part of the deal but it is better to note that they are not included, to meet any possible confusion over interpretation at a later date.

It is usual to include a confidentiality term, that is, both parties agree to keep the terms of the settlement private between themselves. Sometimes, this clause includes the existence of the complaint itself and the fact of a settlement, not just the terms of the settlement. This term can also include a requirement that the complainant refrain from discussing the facts with any other person, except a nominated legal or financial adviser. A mutual non-disparagement clause is common so that each side agrees not to make any negative statements about the other or the incidents giving rise to the complaint.

A signed agreement protects the complainant as if any specific clause has a time line included, such as that money is to be paid, the complainant needs to be assured that there is a proper commitment to meeting those dates.

A signed agreement protects the respondent as there may be obligations imposed on the complainant to maintain confidentiality and possibly meet other terms, such as to not discuss the issue further or return the respondent's property.

The enforceability of the terms of a settlement document depends on its nature and the way it has been structured. Usually, it would be classified as a contract between the parties and would be enforceable in the usual way through a breach of contract or a recovery action for liquidated damages in the courts.

The Victorian Act takes a different approach to the issue, as it registers any signed conciliation agreement with the Registrar of the Tribunal and then the terms are taken to be orders of the tribunal and enforceable as such: *Equal Opportunity Act* 1995 (Vic) s 115. This only occurs at the request of the parties. Arguably, any orders which were later enforced or tried to be enforced could only come within the ambit of the orders that the tribunal could make itself. This means that for that sort of enforceability some of the advantages of the conciliated agreements are lost as other types of issues cannot be included or, if they are, they will not be enforceable if needed. Also, it must be assumed that any confidential terms would not operate either. Obviously, in some circumstances, this is a mechanism which offers many advantages and, in others, it would not be appropriate.

Inquiry and hearing of complaint

Once a complaint is terminated by the President then the complainant has the option of making an application to the court for hearing of the complaint: *HR&EOC Act* s 46PO. The court or tribunal cannot inquire or hear the complaint in the absence of the termination.

Upon terminating the complaint the President is required to produce a written notice to the complainant informing her or him of the decision and setting out reasons for the decision: *HR&EOC Act* s 46PH(2). On request by an affected person who is not the complainant, for example, the respondent, the President must give that person a copy of the notice, although it is standard practice to provide it to the respondent at the same time as to the complainant.

No details of any conciliation proceedings can be included in the report, including any offers for settlement or any admissions by any party about certain facts. This exclusion is designed to protect the integrity of the confidential conciliation process.

Agency as a complainant

Most of the discrimination laws have the capacity for another person, usually the agency involved in complaint handling, to be designated the complainant or to conduct a complaint on their own initiative. Despite the potential and breadth of these provisions they are not often used, with individual complainants responsible for the great majority of complaints lodged both at a State and Federal level.

13

CONDUCTING A HEARING

This chapter looks at the available powers and the conduct of proceedings at a Federal level in the Federal Court and the Federal Magistrates Court.

There is no general or common law in respect of discrimination. The three Federal discrimination laws can only be enforced after a hearing and then a decision from either court. The State laws have established specialist tribunals which follow essentially the same procedures.

To commence the process, it is necessary to lodge a written complaint with the Human Rights and Equal Opportunity Commission ("HR&EOC") and that will trigger a series of steps relating to investigation and attempts at conciliation (see Chapter 12). A minority of complainants commence proceedings in the Federal Court or the Federal Magistrates Court. The processes involved in such proceedings are discussed in this chapter.

The term "agency" is used in this chapter to describe the statutory position and the staff working for that position created specially to handle conciliation of complaints. The formal name varies from "Commissioner" or "Commission" or "Board". The term "tribunal" is used to describe the body set up under State law specifically to hear and determine discrimination complaints through a process of public inquiry and decisions. For factors on choice of law, see Chapter 1.

The term "applicant" is used to describe the person who initiates the process by lodging a complaint and subsequently files an application in either court. The term "respondent" is used to describe the person or organisation which is the subject of the complaint – for example, in an employment complaint the respondent would usually be the employer.

Federal approach

If a complaint cannot be conciliated, is considered a matter of public importance or for a range of other reasons, then the President of the Human Rights and Equal Opportunity Commission may terminate the complaint: *HR&EOC Act* s 46PH.

The applicant is sent a notice of termination and attached to it is a letter from HR&EOC which summarises the complaint and the response and the statutory basis for the termination decision and the complaint, any response and any other relevant documents.

State approaches

Each State tribunal has different procedures and mechanisms for the conduct of cases. This chapter does not detail each of these. It examines the general issues of conducting cases from both the applicant's and respondent's perspectives and the major issues which can arise from a Federal perspective.

Contact with the individual tribunal should be made to obtain information about their procedures. See Appendix E for the contact numbers and addresses of each tribunal and agency.

Commencing proceedings

An applicant has 28 days after a notice of termination issues to commence proceedings in either the Federal Court or the Federal Magistrates Court: *HR&EOC Act* s 46PO(2). An application in the specified form must be filed with an accompanying affidavit and the notice of termination: *FC Rules* O 81 r 5, *FMC Rules* Part 4.01. A copy of the application must be filed with the HR&EOC. A respondent must file a defence to the application, usually before the first directions hearing. There are no formal pleadings and often no points of claim in the Federal Magistrates Court.

There is no general jurisdiction of either court to hear and determine discrimination claims. Without a terminated complaint in existence, there is no basis on which a person can commence proceedings: *Carreon v Vanstone* [2005] FCA 865.

The Federal Magistrates Court is designed to be more informal, speedy and less costly than the Federal Court. Since it commenced operations in April 2000, most Federal discrimination cases have been heard before it. It will conduct hearings in country towns where appropriate.

Proceedings filed in the Federal Court may be transferred to the Federal Magistrates Court either on the application of a party or on the court's own initiative: *FC Act* s 32AB, *FC Rules* O 81, *FMC Rules* Part 8. Proceedings can also be transferred from the Federal Magistrates Court to the Federal Court and one consideration is whether there are broader questions of public importance involving the interpretation of the legislation which would warrant the transfer. More commonly, matters are transferred from the Federal Court, especially where they are not complex and will traverse questions of law already established: *Y v Australian Postal Corporation* [2005] FCA 1396.

At the commencement of proceedings and at other times as prescribed by the Rules, certain fees must be paid unless they are waived by the court.

Content and extent of proceedings

While the hearing and decision are concerned with the terms of the application to the court, this in turn is dictated by the content of the complaint made to the HR&EOC. The unlawful discrimination in the application must be the same or the same in substance as the complaint or arise out of the same or substantially the same acts, omissions or practices that were the subject of the terminated complaint: *HR&EOC Act* s 46PO(3).

Both courts have adopted a broad interpretation of this subsection and have considered that where there is a link demonstrated between the allegations initially made in the complaint and more extensive one being brought before the court, then the revised and broadened allegations may properly become part of the claim to be ventilated in the proceedings: *Charles v Fuji Xerox Australia Pty Ltd* (2000) 105 FCR 573; *Bender v Bovis Lend Lease Pty Ltd* [2003] FMCA 277.

Facts or incidents occurring after the date of the complaint to HR&EOC cannot be included in the proceedings: *Hurst v Queensland* (2006) 151 FCR 562.

Associated jurisdiction

The Federal Court and the Federal Magistrates Court have the power under the "associated" jurisdiction to hear matters that arise from the same sub-stratum of facts as the principal proceedings: *Federal Court of Australia Act 1976* s 32, *Federal Magistrates Act 1999* s 18.

The facts of the discrimination claim and the claim made in the associated jurisdiction must be the same or substantially the same: *New*

South Wales Department of Housing v Moskalev (2007) 158 FCR 206 at [32], *Neate v Totally and Permanently Incapacitated Veterans' Association of NSW Ltd* [2007] FMCA 488 at [24].

The alternate claim may be made out even when the initial discrimination claim is dismissed: *Philip Morris Inc v Adam P Brown Male Fashions Pty Ltd* (1981) 148 CLR 457 at 474.

In employment claims, an action for a breach of contract can be relied on as an alternate or additional claim where it can be argued that the employer has breached or destroyed the trust and confidence that is part of the contract of employment: *Thomson v Orica Australia Pty Ltd* (2002) 116 IR 186 at 224-5.

Extension of time for application

If an application is lodged after the 28-day period from the issue of the notice of termination, then an application for an extension of time must be made to the court: *HR&EOC Act* s 46PO(2). Leave for an extension of time is also required if an appeal from a decision of a single judge is required. Similar principles are applied.

In exercising its discretion, the court needs to be satisfied that there are circumstances warranting the grant of the extension. While strictly the applicant does not carry an onus of proof, an acceptable explanation of the delay is a preliminary requirement. In *Bahonko v Royal Melbourne Institute of Technology* [2006] FCA 1325 at [21]-[23], the Federal Court held:

> The principles to be considered when deciding whether to extend time for the filing of an application were clearly enunciated by Wilcox J in *Hunter Valley Developments Pty Ltd v Cohen* (1984) 3 FCR 344 at 348–9 …
>
> Wilcox J noted that although the section did not place any onus of proof upon an applicant for an extension of time, an application had to be made. Special circumstances did not need to be shown but the Court would not grant the application unless positively satisfied that it was proper to do so. The "proscribed period" (28 days in that case) was not to be ignored. Indeed, it was the prima facie rule that proceedings commenced outside the proscribed period would not be entertained. An applicant for an extension had to show an "acceptable explanation of the delay" and that it was "fair and equitable" in the circumstances to extend time.
>
> His Honour set out other relevant factors, which ought guide the exercise of the Court's discretion. These included the question of prejudice to the respondent. However, the mere absence of prejudice was not enough to justify the grant of an extension. Importantly, he added

that the merits of the substantial application were properly to be taken into account in considering whether an extension of time should be granted.

The prejudice to the respondent occasioned by the delay in lodging an appeal and the initial application is only the period of time between the end of the statutory lodgement period and the date it was actually lodged, and not the entire period in which the discrimination claim has been on foot: *Ingram-Nader v Brinks Australia Pty Ltd* (2006) 151 FCR 524 at [19].

Any other action taken by the applicant needs to be explained to assist the court in assessing the reasons for the delay.

Pursuing other remedies against the same respondent for the same factual matrix is a relevant factor to take into account: *Alamzeb v Director-General Education (Qld)* [2003] FMCA 274.

The merits of the substantive application need to be addressed as an extension will not be granted where the proceedings are without merit or there is some fundamental flaw or the state of the pleadings does not permit a proper assessment of the merits of the case to be made: *Ferrus v Qantas Airways Ltd* (2006) 155 IR 88 at [48].

Discontinuing proceedings

For a variety of reasons, an applicant may want to discontinue proceedings. There may be further negotiations between the parties and a settlement may be reached. The applicant may decide that the time and risks in the litigation process are not worth the potential outcome of a relatively modest amount of compensation. Further facts may be revealed which demonstrate that the case is not going to succeed.

In the Federal Magistrates Court, the application must be filed 14 days before the hearing date or with leave at a later time: *FMC Rules* r 13.01. In the Federal Court, the application must be filed before the first directions hearing with no consent from the parties or after that with consent or by leave: *FC Rules* O 22 r 2.

Costs penalties may arise where the application to discontinue is made without the consent of the respondent. The respondent can apply for costs and, unless there is a good reason for them not to be granted, it can be assumed that they will follow the event. Sometimes an applicant may be able to negotiate with a respondent that each party pays their own costs if the applicant withdraws at an early stage without the respondent having incurred substantial costs. An applicant should not assume that a respondent will waive their rights to a cost recovery just because they are withdrawing or they may find that their withdrawal was based on a false assumption which a respondent does not accept: *Ingui v Ostara* [2003] FMCA 132.

Intervention by Commissioner

The special purpose Commissioners, including the Race, Sex and Disability Commissioners created under the *HR&EOC Act*, have a statutory right to assist both courts in an *amicus curiae* role where there is a matter of broader application or public interest: s 46PV(1). The court must grant leave and so the Commissioner makes a formal application setting out the reasons they seek to intervene, such as involvement in the legal policy area which will be interpreted during the proceedings or that the implications of the interpretation of a particular legislative provision need to be properly considered from an independent impartial standpoint rather than from one dictated by a view of the facts adopted by one party. The Commissioner has intervened in a number of proceedings where a broader public interest in the outcome of an individual case is shown.

Constitution of hearing

In the Federal jurisdiction, in either court there is a single judge who hears and determines the case. On appeal to the Full Federal Court, there may be three or one judge depending on the nature of the appeal.

In some States, the tribunal is constituted by three members, the chair person being a practising lawyer. The legal member has the capacity to make decisions alone on questions of law, and questions of fact are determined by a unanimous decision of all three members or a majority of two. In other States a judicial member sits alone. Appeal provisions vary between States.

Onus of proof

In all cases of direct discrimination and most cases of indirect discrimination, the applicant carries the onus of proof. The respondent carries the onus when seeking to rely on an exemption or exception (see Chapter 11).

When establishing discrimination itself, the only variation arises where there is a shift in the onus in the statutory definition of indirect discrimination which requires the respondent to demonstrate that the alleged act was "reasonable" (see Chapter 3). If the applicant does not establish sufficient facts which even if accepted would demonstrate a breach of the legislation, then the complaint necessarily must fail.

While the respondent does not carry any onus as such, the reality of the conduct of cases is that a prudent respondent provides as much information to the tribunal determining the issues between the parties as it can to assist the tribunal to reach the "correct" decision, that is, one in the respondent's favour. Strictly, this is not necessary but is the sensible course of action for any respondent to follow. An argument that the applicant has not discharged her or his onus may be valid and successful in some circumstances, but where there are complicated or confused facts asserted by an applicant, then it is better to anticipate that an application to prematurely dispose of the matter may not find favour and hence all necessary points for the defence should be mounted.

Standard of proof

The standard of proof is the *Briginshaw* test:

> The seriousness of an allegation made, the inherent unlikelihood of an occurrence of a given description, or the gravity of the consequences flowing from a particular finding are considerations which must affect the answer to the question whether the issue has been proved. (*Briginshaw v Briginshaw* (1938) 60 CLR 336 at 362)

This test has been applied in all jurisdictions as the basis for assessing the evidence and the allegations. As the Full Federal Court noted:

> It is for the applicant who complains of racial discrimination to make out his or her case on the balance of probabilities. It may be accepted that it is unusual to find direct evidence of racial discrimination, and the outcome of a case will usually depend on what inferences it is proper to draw from the primary facts found ... There may be cases in which the motivation may be subconscious. There may be cases in which the proper inference to be drawn from the evidence is that, whether or not the employer realised it at the time or not, race was the reason it acted as it did ... It was common ground at first instance that the standard of proof for breaches of the RDA is the higher standard referred to in *Briginshaw v Briginshaw* ... Racial discrimination is a serious matter, which is not lightly to be inferred ...
>
> In a case depending on circumstantial evidence, it is well established that the trier of fact must consider "the weight which is to be given to the united force of all the circumstances put together". One should not put a piece of circumstantial evidence out of consideration merely because an inference does not arise from it alone ... It is the cumulative effect of the circumstances which is important provided, of course, that the circumstances relied upon are established as facts. (*Sharma v Legal Aid (Qld)* (2002) 115 IR 91 at 98)

As the Federal Court has noted:

> It is generally accepted ... that there is a need to distinguish between identification of the appropriate standard of proof (on the balance of probabilities in a civil case) and the quality of evidence which will satisfy the standard in a particular case. That is a matter which may vary according to the gravity of the accusations or contentions to be evaluated. Although the balance of probabilities remains the civil standard of proof, what may be required to satisfy that standard of proof in a given case, and satisfy it to the 'reasonable satisfaction' of the court, is not fixed. (*Penhall-Jones v New South Wales* [2007] FCA 925 at [118]).

Injunctions

The applicant, respondent, an affected person or the HR&EOC may apply to the Federal Court or the Federal Magistrates Court for an interim or interlocutory injunction at any time after a complaint is lodged with the HR&EOC: *HR&EOC Act* ss 40PO(6), 46PP. The basis for an application must be to maintain "the "status quo, as it existed immediately before the complaint was lodged" or "the rights of any applicant, respondent or affected person". The court cannot grant an interim injunction conditional on the applicant giving an undertaking as to damages: *HR&EOC Act* ss 46PO(8), 46PP(5).

Such an order can provide a powerful tool for a person who considers that they are about to lose their job due to an act of discrimination such as dismissal due to pregnancy. Only the initial procedural step of lodging a complaint is required (see Chapter 12).

An interim injunction may be more far reaching than just maintaining the status quo as to maintain "the rights" of the parties may require some form of active intervention in the relationship between the parties. It may be of a mandatory or prohibitive nature to prevent one party taking action which will prejudice the other party in some way: *Business World Computers Pty Ltd v Telecom* (1988) 82 ALR 499 at 501-4. The application must be clearly set out with the applicant's objectives and also there must be evidence that the respondent intends to alter the status quo: *Cox v Said* [2006] FMCA 1300.

An ex parte injunction to stop a criminal trial due to start in three days was refused by the Federal Court and a major factor was that, while a race discrimination complaint had recently been lodged with HR&EOC, it could have been lodged at a much earlier time: *Wotton v Queensland* [2007] FCA 280.

There are two tests to be applied before an interim injunction is granted. The first test is whether there is a genuine or serious question of fact to be tried eventually during the court hearing. The court must be satisfied that a dispute exists which is capable of being conciliated by the HR&EOC and that "the dispute itself is not fanciful or so lacking in merit that no reasonable commission invested with the powers of the Human Rights & Equal Opportunity Commission would decline to entertain it": *Beck v Leichhardt Municipal Council* [2002] FMCA 331 at [16].

In the circumstances where the respondent relies on a statutory defence such as unjustifiable hardship in a disability complaint, then that will be a factor taken into account also in the general assessment of the serious issue to be tried test: *P v Minister for Education* (1996) EOC ¶92-795.

The second test is an assessment of where the balance of convenience falls. If either party intends to rely on this test as a basis for opposing or supporting the grant of an interim injunction, then evidence needs to be led to demonstrate the utility of the order or, conversely, that the granting of the order would lead to results which would have a wider detrimental impact than just on the applicant.

An interim injunction can be granted to maintain a person in a position pending either the conciliation processes or until the determination of a final court hearing. An employment-related order may go beyond the usual common law principle that specific performance will not usually not be granted in relation to employment contracts. This arises as the statutory provisions provide a broader compass. An injunction will not be granted where the working relationship has already broken down and is unlikely to be able to be restored.

An interim injunction cannot be used to create a right that did not exist at the time the complaint was made. Therefore, if a person is not appointed to a position or fails to achieve a promotion, or is unable to secure a position as certain conditions cannot be met then an interim injunction will not be granted to produce that result: *AB v NSW Minister for Education* [2003] FMCA 16. In those circumstances, the award of financial compensation at the end of the proceedings is seen as an appropriate remedy.

A short term interim injunction to prevent a respondent from disposing of real estate assets being the conciliation of a complaint may be granted: *A v B* [2006] FMCA 454.

In appropriate circumstances, the court may be prepared to accept an undertaking that a respondent will not take certain steps instead of granting an interim injunction even if the order was appropriate to be granted.

An injunction at the end of a case after disability discrimination in education had been established was refused by the Full Federal Court as there was no evidence to establish that the likelihood that the educational authority would contravene the student's rights in the future and the obligations that the student was seeking to impose went beyond the breaches established by the evidence: *Hurst v Queensland (No 2)* [2006] FCAFC 151.

Representation

Parties have the right to appear themselves and they may have legal representation: *HR&EOC Act* s 46PO. Also, they may be represented by a non-lawyer unless the court is of the opinion that it is "inappropriate" for the person to appear.

A frequent difficulty in the discrimination jurisdiction is that applicants are self-represented. To a lesser extent, an individual respondent may also appear without legal assistance. This can raise certain problems for a legally represented respondent as the court has to balance the interests of all parties when facing the obvious deficiencies in an applicant's case both as to the procedural aspects and then the substantive issues where merit is difficult to readily ascertain.

An impecunious applicant may have little regard for the potential outcome of costs orders against them as they have no financial means and no intention of paying such orders. A successful respondent can be left with an unpaid costs bill.

Procedural difficulties can arise when an applicant has to cross-examine the respondent's witnesses when they are unaware of the usual methods of the process and make serious but unsubstantiated allegations or use the opportunity to vent their general frustrations about their situation. On some occasions, they have been permitted to continue asking irrelevant and contentious questions as an attempt to allow them an opportunity to ventilate their propositions. This can be a complete waste of time and costs and only adds to their suspicions and hostility. A real dilemma arises for the presiding judicial officer when confronted with the alleged perpetrator of sexual harassment being permitted to cross-examine the victim/applicant and in one way repeating or refreshing the alleged harassment.

Both courts operate a pro bono system where cases may be referred to a panel for assistance. Only cases where there is some appearance of merit and a substantial reason for the person not being able to gain access to their own paid lawyer will result in a referral.

Evidence of witnesses

Usually, evidence from witnesses is in affidavit form: *FC Rules* O 14, *FMC Rules* Part 15.4. Affidavits are filed some time before the hearing following court orders setting out the timetable made at a directions hearing. Often, the applicants have their own evidence of events and some minor supporting evidence such as evidence supporting a damages claim for pain and suffering. The majority of the evidence is put on by respondents as they endeavour to explain the factual situation presented by the applicant. This means that the bulk of the hearing can be spent on evidence from the respondent's witnesses.

If a witness is uncooperative, then they may be able to be subpoenaed for the hearing without the advantage of the other side being able to peruse their evidence and respond appropriately. This is an unusual circumstance.

An affidavit will not be accepted for filing if longer than 50 pages, without the leave of the court. Where there are lengthy documents referred to in an affidavit, then they should be exhibited in a separate bundle. If one party's documents are lengthy, then they may elect to prepare a bundle which is put in volumes and paginated. Each witness can then refer to the common bundle in their affidavit and the hearing proceeds on a more efficient basis as repetition is significantly reduced. This is more commonly a convenient mechanism for respondents.

Except in the most exceptional of circumstances, a judge cannot rely on evidence that was filed but not tendered by a party as this can give rise to a reasonable apprehension of bias: *Huang v University of New South Wales (No 3)* (2006) 154 FCR 16.

Production of documents

Both the Federal Court and the Federal Magistrates Court have the power to require witnesses to attend and answer questions and to require the production of documents. Parties may issue a notice to produce to other parties: *FC Rules* O 33 r 12*, FMC Rules* r 15.24.

In the Federal Magistrates Court, there is a limit of five subpoenas for each party for a proceeding. If more than five are needed, then the party must approach the court to obtain an order. When doing so, an affidavit setting out the reasons for the extra ones should accompany the application. Usually, such applications are considered in chambers. Copies of subpoenas issued with the return date noted should be provided to the other side. Where the costs of complying with a subpoena involve substantial loss or expense, then an application may be made for the payment of those costs to the person issuing the subpoena.

Once documents are produced, then an order for inspection and copying is needed. These matters are usually dealt with by a registrar. If a person wants to set aside a subpoena, they must apply to the court and have some valid reasons, such as the breadth or the oppressive nature of the request or that a fishing expedition is being conducted in the hope of turning up some documents to prove the case.

Often, the documents that an applicant needs to establish part of the claim are in the possession of the respondent. Sometimes it will be in the interests of the respondent to produce them as they may disprove the allegations made by the applicant and establish an alternate scenario. The preparation of a properly crafted subpoena to produce documents can be a crucial step for an applicant.

An employer or other type of respondent may need to put into evidence their policies in relevant areas or other documents showing the approach they adopt in relevant circumstances. A range of documents may be needed to establish a position, such as job descriptions, corporate structures, employment profile, product information and background to the corporate development and history.

An order for discovery may be the most suitable mechanism for an applicant to obtain these documents. Notices of discovery listing the categories of relevant documents may be issued in the Federal Court following the usual court rules: *FC Rules* O 15. In the Federal Magistrates Court, interrogatories and discovery are only allowed when the court makes a declaration that it is appropriate "in the interests of justice": *FMC Act* s 45, *FMC Rules* Part 14.2.

Joinder of other parties

Both courts have the power to join other parties: *FC Rules* O 6 r 2, *FMC Rules* Part 11.1.

Sometimes other persons or organisations are joined as respondents. This can occur in a variety of circumstances. The court rules require all parties to be joined for the complete and final determination of all matters in dispute. Parties may apply to be included or removed as a party or this may occur on the court's own motion.

In the Federal Magistrates Court, the joinder of other parties can occur on a party's own action before the first directions hearing and after that, a court order is required. Obviously, a relevant link will need to be demonstrated between the complaint and the person or organisation. The refining of the focus of a complaint or some information from the nominated respondent may clarify the identity of those responsible for the alleged discriminatory act. The corporate structure may change and the nomenclature of the respondent may need some alteration. A respondent may indicate that they dispute the assertion of vicarious responsibility and so it may, in some circumstances, be prudent to join the individuals alleged to be responsible for the breaches of the discrimination law.

Closed hearings and non-publication orders

There are powers to close hearings or suppress the publication of certain, identified information: *FC Act* ss 17, 50, *FMC Act* s 61.

Generally, the approach to the closure of a hearing is that it should not occur at all as "justice must be seen to be done": *ABC v Parish* (1980) 29 ALR 228. Courts are reluctant to order that people cannot enter the courtroom during a hearing and do so only in the more extreme cases where the evidence to be given cannot properly or adequately be given by the witness in front of unnecessary or unknown people.

The preferred approach is for the court to make an order prohibiting the publication of any information which will identify the witness, a document or the evidence itself, including any sensitive or personal information such as lewd acts of sexual harassment or non-consensual sexual intercourse, where prejudice and embarrassment to the applicant may arise from publication of those details: *E v Australian Red Cross Society* (1991) 27 FCR 310 at 313.

Such orders are not common and require a substantial basis to be made out, as:

> [T]he need for substantial and serious grounds of a high order before departing from the principle that justice should be administered with full transparency so far as practicable. Underlying this principle is the need for public confidence in, and public understanding of, the process by which justice is administered. There is a significant public interest in being able to follow the way in which disputes are resolved in the court and the suppression of allegations, evidence, or identity may result in loss of confidence or community mistrust of the process of the administration of justice. For that reason, a strong basis for departure from the prima facie rule must be established ... [T]he issue for the court to consider is whether members of the public need to know the details of the information sought to be suppressed ... [I]n determining whether to make a suppression order, the court must proceed on the assumption that the public are entitled to see justice administered with full access to the evidence unless it is necessary that, in order for justice to be done, the material ought be kept confidential. (*Johnston v Cameron* (2002) 195 ALR 300 at 316)

In some cases, a suppression order may be granted for the identity of the applicant or a witness. This means that any media or legal reporting of the case refers to the applicant in an anonymous way but the allegations in the complaint and the evidence are revealed. This protects the public interest in an open justice system while keeping the individual away from some degree of public scrutiny.

The publication of the name of a party could be prevented if some significant degree of commercial sensitivity or potential economic loss arising from media exposure of the complaint can be established to demonstrate a public interest that needs to be protected: *Versace v Monte* [2001] FCA 1565. The test is a high one and is rarely satisfied. If the name of the respondent is suppressed, it may only be until the outcome of the case is determined and, if the respondent is found to be in breach of the legislation, then the name is released.

Some of the difficulties and sensitivities for respondents arise when the media attend the first day or two of a hearing and the applicant's allegations are given substantial media attention but, when the response is provided, there is not a similar degree of coverage. When a decision is handed down, there may be no or minimal media attention which does not equate with the coverage of the initial allegations. Some respondents have found that their "trial by media" far outstrips the impact of any eventual decision. This is one factor taken into account when balancing the competing interests and priorities for a respondent trying to settle a complaint before a hearing commences and any publicity is generated.

First directions hearing

Some cases involve complex interlocutory matters and many hearing days while a minority are heard in a day on the basis of the documents annexed to the HR&EOC notice of termination and some submissions.

Usually at the first directions hearing in both courts, orders are made for the further conduct of the proceedings and often hearing dates are set. The directions given set out the date for the applicant to file and serve any evidence and then a further period for the respondent to do the same and for any reply from the applicant. The usual period for each step is 28 days. The Federal Magistrates Court endeavours to have only one directions hearing. The Federal Court usually requires the parties to attend a further directions hearing once all the evidence is filed and served to set a hearing date and make any preliminary orders.

While there are no formal pleadings in either court in these matters, sometimes an order is made for a points of claim or some further formal documentation setting out the claim to clarify the issues before the court.

Representative complaints

While representative complaints can be lodged under the terms of the *HR&EOC Act*, the Federal Magistrates Court does not have any particular rules or procedures for the conduct of such matters. It appears that they would be conducted in the same manner as proceedings with a single applicant.

There are complex procedures in the Federal Court under Part IVA of the *FC Act* and O 73 of the *FC Rules* where there are seven or more applicants. These have not been used in any discrimination cases as yet. Some employment cases could involve large groups of employees all affected by a restructure, pay arrangements or other internal mechanisms which are alleged to be discriminatory on the ground of sex or disability. A trade union can lodge a discrimination complaint on behalf of its members and this is another way of incorporating a group of people under the one complaint: *HR&EOC Act* s 46P(2)(c); *Commonwealth Bank v HR&EOC* (1997) 80 FCR 78.

Evidence

Both courts are bound by the *Evidence Act* 1995 (Cth). The Federal Magistrates Court is required to act as informally as possible when exercising judicial power: *FMC Act* s 3. This means that some judges sometimes adopt a less rigid view about the admissibility of certain evidence which may strictly be inadmissible. A broader brush approach to relevance can assist applicants in presenting all the material they consider necessary while still maintaining proper boundaries from straying into areas completely unrelated to the allegations which are the subject of the proceedings. This flexibility is one advantage of the Federal Magistrates Court over the Federal Court for an applicant. In the Federal Court, the rules of evidence are applied consistently and with little variation. As all the evidence is usually in affidavit form, tables of objections and related oral arguments can take some of the first part of the hearing to resolve.

A preliminary application by a respondent to strike out some of the applicant's affidavit material may be appropriate:

> [T]he Court clearly needs to ensure that affidavit material before the Court properly identifies issues relied upon which can be regarded as issues which are the same as or the same in substance as the unlawful discrimination that was the subject of the terminated complaint or must arise out of the same or substantially the same acts, omissions or practices that were the subject of the terminated complaint. It is within the power of the Court to determine those parts of affidavit material

which should be struck out. To do so is not to embark upon a process which might be better left to the trial of action but rather to ensure that issues are properly identified consistent with the obligations of the Court in considering the unlawful discrimination alleged in this application compared with the discrimination which was the subject of the terminated complaint. It is appropriate for that matter to be considered at an early stage of the proceedings particularly where there is a potential for voluminous affidavit material raising numerous issues perhaps not raised before the Commission and therefore not subject to the conciliation procedures of the Commission. To allow the affidavit material to be dealt with at trial may involve additional expense to a Respondent in meeting allegations not previously made the subject of a complaint before HREOC. (*Bender v Bovis Lend Lease Pty Ltd* [2003] FMCA 277 at [21])

Usually there is no direct evidence of discrimination and so it is necessary for the court to look at all the evidence and determine whether it can draw an inference from the combination of facts even if none of the facts when viewed alone would have supported the inference: *Chamberlain v The Queen (No 2)* (1984) 153 CLR 521; *Khanna v Ministry of Defence* [1981] ICR 653 at 658. This may form an essential part of an applicant's case as it is unusual for there to be uncontroverted direct evidence of the acts alleged to be discrimination or harassment.

Some witnesses, especially the applicant, can be in the witness box for a substantial period. This arises particularly in employment cases where there is a lengthy period covered by the complaint and numerous allegations identifying many conversations and documents, each of which must be explored separately. Those types of cases usually have a substantial number of respondent witnesses as the range of allegations often involves many people not only in direct contact in the workplace but also throughout the management structure.

Evidence may be adduced which demonstrates or raises an inference that the decision-makers had a particular intention or motive at the time of making the decision or that they were following a particular policy that led to a discriminatory result. Alternatively, the evidence may demonstrate that there was no less favourable treatment or that there in fact was, but it was not on the ground alleged to give rise to the discrimination claim when a particular policy was implemented.

Frequently, applicants keep a diary of events and these can be detailed and cover a substantial period. Their contents can give rise to a significant body of other evidence such as minutes of meetings and supporting documents as well as the work documents being produced by the applicant and others.

The identification of a comparable employee to establish the less favourable treatment component of a direct discrimination complaint may require a detailed analysis of the employment records and work performance data of other employees. Obtaining this evidence from the respondent and then analysing it to present to the court can be a time-consuming exercise for an applicant. The creative use of discovery or subpoenas can be a significant pre-hearing focus.

An indirect discrimination complaint will usually require substantial evidence to provide the basis for the claim and a detailed analysis of factors such as workforce composition may be required: *Wollongong City Council v Bonella* (EOD) [2002] NSWADTAP 26. Such evidence may be required from properly qualified experts.

In all the State tribunals, the rules of evidence do not apply. This means that there is some more flexibility than can arise from a strict application of the *Evidence Act*.

Expert evidence

Expert evidence can be called by either party to provide relevant information to the court. Such evidence can cover a range of issues such as the nature and impact of a particular disability on either the individual applicant or on a group of people with that disability. In more complex areas such as establishing an unjustifiable hardship defence, there may be some professional evidence from architects and engineers on the difficulties to be encountered in altering a building to make it fully accessible or the costs which will be incurred for an immediate alteration or the long-term plans to alter premises over time. An applicant may then need to provide some expert evidence to counter this evidence and so be required to call their own expert architects or engineers to explain a different planning process to the court.

An applicant may call expert evidence of their psychological state and that expert may be able to attribute a casual nexus between the acts of discrimination or harassment and the person's current health status. A respondent may require an applicant to attend for psychiatric or psychological testing and reporting from an independent expert not involved in their treatment. Questions of causation assist a tribunal in determining the level of financial compensation to be awarded to a successful applicant.

An indirect discrimination complaint involving statistical analysis to determine the pool for the "substantially higher proportion" test to be met may require expert evidence on the identification and construction of the group itself and the proper approach to determining the various factors to meet the statutory formulae. The direct discrimination test of a comparator between the applicant and others not in the same group as the applicant, such as men or people without a disability, may require expert evidence to establish the parameters of the group.

Both courts have formal requirements for expert witnesses: *FC Rules* O 34, *FMC Rules* Part 15.2. In June 2007, the Federal Court issued a revised Practice Direction which sets out the guidelines for expert witnesses including the form of the evidence or report and the way it must be set out.

Submissions

The applicant must bring the elements of the case together at the conclusion of the evidence by summarising and analysing the facts and the law in support of their complaint, using the transcript of the evidence when it is available. The respondent then adopts the same process by trying to meet the contents of the applicant's submissions and raise any other material which is beneficial to the position they put to the court. The applicant then makes a short reply.

In some cases, these submissions are oral and, in a straightforward case, may take little time. In more complex cases, these can take considerable time and can be written. The analysis of the law can be detailed as there may be a number of separate and substantial legal issues to be determined by the court or tribunal.

Decision

At the conclusion of the hearing, the court forms a view on the facts and the law and determines whether the allegations of unlawful discrimination have been substantiated and, if so, the orders to be made.

If a finding for the applicant is made, that decision may involve rejecting the respondent's submissions or any defence they may have raised. If the finding is for the respondent, then it may be that the applicant has not been able to make out their case to the satisfaction of the court or the applicant's evidence or some parts of it may be specifically rejected.

The court then must issue a decision which adequately covers the questions of fact and law before it and on which it relies to make the decision itself. The process must be set out to enable the parties to understand the route taken by the court to make the decision and the components of the decision. It is "necessary that the essential ground or grounds upon which the decision rests should be articulated. In many cases the reasons for preferring one conclusion to another also need to be given": *Soulemezis v Dudley (Holdings) Pty Limited* (1987) 10 NSWLR 247 at 280, *Martin v Queensland Electricity Transmission Corporation* [2003] QSC 309 at [43].

Once a complaint is found to be substantiated, then a range of remedies are available (see Chapter 14). An order for costs is usually made (see Chapter 14).

Separate questions should only be answered in a preliminary decision where the necessary findings of fact have been made by the judge, otherwise a mechanism designed to shorten proceedings and reduce costs may have the opposite effect: *Rainsford v Victoria* (2005) 144 FCR 279.

Summary dismissal of complaints

One area that has been frequently used by respondents to avoid conducting a full hearing when there is an application without merit of fact or law is to apply for a summary dismissal of the complaint at some point during the hearing. This application may be made at any time.

One convenient time is at the conclusion of the applicant's case as, at that time, given the applicant carries the onus of proof, the applicant's case should be at its highest before any evidence led by the respondent can undermine its effectiveness.

Another appropriate time may be when all the applicant's affidavits and documents have been filed and the respondent's submission to the court is that, taking the applicant's case at its highest and as put by the applicant, there is no breach of the discrimination law demonstrated and so the case should be terminated at that point.

Generally, the approach is that while an applicant cannot be denied an opportunity to put forward their case to the best of their ability, they cannot be permitted to pursue a complaint that is without merit or substance or is vexatious. Dismissal will not be ordered where it is demonstrated that there are genuine issues to be tried and these could properly form the basis of a substantiated discrimination claim: *Ilian v Australian Broadcasting Corp* [2005] FMCA 1143.

Both courts have specific procedures for making an application where no reasonable cause of action is disclosed or where the proceedings are frivolous or vexatious or an abuse of process: *FC Rules* O 20 r 2, *FMC Rules* Part 13.3.

Most applications are dismissed on the basis that the complaint is lacking in substance or is misconceived: *Perry v Howard* [2005] FCA 1702. Both can arise as a genuine misunderstanding of the events by the applicant, a failure (albeit a persistent one) to accept an alternative explanation proffered by a respondent for the result being queried, or a misapprehension about the ambit and objectives of the discrimination law.

The major consideration by either court is that proceedings should not be permitted to continue where it is apparent that they will fail: *Webster v Lampard* (1993) 177 CLR 598. The question to be addressed is:

> The true inquiry is not whether the appellant's claim lacked merit, but whether the appellant's claim failed to disclose a reasonable cause of action. (*Rana v University of South Australia* (2004) 136 FCR 344 at [79])

A summary dismissal should not be made where the judicial officer evaluates and weighs the evidence as that is a process that can only be performed after a fully contested hearing: *Penhall-Jones v New South Wales (Ministry of Transport)* [2006] FCA 934 at [26].

A subjective view by the applicant that they have been discriminated against in the absence of any evidence capable of sustaining that view will not be sufficient and the proceedings will be summarily dismissed: *Paramasivam v University of New South Wales* [2007] FCA 875.

Summary dismissal is an interlocutory decision and so an appellant needs leave to appeal before an appeal can be pursued: *FC Act* s 24(1A), *Joyce v St George Bank Ltd* [2005] FCA 916.

Costs

The usual practice is that costs follow the event and so an unsuccessful party is ordered to pay the party-party costs of the successful party or parties: *Fetherston v Peninsula Health (No 2)* (2004) 137 FCR 262 (see Chapter 14).

Schedule 1 to the *FMC Rules* sets out the costs usually recoverable in the Federal Magistrates Court. Where counsel is used, it is necessary to seek an order that this was required to gain the increased amount of costs.

In Queensland, a costs order made in the absence of the applicant was overturned on appeal as it was a breach of procedural fairness: *N v Queensland* [2006] QSC 062.

Indemnity costs

Where one party considers that they have a substantial chance of a successful outcome when the other party persistently refuses to enter into negotiations to end the case before the hearing, then a formal offer of compromise should be considered.

The Federal Court has formal procedures for applications for offers of compromise: *FC Rules* O 23. These procedures apply to the Federal Magistrates Court also. Under this provision, a judge or magistrate exercises her or his discretion and takes account of all relevant factors including the final outcome of the proceedings, the amount offered in any offer of compromise and the rejection or non-response of the applicant and date on which it was made: *Batzialas v Tony Davies Motors* [2002] FMCA 243.

The more informal processes of a "Calderbank letter" (see Chapter 14) remain available and may be more convenient as only an exchange of correspondence is required to demonstrate that reasonable efforts were made by one party to settle the case: *Caratti v Weininger (No 2)* [2007] FMCA 783. There are some formalities which need to be followed, principally so the applicant can distinguish between an amount for costs and the amount which she or he may end up with. Such a letter is admissible into evidence: *Evidence Act* 1995 s 131(2)(h).

Where a reasonable offer is rejected and the final court orders are above or below any amount offered, then the party making the offer is entitled to indemnity costs from the date of the offer and party-party costs before that date unless the court orders otherwise: *FC Rules* O 23 r 11(4), (5). Indemnity costs are the full legal costs incurred during the conduct of the proceedings. This is an advantage as the usual costs order only covers between 65 to 80 per cent of the full legal costs.

Security for costs applications

In some circumstances, an application for a security for costs order may be appropriate, particularly where the case is manifestly without merit: *FC Act* s 56, *FC Rules* O 28, *FMC Rules* r 21.01. The Federal Magistrates Court can order that costs be paid by a party before the proceeding is concluded: *FMC Rules* r 21.02(2)(d). An application can be made when an appeal to the Full Court has been lodged even when one was not made in the initial proceedings: *FC Rules* O 52 r 20.

A variety of factors may be relevant including the prospects of success and the quantum of any costs orders. Whether the making of the order will stifle the further conduct of the proceedings can be relevant as can whether the financial status of the applicant has arisen as a result of the conduct complained of in the litigation: *Wyong-Gosford Progressive Community Radio Incorporated v Australian Communications and Media Authority* [2006] FCA 625 at [11]-[12].

This application can be appropriate where there is an impecunious applicant who has a history of not paying costs orders after unsuccessful litigation and the case is one with no obvious basis to succeed: *Croker v Sydney Institute of TAFE* [2003] FCA 942.

Order limiting amount of costs

One available procedure is the power of the court, by its own motion or on application by the parties, to set the maximum costs that may be recovered on a party-party basis: *FMC Rules* r 21.03. The Federal Court can only do so at a directions hearing: *FC Rules* O 62A r 1. In such a way an applicant can seek to protect themselves from a large costs order. The application may be warranted where the applicant intended to run a relatively simple proceeding but the respondent is making a substantial response by using a large number of witnesses or extensive documentation, resulting in the proceedings being longer than the applicant thought when initiating them.

The Federal Magistrates Court as held that the legal and factual complexities of the matter were relevant considerations as were:

> Thus it is relevant as part of all the circumstances of the particular case to consider matters such as the timing of the application, whether the order sought is proposed to apply for the benefit of both parties, the nature and likely complexity of the claim and the extent of the remedies sought, the costs likely to be incurred as well as any other matters which may go towards establishing that there should be a departure in advance from the usual rules as to quantification of the amount of costs to be payable by the ultimately unsuccessful party. (*Flew v Mirvac Parking Pty Ltd* [2006] FMCA 1818 at [48])

The Federal Court has ordered a set maximum amount after the conclusion of proceedings due to the "delay, expense and inconvenience" of taxing a substantial costs amount and the lack of financial capacity for the person paying the costs such that they would be unable to pay these significant extra costs arising from the taxation process: *Dunstan v Human Rights and Equal Opportunity Commission (No 3)* [2006] FCA 916.

Appeals

If either party is dissatisfied with a decision of a single judge of the Federal Court or the Federal Magistrates Court, then they can appeal to the Full Federal Court: *FC Act* s 24, *FMC Act* s 20. On an appeal from the Federal Magistrates Court, a single judge may exercise appellate jurisdiction where the Chief Justice considers it appropriate: *FC Act* s 25(1A). If a single judge exercises the appellate jurisdiction, then there is no further appeal to the Full Court: *FC Act* s 24(1AAA).

An appeal must be lodged within 21 days of the date the decision was pronounced: *FC Rules* O 52 r 15. An application for leave to appeal must be made if the appeal is lodged later than 21 days and must demonstrate that there is sufficient merit for the appeal to be permitted to continue. There must be a demonstrable prejudice to the respondent for leave to be refused, especially where the period after the 21 days is a relatively short duration: *Joyce v St George Bank Ltd* [2006] FCA 257. An extension of time will not be granted where the appeal is without any merit and so has no prospects of success: *SZGAP v Minister for Immigration and Multicultural and Indigenous Affairs* (2005) 227 ALR 683, *Mandic v Phillis* (2005) 225 ALR 760.

An application to the High Court for special leave to appeal is the only further avenue for appeal if a party is unsuccessful before the Full Federal Court. If special leave is granted, then the matter goes to a full hearing before the High Court.

An appeal where a Federal Magistrate has dismissed an application without a full hearing will further examine the statutory basis for the claim and the facts as asserted by the applicant and it will be dismissed if no sustainable claim can be identified. The link or causal nexus between the acts and the ground of discrimination must be able to be demonstrated.

14

REMEDIES

This chapter examines the type and range of orders made in discrimination and harassment cases. The primary focus is on the outcome of cases conducted in the Federal Court or the Federal Magistrates Court. The equivalent State laws are referred to briefly. The range of orders is similar across Australia.

At the conclusion of the hearing, the Federal Court or the Federal Magistrates Court hands down a decision and makes formal orders.

The court has the power to make certain orders as set out in s 46PO(4) of the *Human Rights and Equal Opportunity Commission Act 1986*:

> If the court concerned is satisfied that there has been unlawful discrimination by any respondent, the court may make such orders (including a declaration of right) as it thinks fit, including any of the following orders or any order to a similar effect:
>
> (a) an order declaring that the respondent has committed unlawful discrimination and directing the respondent not to repeat or continue such unlawful discrimination;
>
> (b) an order requiring a respondent to perform any reasonable act or course of conduct to redress any loss or damage suffered by an applicant;
>
> (c) an order requiring a respondent to employ or re-employ an applicant;
>
> (d) an order requiring a respondent to pay to an applicant damages by way of compensation for any loss or damage suffered because of the conduct of the respondent;
>
> (e) an order requiring a respondent to vary the termination of a contract or agreement to redress any loss or damage suffered by an applicant;
>
> (f) an order declaring that it would be inappropriate for any further action to be taken in the matter.

Orders in favour of respondent

If the respondent is successful and the proceedings are dismissed as not being made out, then the order records that outcome and usually a costs order is made (see below). A significant proportion of cases before the Federal Court and the Federal Magistrates Court are dismissed. Both courts apply technical interpretations to the terms of the discrimination laws and the factual matters in each case. A number of cases are unsuccessful as they are not made out on a factual basis. Others fail the test of establishing that the facts as asserted actually meet the various legal requirements, which can be complex and have narrow application. Legal advisers need to make a realistic and proper assessment of the merits of a complaint before either filing an application or a defence as the costs of some cases can be high while the amount of damages awarded is relatively small. Applicant's legal costs of $80,000 for a damages award of $15,000 are not unusual. Fruitful negotiations or an offer of compromise can be an essential part of a respondent's defence tactics.

Orders in favour of applicant

There are a range of orders the Federal Court or the Federal Magistrates Court can make when an applicant successfully establishes that there has been an act of unlawful discrimination in breach of the federal discrimination laws. This requires a finding from the court that the respondent has committed an act of racial, sex, disability or age discrimination and then further orders are made. These usually reflect the type or tenor of orders sought by the applicant but the court is not restricted and can make any orders that it considers appropriate. This can occur where matters have been revealed during the proceedings that go beyond the original allegations and serve to put the respondent's actions or decisions in a poor light.

Damages

The remedy most commonly sought and awarded is for the payment of an amount of financial compensation. The principles of assessment of damages are flexible, while generally based on the principles applied when assessing damages in tort: *Hall v A & A Sheiban Pty Ltd* (1989) 20 FCR 217. Any damages to be awarded are statutorily based and it is the wording of the statute which is the principal basis for assessment for this head of damage: *Stephenson v HR&EOC* (1995) 61 FLR 134 at 142-3.

As Wilcox J has noted:

> [T]he task of determining the appropriate levels of damages in a case of sex discrimination or sexual harassment is not an easy one. Where it appears that a claimant has incurred particular expenditure or lost particular income as a result of the relevant loss, that economic loss may readily be calculated. But damages for such matters as injury to feelings, distress, humiliation and the effect of the claimant's relationships with other people are not susceptible to mathematical calculation … To ignore such items of damage simply because of the impossibility of demonstrating the correctness of any particular figure would be to visit an injustice upon a complainant be failing to grant relief in respect of a proved item of damage. (*Hall v A & A Sheiban Pty Ltd* (1989) 20 FCR 217 at 256)

Damages are designed to place applicants in the position in which they would have been if there had not been an act of unlawful discrimination committed against them: *Haines v Bendall* (1991) 172 CLR 60 at 63. The task of assessing damages is for compensation for the applicant and it is not to "impose punishment" on the respondent: *Commonwealth v Evans* (2004) 81 ALD 402 at [80].

The damages fall into three categories, special damages covering economic loss, general damages covering non-economic loss and exemplary or aggravated damages.

An award of damages should not be seen as a replacement for other orders. Alternatively, other orders such as to appoint a person to the job in question is not a replacement for an order for damages for the injury to feelings and humiliation felt by the complainant before that decision and both orders can be made.

It is essential that evidence of loss or damage be adduced during the hearing and, if it is available and appropriate, then that part of the claim must be supported by any necessary expert evidence such as a psychiatrist for evidence of hurt and humiliation suffered as a result of the unlawful conduct. In the absence of any evidence of loss or damage, then no damages will be awarded: *Hurst v Queensland (No 2)* [2006] FCAFC 151 at [26].

Aggravated damages

Aggravated damages will only be awarded in limited circumstances.

Responding to a certain train of events will not demonstrate the basis for an aggravated damages award. There needs to be an extra element of malevolence or spite or ill will also: *Hewett v Davies* [2006] FMCA 1678 at [20]. Where an employer initiates internal policies on discrimination once a situation comes to their attention, these responses cannot form the basis of an aggravated damages claim even if they were not ultimately successful and added to the distress suffered by the complainant. They will lack the extra essential ingredient needed.

Aggravated damages may be awarded when the respondent's conduct after the complaint was made and up to the time of the hearing added to the applicant's distress and hurt: *Cross v Hughes* (2006) 233 ALR 108 at [30], *Elliott v Nanda* (2001) 111 FCR 240. Aggravated damages may be awarded where the respondent during the proceedings had acted in a way that was "inappropriate, lacking bona fides, improper or unjustifiable": *Oberoi v HR&EOC* [2001] FMCA 34 at [44].

Exemplary damages are not available under this legislative scheme: *Hughes v Car Buyers Pty Ltd* (2004) 210 ALR 645, disapproving of an earlier decision in *Font v Paspaley Pearls* [2002] FMCA 142. The preferred view is that exemplary damages are not available: *Frith v Glen Straits Pty Ltd (t/as The Exchange Hotel)* (2005) 218 ALR 560 at [99].

Special damages for economic loss

Special damages for economic loss covers the loss of earning capacity where there is a financial loss directly attributable to the discrimination. If an applicant leaves her job because of harassment and then is unable to find another job for some period, the damages can cover the period during which she was unemployed. Damages can include a loss of opportunity to work overtime or shift work and earn extra wages: *Trindall v NSW Commissioner of Police* [2005] FMCA 2.

If an applicant cannot seek other work due to her psychological state arising from the harassment or discrimination, then she must ensure that there is sufficient professional medical evidence of the reasons for failure to mitigate: *Lee v Smith* [2007] FMCA 59 at [215].

An applicant has a duty to mitigate her damages, that is, actively seek other work to reduce her loss, and any money earned or sick leave payments will be off-set against the amount of damages otherwise awarded: *Power v Aboriginal Hostels Ltd* [2004] FMCA 452 at [81].

This head of damages can also cover any differences that arose during the discrimination or harassment period which can be shown to be unlawful acts, for example, different pay rates when the woman was paid a lower, and discriminatory, rate or the financial assessment of the denial of opportunities for training, transfer or promotion.

This loss can cover future loss also, where the loss is able to be ascertained by some reasonable mechanism and is causally linked to the discrimination. This can include an estimation of a loss of opportunity for further work where a probation period was involved: *Dare v Hurley* [2005] FMCA 844. The future costs of counselling may be included, supported by evidence of the anticipated length of the counselling treatment and the cost per hour.

Few cases have resulted in orders for economic loss greater than $50,000. Applicants making claims for millions of dollars for real or imagined wrongs are bound to be further disappointed even if the outcome is successful for them. When a claim for breach of contract is successful either in addition to or as an alternate to the discrimination claim, the damages for economic loss remain the same.

General damages for non-economic loss

General damages for non-economic loss covers issues such as hurt, humiliation, injury to feelings and the range of damages available depends on the nature and degree of the loss which can be established in an appropriate evidentiary form. The damages in the discrimination arena under this head are relatively modest and amounts between $8000–$20,000 are common. It appears that the courts have not accorded much weight or significance to the emotional loss and turmoil to an applicant occasioned by acts of unlawful discrimination and harassment. On some occasions, there was not sufficient or any evidence to support a claim for such damages.

As a Federal Magistrate observed:

> At some point judicial officers are required to assess damages having regard to the individual circumstances before them. A degree of comparison between decided cases is both unavoidable and appropriate. However care needs to be taken to ensure that particular acts are not "rated". To do so ignores the requirement to "consider the effect on the complainant of the conduct complained of": *Hall v Sheiban* ... at 570. The award of general damages in discrimination matters is not intended to be punitive but rather to place complainants in the situation that they would otherwise have been in had the harassment not occurred: *Howe v Qantas* (2004) 188 FLR 1; *Hall v Sheiban*. To do so clearly requires specific reference to a person's individual circumstances. (*Phillis v Mandic* [2005] FMCA 330 at [26], leave to appeal out of time refused: (2005) 225 ALR 760)

Another Federal Magistrate has observed:

> The exact determination of the appropriate amount of compensation for the applicant's personal distress is never easy in these cases. Account must be taken of my assessment of the likely personal effects on this particular applicant of the discriminatory conduct, and an award should

be arrived at which is "restrained" but not "minimal", taking into account the intangibility of an injury by way of hurt feelings and mental distress without an established medical injury. (*Rankilor v Jerome Pty Ltd t/as Barkers Discount Furniture Store* [2006] FMCA 922 at [41])

Interest

Interest may be added into an award of damages, covering the period from when the act of discrimination occurred to the date of the decision as a fair measure of compensation. Both the Federal Court and the Federal Magistrates Court use the interest rate set out in the *Federal Court Act* and *Rules*: *Forest v Queensland Health* [2007] FCA 1236; *FMC Rules* r 26.01.

Recent damages awards

Some recent awards in discrimination cases are:

- after suffering multiple acts of sexual harassment and victimisation and one act of serious sexual assault, the applicant was unable to work for several years due to the impact of the unlawful conduct and she was awarded $100,000 for general damages suffered over a period of five years, $232,163.02 for economic loss, with the court noting that she would be required to repay $178,615.30 for worker's compensation payments for the same illness and same period, $5000 for future medical expense, $30,000 for future economic loss plus interest on some sums: *Lee v Smith (No 2)* [2007] FMCA 1092 and [2007] FMCA 59 at [215];

- a disabled man and his assistance animal were discriminated against when they were barred from entry to two different health facilities because of the presence of his dog – damages of $5000 for one facility and $3000 for the second one plus interest: *Forest v Queensland Health* [2007] FCA 1236;

- a single parent was discriminated against on the ground of family responsibilities by taking leave to care for a six-year-old child, and being involuntarily moved from one team to another – $12,000 for pain and suffering, reduced from $25,000 on appeal, and $16,000 for lost wages plus interest and lost superannuation for five months: *Commonwealth v Evans* (2004) 81 ALD 402;

- an act of victimisation by refusal to offer further work after a disability complaint to HR&EOC and a threat to make a further complaint – damages for hurt feelings of $5000 and lost wages: *Drury v Andreco Hurll Refractory Services Pty Ltd (No 4)* (2005) 225 ALR 339;

- disability discrimination against an employee by failing to provide work opportunities resulting in two periods away from work – damages of $24,000 for loss of wages and $15,000 for humiliation and injury to feelings: *McKenzie v Department of Urban Services* (2001) 163 FLR 133.

Some recent awards of damages for pain and suffering in sexual harassment cases are:

- there was a single act of sexual harassment by an employer placing a pay packet into his fly for the applicant to collect it and where she suffered no loss of wages and there was no expert evidence of psychological damages, only the applicant's evidence of her distress – general damages of $2500: *Hewett v Davies* [2006] FMCA 1678;

- there were several acts of sexual harassment including requests to attend a live sex show and entering into her hotel bedroom in his underwear and carrying a pillow while on work-related travel – damages totalling $11,822, including $5000 general damages and economic loss of $3300: *Cross v Hughes* (2006) 233 ALR 108;

- a work colleague made sexually suggestive remarks including requests to view the applicant's naval piercing and some acts of physical touching, and there was some evidence of mild depression and a favourable future prognosis – general damages of $4000: *Phillis v Mandic* [2005] FMCA 330, leave to appeal out of time refused: (2005) 225 ALR 760;

- a work colleague sexually harassed the applicant on two occasions in the accommodation provided by the employer – damages for hurt and humiliation were "modest", amount of $5000 ordered against the employer: *South Pacific Resort Hotels Pty Ltd v Trainor* (2005) 144 FCR 402;

- a waitress was repeatedly sexually harassed by the chef over a period, including being physically touched and subjected to repeated sexually explicit remarks – general damages of $20,000: *Bishop v Takla* [2004] FMCA 74.

Promotions or transfers

Other remedies available include ordering that the person be employed, transferred or promoted to the position which they were denied due to the unlawful discrimination. This is a practical and desirable outcome from such litigation as the remedy directly relates to the cause of action. An alternate version of such orders is that the applicant be considered for the next promotion or transfer without any discriminatory considerations being part of the decision-making process. This provides the applicant with a fair opportunity to compete for the promotion or transfer without the process being polluted by any unlawful acts of discrimination.

Not to repeat unlawful act

An order can be made that identifies an unlawful act and that the act not be repeated or continued. This can be a useful basis for an order when there is a continuing course of conduct and which, without any specific mechanism to make it stop, will continue.

If the act of discrimination arose because of the application of a policy which incorporates systemic discrimination, then the application of the policy in areas such as recruitment and selection or promotion can be ordered to cease operating.

A woman found to have breached the *Racial Discrimination Act* by the racially discriminatory material in the pamphlets she distributed in letterboxes and at the Launceston market was ordered to cease such activities and from distributing, selling or offering to sell any leaflet or other publication of a similar kind: *Jones v Scully* (2002) 120 FCR 243. Orders shutting down all internet sites containing Holocaust denial material run or controlled by an individual have been made: *Toben v Jones* (2003) 129 FCR 515; *Jones v Bible Believers' Church* [2007] FCA 55.

Apology

One form of order available to the court is that the respondent or an individual apologise to the applicant for the discrimination or harassment. However, as a Federal Court judge observed:

> I do not consider it appropriate to seek to compel the respondent to articulate a sentiment that he plainly enough does not feel. As Hely J pointed out in *Jones v Scully* at [245], "prima facie the idea of ordering someone to make an apology is a contradiction in terms". (*Jones v Toben* (2002) 71 ALD 629 at [106])

While following the same principle, a Federal Magistrate noted after finding indirect discrimination on the ground of disability that:

The applicant's distress at the failure to be offered an apology is, however, a matter which I propose to take into account in a minor way when awarding compensation. (*Rawcliffe v Northern Sydney Central Coast Area Health Service* [2007] FMCA 931 at [101])

Other redress

A court can order that the respondent perform any reasonable act or course of conduct to redress any loss or damage suffered by the complainant. This is a broad power which is not often used. Any order must be directed specifically at the redressing of loss or damage and not to punish or discipline those who committed the unlawful discriminatory acts: *Commissioner of Police, NSW Police Service v Estate of Russell* [2001] NSWSC 745 at [46]-[53].

Variation of contract

An order that the termination of a contract should be varied to redress any loss or damage to the complainant can be made. The circumstances for such an order would not arise often.

No further action

In some circumstances, a finding that the complaint has been substantiated and that there has been an act of unlawful discrimination may be sufficient. Where the actual act is of a relatively minor nature but the finding is in the public interest, then no further action may be appropriate.

Costs

In both the Federal Court and the Federal Magistrates Court, costs usually follow the event. This means that an unsuccessful party has costs awarded against them: *Bropho v Western Australia (No 2)* [2007] FCA 1048; *Hollingdale v North Coast Area Health Service (No 2)* [2006] FMCA 585.

In the Federal Magistrates Court, costs orders are usually made on the basis that costs are to be assessed against the Court's scale of costs in Sch 1 to the *Federal Magistrates Court Rules 2001*. This scale relates to the conduct of the proceedings and, pursuant to r 21.15, the court may order that it was reasonable to engage counsel in the proceedings, thus increasing the costs allowable under Sch 1.

Where a summary dismissal application brought by the respondent is successful, then usually costs will be awarded against the unsuccessful applicant: *Artinos v Stuart Reid Pty Ltd* [2007] FMCA 1141; *Neate v Totally and Permanently Incapacitated Veterans' Association of New South Wales* [2007] FMCA 488.

In some circumstances, the court will examine the substantial outcome of the case. It may the award full costs to the applicant even though only part of the case was successful. It may apportion costs where an applicant is only partially successful in sustaining the claims put against the respondent: *Ho v Regulator Australia Pty Ltd (No 2)* [2004] FMCA 402. Where a respondent is only partially successful in a motion to dismiss the proceedings or other interlocutory applications, then only part of the costs may be awarded to them: *Paramasivam v New South Wales (No 2)* [2007] FMCA 1033.

A Federal Magistrate observed that the factors to be taken into account when determining costs can be summarised as:

- where there is a public interest element to the complaint;
- where the applicant is unrepresented and not in a position to assess the risk of litigation;
- that the [successful] party should not lose the benefit of their victory because of the burden of their own legal costs;
- that litigants should not be discouraged from bringing meritorious [actions] and courts should be slow to award costs at an early stage; and
- that unmeritorious claims and conduct which unnecessarily prolong proceedings should be discouraged. (*Wiggins v Department of Defence – Navy (No 3)* [2006] FMCA 970 at [35])

The assessment of public interest may lead to no order being made for costs so that, even though the respondent is successful, they do not recover their costs: *AB v New South Wales (No 2)* [2005] FMCA 1624.

The impecuniosity of an unsuccessful applicant is not a reason for the court to refrain from making a costs order where one would usually be made: *Joyce v St George Bank Ltd* [2005] FMCA 868 at [23].

Where an offer to settle proceedings is made by a respondent, there needs to be a clear delineation between the amount being offered as compensation and the amount for costs: *San v Dirluck Pty Ltd (No 2)* [2005] FMCA 846. In the alternate, the offer should be for an amount for compensation and costs as agreed or assessed. If the court then orders an amount that is lower than the amount offered, the respondent may be able to apply for costs even though they were unsuccessful as a "Calderbank" letter or an offer of compromise under the court rules was made.

If an applicant rejects an offer and then the respondent is successful in having the application dismissed, the court may order indemnity costs from the date that the applicant rejected the offer: *Meka v Shell Company Australia Limited (No 2)* [2005] FMCA 700. Indemnity costs are the full costs and are likely to be significantly higher than costs under the FMC Schedule.

The State discrimination jurisdictions are usually "no costs" jurisdictions in that the tribunal hearing and determining the inquiry will rarely make orders as to costs even when the complainant is successful. This means that each party pays their own costs. When a complainant is self-represented, they may incur no financial outlay apart from their own time and the respondent may be faced with a substantial legal bill from the conduct of the proceedings.

Enforcement

The Federal Court and the Federal Magistrates Court can make a variety of orders including an award of financial compensation and costs. In some cases, the respondent refuses to pay any award made and the applicant is required to go through further steps to obtain the remedy by enforcement proceedings. These orders can be enforced through the usual mechanisms for enforcing civil debts under the relevant state or territory law: *FC Act* s 53, *FMC Act* s 78.

15

INDUSTRIAL LAWS

One important development in relation to discrimination law is where the principles overlap or intersect with the industrial law system. In the industrial law context, discrimination issues can arise in the system setting the general terms and conditions of employment across a group of employers or for an individual employer and in the termination of an employment contract.

The main area of overlap within the general industrial law system is between discrimination laws and unfair dismissal claims. Allegations that discrimination or harassment is the basis for a termination are an area of growth especially since the former Federal Government's Work Choices legislation and are discussed in this chapter. A person alleged to be a harasser may be dismissed because of the allegations and the relevant principles and law are discussed in this chapter.

The current contents of Australian Workplace Agreements (AWAs) and certified agreements and their discriminatory impact is another area of overlap of the principles of discrimination laws and the operation of industrial laws. One issue of potential significance is the role of the President of the Human Rights and Equal Opportunity Commission ("HR&EOC") and her or his statutory powers to intervene in certain industrial law proceedings and to have a role in reviewing sex discriminatory awards. These issues are discussed in this chapter.

Different factors can arise within the two systems and sometimes they are in conflict and can give rise to apparently irreconcilable positions. Key issues are the rights of employees who may be in conflict with each other and who may each have claims against their employer that different laws have been breached within the context of their individual employment relationship.

The unfair dismissal laws are based on a system designed to protect the interests of an individual worker and focus on one part of the employment contract only – the act of termination. Unlike a discrimination case, the legal issue to be examined in such litigation has a narrower circumference as it addresses a particular act rather than the context and structure of the entire working relationship. The balance of interests between an employer and the individual employee is through an analysis of the question of whether the termination was "harsh, unjust or unreasonable".

Since the passage of the *Workplace Relations Amendment (Work Choices) Act 2005*, amending the *Workplace Relations Act* 1996 ("the *WR Act*"), there are limitations on claims for unfair dismissal that can be brought and this has increased the number of claims of discrimination in the dismissal process itself. The Rudd Labor Government has announced significant changes to the industrial relations legislation. Transitional arrangements will be enacted in 2008. Consultation processes for the development of new national employment standards, including new unfair dismissal laws, will be conducted during 2008 and it is proposed that broad-sweeping changes will be enacted in 2010.

The Work Choices amendments commenced operation on 27 March 2006. They cover most private sector employees, through the use of the constitutional corporations power, and Australian Government employees and employees in the NT and ACT and all Victorian employers and employees. Also covered are waterside workers, flight crew and seamen.

The transitional amendments to be passed in early 2008 will prevent the creation of new AWAs, abolish the "fairness test" and introduce a no disadvantage test.

The Australian Industrial Relations Commission "shall take account of the principles embodied in" the *Racial Discrimination Act*, the *Sex Discrimination Act* and the *Disability Discrimination Act* relating to discrimination in employment: *WR Act* s 105. Also, the Commission is required to take account of the *Families Responsibilities Convention* (s 106) when performing its functions. There is an open question on the interpretation of these sections as the Commission is only required to "take account" and, having taken account of those principles, it could proceed to ignore them and make an award which contains discriminatory terms.

The constitutional basis of an earlier federal industrial law was closely analysed by the High Court in 1996: *Victoria v Commonwealth* (*Industrial Relations Act case*) (1996) 187 CLR 416. A majority of the High Court (Gleeson CJ, Gummow, Hayne, Heydon and Crennan JJ) upheld the constitutional validity of the Work Choices amendments when they interpreted the corporations power broadly to cover labour relations by "constitutional corporations": *New South Wales v Common-wealth* (2006) 231 ALR 1.

One object of the *WR Act* is to give effect to several international Conventions providing for equal remuneration for work of equal value between women and men: s 620. The Commission has the power to make orders to ensure that the equal remuneration principle operates in the workplace.

Unfair dismissal

There is now one unfair dismissal law for most Australian employers and employees – the *WR Act*. The main impact of the 2006 Work Choices amendments was to impose limitations on the unfair dismissal jurisdiction. The Rudd Labor Government proposes to introduce significant amendments to the unfair dismissal laws in 2010.

The main current limitation is that there is no ability to bring an unfair dismissal claim against an employer with 100 employees or less: s 643(10). This limitation will probably be changed in amendments to be enacted in 2010.

An employee can be dismissed in the first six months of their employment: s 643(6),(7). Other employees can be dismissed or made redundant for "genuine operational requirements": s 643(8), *Perry v Savills (Vic) Pty Limited* [2006] AIRC 363. "Operational reasons" is defined and actually means termination by way of redundancy: s 643(9).

Previous State and Territory laws are excluded from operation where the employer is a "constitutional corporation": s 16.

The *WR Act* provides mechanisms for reinstatement or damages where the termination of a person's employment was "harsh, unjust or unreasonable" or where the discrimination or notice provisions are breached: s 643(1). The Commission is required to examine a number of factors including whether there was a "valid reason" for the termination relating to the conduct of the employee or to the "unsatisfactory perfor-mance" of the employee and any warnings having been given: s 652(3). The Commission is required to dismiss an application when it is satisfied that the reason for the termination was for genuine operational require-ments or for reasons that include genuine operational requirements: s 649.

Generally, there are no longer State unfair dismissal jurisdictions or unfair contract jurisdictions in most instances and there are some technical minor exceptions where specialist advice is required.

Unlawful termination

Section 659 of the *WR Act* sets out various grounds on which an employer must not terminate an employee's employment. These overlap with some of the discrimination areas and include a bar on termination for race, sex, age, disability, family responsibilities and pregnancy.

Other reasons that cannot be relied on as the reason for a termination are absence from work for maternity leave or other parental leave and some absences from work because of illness or injury.

There are two exceptions to these provisions. The first is where the reason for termination was based on the inherent requirements of the job: *Qantas Airways Ltd v Christie* (1998) 193 CLR 280; *X v Commonwealth* (1999) 200 CLR 177. The second exception is where a person is terminated when working as a member of staff of a religious institution if the termination was to avoid injury to the religious susceptibilities of adherents of that religion or creed: *Hozack v Church of Jesus Christ of Latter-Day Saints* (1997) 79 FCR 441.

An employer has the onus of proof in establishing a defence to a claim for termination in breach of s 659 that the termination was for a reason other than one or more of the proscribed reasons: *WR Act* s 664.

Making a choice – dismissal or discrimination claim?

Issues of discrimination and harassment arise in the unfair dismissal jurisdiction in two ways. One way is where the applicant claims a ground of discrimination or harassment that is also covered in the discrimination law as the basis for their unfair dismissal. The second way is when a person claims to have been unfairly dismissed because the employer has acted on the principles of discrimination law and the employer's related policies, and the perpetrator has been dismissed after allegations of discrimination or harassment have been established.

A discrimination case can have a considerably broader focus than an unfair dismissal claim as the entire history of the employment relationship may be examined. A complainant may be seeking some remedy for working in a hostile environment or for acts of unlawful discrimination. The emphasis in any discrimination litigation is on facts and legal tests which give rise to fundamentally different issues than litigation examining a dismissal.

It may be that the two systems appear to be irreconcilable, at least on occasions, because of their different focus. Where they appear to be in conflict currently is in the setting of acceptable work practices and standards of behaviour so the same general principles are applied in both jurisdictions. Some industrial law tribunals are more accepting of poor standards of workplace behaviour such as harassment than are the specialist discrimination tribunals.

This can lead to a result that behaviour by an employee against another employee can be the basis of a breach of the discrimination laws and result in an award of damages or other relief against an employer through the vicarious liability provisions. The same behaviour can be found not to be the proper basis for dismissal and the perpetrator can be reinstated.

While broad discrimination principles are generally known and acknowledged by industrial tribunals, the intricacies of issues such as vicarious liability and the potential legal consequences for a breach of an employer's duty of care towards all employees, not just the dismissed employee, are not factors necessarily taken into account by those administering the industrial laws. While a worker is protected from some acts of discrimination by an employer by the terms of s 659(2)(f) of the *WR Act*, there is no reverse provision which makes a breach of the discrimination laws a valid reason for termination.

To ensure that they can confidently operate and not be in breach of either law, employers should ensure that they have policies on acceptable workplace standards of behaviour and enforce them consistently. They need to ensure that their employees are aware of the policies and clearly understand that any breaches will not be tolerated and could lead to dismissal. Further, they need a grievance or complaints policy which provides an effective internal process for addressing any issues about discrimination and harassment which employees want to raise.

Discrimination issues can arise in other ways within the industrial law system also. One example involved a long standing but later eliminated discriminatory employment practice giving rise to a conflict between two groups of employees after one group instituted a discrimination action and the second group later resorted to an industrial law action. As Wilcox CJ noted in the industrial law action, "discrimination casts a long shadow". That case arose as 29 Qantas women flight attendants left work before 1983 due to discriminatory promotion practices. They returned to work during the 1990s following a successful case under the NSW sex discrimination law. Subsequently, there was conflict between a group of 24 women who returned to Qantas and 823 female and male flight attendants who had maintained continuous service. The case addressed the way the seniority of those returning was to be worked out and recognised them as being reinstated with their previous seniority despite having resigned voluntarily rather than be dismissed: *Barlow v Qantas Airways Limited* (1997) 75 IR 100.

Another less common area of overlap is where the actions which constitute acts of unlawful discrimination on various grounds such as sex, pregnancy or sexual harassment against other employees can trigger the termination of another employee who refuses or declines to participate in the discrimination or is involved at some other level: *David v Portseal Pty Ltd* (1997) 72 IR 414.

Unfair dismissal of complainant

A complainant can be dismissed from their employment in a manner directly related to acts of discrimination or harassment in various different ways.

One mechanism to protect an employee in those circumstances can be the use of s 659 of the *WR Act* which is designed to give effect to two international treaties – the *Convention concerning Discrimination in respect of Employment and Occupation* and the *Family Responsibilities Convention*. Under this section, employment cannot be terminated on certain specified grounds, including:

- temporary absence from work because of illness or injury: *Gordon v Express Gas Operations Pty Ltd* [2007] FMCA 1059, *Sperandio v Lynch* [2006] FCA 1648, *Lee v Hills Before and After School Care* (2007) 160 IR 440;

- membership or non-membership of a trade union or participating in trade union activities: *AFMEPKIU v Australian Health & Nutrition Association Ltd* (2003) 147 IR 380, see generally *CPSU v Commonwealth* (2007) 165 IR 335, *McIlwain v Ramsey Food Packaging Pty Ltd* (2006) 154 IR 111 and (2006) 158 IR 181;

- the filing of a complaint, or the participation in proceedings, against an employer involving alleged violation of laws or regulations, or recourse to competent administrative authorities: *Crowley v Parker Hannifin (Australia) Pty Limited* [2006] FCA 901, *Wang v University of New South Wales* [2005] FCA 1040, *Zhang v Royal Australian Chemical Institute Inc* [2005] FCAFC 99;

- race, colour, sex, sexual preference, age, physical or mental disability, marital status, family responsibilities, pregnancy, religion, political opinion, national extraction or social origin: *Sallehpour v Frontier Software Pty Ltd* [2005] FCA 247, *Cucanic v IGA Distribution (Vic) Pty Ltd* [2004] FCA 1226, *Vickery v Assetta* [2004] FCA 555;

- absence from work during maternity leave or other parental leave: *Mifsud v Skye Children's Co-Operative Ltd* (2007) 164 IR 218.

The restrictions on other proceedings apply to termination proceedings also. The employer must be a "constitutional corporation" employing more than 100 people and the employee must earn below the cap of around $95,000. The "operational requirement" exemption applies also.

When a termination application is based on s 659, then, during the conduct of the case, evidence more usually found in a discrimination case such as allegations of harassment or victimisation may be led. A number of different grounds may be relied on in the one application.

The initiating process can be lodged in the Commission instead of in the discrimination arena. It may be brought in both jurisdictions as there may be some parts of the discrimination claim not mirrored in the unfair dismissal claim. The legal issues to be determined in each proceeding are different. Whether a dismissal was harsh, unjust or unreasonable requires the application of different legal tests compared with those applied where there was an unlawful act of discrimination either during the course of employment or in the dismissal decision.

There is a bar to commencing or pursuing termination proceedings where a complaint has been made with the HR&EOC relating to that termination: *WR Act* s 672.

The President of the HR&EOC may terminate a complaint where she or he is satisfied that some other remedy has been sought and that therefore the subject matter had been adequately dealt with or some other remedy is reasonably available to the complainant: *HR&EOC Act* s 46PH(1)(c), (d).

The relief provided may not be the same. One crucial issue is that the relief available in the industrial relations proceedings is based on a breach of contract and no remedy is available for general damages such as shock, distress or humiliation: *WR Act* s 654(9). The only remedies are reinstatement or compensation for lost wages.

On some occasions, more immediate and appropriate remedies for structural changes giving rise to indirect sex discrimination may be properly pursued in the industrial jurisdiction.

Two actions by the same person have been pursued and the discrimination court or tribunal has taken into account the compensation for financial loss and damage previously awarded for the dismissal by the Australian Industrial Relations Commission: *Wilson v Budsoar Pty Ltd* [1999] NSWCA 228.

Previous AIRC proceedings do not raise a bar to later discrimination proceedings as the causes of actions are different, even when based on the same facts, as any previous judgment or decision is not in relation to the same cause of action: *Gibbs v Commonwealth Bank of Australia* (1997) EOC ¶92-877.

In all State laws except Western Australia, the possibility of two simultaneous actions on the same facts has been recognised. Given the almost blanket coverage of the current Work Choices legislation, these provisions have fallen away in most situations.

There can be advantages to a complainant in bringing an action in both jurisdictions. It can broaden the outcome as the discrimination claim may provide a remedy such as damages for the period of employment and the unfair dismissal claim may focus just on the events surrounding the dismissal and may more easily lead to reinstatement if sought. The unfair dismissal jurisdictions are usually faster than the discrimination jurisdictions and so it is possible to resolve one part of a complaint before the other issues are addressed. It is common when settling an unfair dismissal claim for the discrimination claim to be included. This enables all the matters at issue between the parties to be disposed of in one deed of release. The basis for the deed is that the complainant withdraws the complaint to the discrimination agency as well as terminating the industrial law proceedings.

There have been some claims of unfair dismissal based on constructive dismissal, that is, when the employee had to leave the place of employment as a direct result of the harassment or discrimination. (For a discussion on constructive dismissal, see Chapter 4.) An employee's resignation is taken to constitute a termination where, on the balance of probabilities, the employee proves that their resignation was not voluntary but the employee "was forced to do so because of the conduct, or course of conduct, engaged in by the employer": *WR Act* s 642(4).

Where there has been a course of conduct which amounts to discrimination or harassment, the complainant may reach a point where she decides she can no longer tolerate the situation. There may be one particular incident that is the trigger or the "final straw" that leads to the person's resignation.

Alternatively, the employee may be dismissed after complaining about the discrimination or the harassment to either the perpetrator or another person in the company. The dismissed employee may claim that the dismissal arose as a direct result of the complaint and was not for a valid reason: *Jones v Armas Nominees Pty Ltd t/a Network Rent A Car* (1994) 59 IR 61. Such a claim may constitute a valid complaint of victimisation under the discrimination law too (see Chapter 9).

The failure of an employer to investigate and stop the acts of sexual harassment against an employee and then forcing her to resign was harsh, unjust and unreasonable as the employer was requiring her to put up with the sexual harassment on an on-going basis with no resolution offered: *Groves v Benlor Real Estate Pty Ltd* (2001) EOC ¶93-152.

Refusal by an employee to participate willingly in sexual conduct initiated by an employer towards that employee which then amounts to acts of sexual harassment can be the main or one reason for the termination and this can mean that the termination was not made for a valid reason: *Eggleton v Kingsgrove Medical Centre Pty Ltd* (1997) 72 IR 434

A termination during maternity leave or a significant alteration of duties after a return from maternity leave and then a termination may constitute discrimination on the ground of parental responsibilities and be in breach of the relevant industrial law: *St Vincent's Hospital of Sydney Limited v Harris* (1998) EOC ¶92-925.

Where there has been a restructure and the new position is substantially the same as the previous one, then constructive dismissal does not arise where the employee is pregnant but she refuses to discuss the new position or canvass other options: *Roeske v Moffat Pty Ltd* [2007] AIRC 45.

The High Court examined the operation of the discrimination provisions in the industrial law when it held that age was not the basis for a termination as being under 60 was an inherent requirement for the job of a pilot: *Qantas Airways Ltd v Christie* (1998) 193 CLR 280.

There have been a number of cases where a person has claimed that the termination of their employment was on the basis of their disability: *Patterson v Newcrest Mining Ltd* (1996) 67 IR 101. These claims are sometimes linked to related worker's compensation claims as the disability which is being relied on has arisen from a workplace injury: *Brown v Power t/a Royal Hotel Tumut* (1996) 66 IR 1; *Rosi v Donfield Constructions Pty Ltd* (1996) 72 IR 106. An absence from work due to illness may be perceived by the employee as the reason for the termination, but it may have been a valid reason for the operational requirements of the employer and not linked to the illness or disability: *Rus v Girotto Precast Pty Ltd* (1996) 71 IR 207.

A music lecturer's behaviour, including sexually harassing five students and repeatedly telephoning another student, was improper and inappropriate and, while his bipolar condition may have contributed to the misconduct, the conduct was unacceptable regardless of the cause and so the majority of the Full Bench of the AIRC found that his dismissal was justified: *Shanahan v University of Western Sydney* [2005] AIRC 473.

A male employee had obtained a three-year extension of his posting to Cairns to remain in the same city as his children for whom he had a shared parenting arrangement. His employer could no longer continue this arrangement. The AIRC found:

> The respondent has met its obligations to the applicant in relation to the applicant's family responsibilities. The respondent still has a service to run and budgets to meet. The family responsibilities of employees are important matters to be considered by employers, however they are not the only matters that need be considered. In the Commission's view the respondent considered the competing interests and in the final offer produced a balance that was about right. The applicant acted unreasonably in refusing the respondent's final offer. It seems that the applicant was prepared to accept that the respondent could "fix" all of the employment problems which arose from his unfortunate family circumstances provided the applicant's employment problems were "fixed" by the respondent on the applicant's terms. The direction given to the applicant to relocate to Brisbane in accordance with the terms of his contract of employment is considered in the context of the applicant's unreasonable refusal of the arrangements proposed by the respondent that would allow the applicant to remain in Cairns. The Commission has concluded that, in the foregoing context, the direction was reasonable. As the applicant refused to comply with the respondent's reasonable direction, the Commission is satisfied that there was a valid reason for the termination of the applicant's employment. (*Webb v Australian Customs Service* [2004] AIRC 625 at [52]-[53])

A person on light duties arising from a work-related injury may have a claim in relation to any termination, even if it is not cast in the discrimination manner but in relation to the capacity to perform other work reasonably available from the employer and within the employee's skills, training and qualification: *Mitchell v Macquarie Health Service* (1995) 67 IR 107.

An employee dismissed on the ground of race as employer preferred a Japanese person to sell opals in a tourist area and after making a race discrimination complaint to the discrimination agency was found to have been unfairly dismissed: *McElwaine v Charles F Grimes (Management) Pty Ltd* (unreported, 28/08/1998 IRC(Qld) B1477/97).

For a claim of discrimination to be successful in termination proceedings, then some evidence must be led which would sustain the basis of the claim. Mere assertion of a breach of s 170CK will not be sufficient to enable the Commission to make the relevant finding: *Monaghan v Wiluna Gold Mines Pty Ltd* (1996) 69 IR 108 at 113.

Dismissal after complaining on behalf of a female co-worker about the sexual harassment she was suffering from a male chef was unfair: *Four Sons Pty Ltd v Sakchai Limsiripothong* (2000) 98 IR 1.

Unfair dismissal of perpetrator

The second area of overlap between the two laws is in the application of the principles established by discrimination laws in the industrial law arena, especially in relation to unfair dismissals. This arises where an employee claims unfair dismissal when they were sacked after a complaint of harassment or discrimination was made against them. These dismissals can arise after the employer has conducted some form of internal investigation and has been satisfied that there were acts of discrimination or harassment committed by the person dismissed. The most common complaints have related to sexual harassment by the person dismissed against a co-worker.

There has been some inconsistency between the principles of industrial law coming into conflict with those of harassment law. In the past few years, the specialist industrial commissions have been more willing to find a termination was not in breach of the legislation after acts of sexual harassment were found to have occurred. Other acts of discrimination or intimidation are generally found not to sustain a dismissal.

When the AIRC finds for an employee, they are required to take into account any "misconduct of the employee that contributed to the employer's decision to terminate the employee's employment": *WR Act* s 654(9)(e).

On appeal, a male prison officer was reinstated by the Full Bench of the AIRC when the sexual harassment was found not to be employment-related as:

> The nub of [the employer's argument] is that the harassment conduct took place while the respondent was on duty and the Commissioner should have treated it as such. After quite a deal of consideration we have decided to reject this ground ... the relevant inquiry is whether the finding that the harassment conduct was private rather than employment-related was reasonably open. We have concluded that it was. The case is not a clear cut one. Reasonable minds might differ on the question of whether the conduct was employment related. We are influenced, however, by a number of considerations. The first is that on the night in question, although in Sale at their employer's expense, the prison officers were clearly not on duty in any formal sense, were enjoying an evening meal, drinks and engaging in purely social activities on licensed premises and in public places. In the circumstances it might be thought an unreasonable infringement on personal liberty to characterise the behaviour as other than private in character. There is no suggestion that members of the public were aware of the conduct. While it is clear the behaviour had the capacity to reflect adversely on the appellant as the employer the same might have been

said if the conduct had occurred in Melbourne while colleagues were socialising after work. This is not to say that private conduct can never be relevant to termination of employment. But in our view it would be wrong to think one could adopt a formula or set of criteria by the application of which conduct can readily be classified as private or work related. It is the whole of the circumstances which must be taken into account in each case. (*Tichy v Department of Justice* [2005] AIRC 592 at [16])

A female employee was reinstated by the AIRC when it found that she had not sexually harassed three female colleagues by engaging in an act of sexual intercourse in their presence while they slept in a hotel room and also being in a bath naked with two co-workers. The Commission found:

> The conduct took place in a hotel room, with the lights out, in the early hours of the morning, when Ms Streeter thought – not entirely unreasonably – that the other employees were asleep ... Most of the impugned behaviour occurred well away from the workplace, after rather than during a work function, in a hotel room that was booked and paid for privately. (*Streeter v Telstra Corporation Ltd* [2007] AIRC 679 at [141], [149])

The dismissal of a male who sent a highly offensive email containing vulgar sexually explicit images which breached the employer's email and internet usage policy to a colleague was upheld: *Rogers v State Rail Authority of NSW* [2005] AIRC 617.

An employee who persistently breached the sexual harassment policy by repeatedly making derogatory remarks about women which were overheard by fellow employees, despite a clear warning to cease such conduct by the CEO, had his dismissal upheld: *Silvan v Commonwealth Club Ltd* [2005] AIRC 176.

A male employee's shouting abusive comments with derogatory sexual references outside the hotel room of a female co-worker during a company training program, either thinking that she heard the threats or not caring whether she did or not, was a deliberate act of intimidation and although at night was not of a private nature and justified the employer terminating his employment: *GrainCorp Operations Ltd v Markham* (2002) 120 IR 253.

The standards of acceptable workplace behaviour need to be clearly defined. In some workplaces, a level of "skylarking," sexual banter or sexual jokes has been accepted by management as part of the workplace culture. Crossing the line can result in claims of sexual harassment where there is a company policy that sets out that such conduct is not acceptable in the workplace and this can lead to dismissal by the perpetrator:

Clarke v Burson Automotive Pty Ltd [2003] AIRC 979. Physical attacks in the guise of a "joke" or "initiation ceremonies" against apprentices and other junior employees can provide the basis for a claim of discrimination on the ground of age.

While once some level of "skylarking" may have been condoned by an employer as an acceptable workplace practice, it is increasingly clear that such behaviour cannot be tolerated as it can lead to allegations of discrimination or harassment. Any change of employer policy to a position where any level of skylarking or physical interaction between employees, even if designed to be a joke, will not be tolerated and can lead to dismissal needs to be clearly communicated to the employees.

The long-term existence of a "blokey culture" with a preoccupation with sexual matters is not an answer to allegations of sexual harassment and intimidation against a young female recruit and can properly lead to a dismissal which is not unfair: *Coughran v Public Employment Office, Attorney-General's Department* [2003] NSWIRComm 181. Unfortunately, some industrial presiding officers consider excessive consumption of alcohol as a factor to be taken into account in favour of the perpetrator of acts of sexual harassment as an excuse for their behaviour or demonstrating some peculiar form of self-destruction, particularly where the harassment occurred away from the workplace although obviously work connected: *Cassel v Commissioner of Police* [2003] NSWIRComm 73. Such findings side-step the operation of policies designed to protect employees against such acts and undermine the focus on equity in the workplace by providing an "excuse" for behaviour that should not be tolerated in the workplace.

Where an employee had a long and repeated pattern of conduct of bullying behaviour and refusing to take supervisor's directions, this was relevant when assessing whether the last incident threatening violence that gave rise to the dismissal was a proper basis for a termination: *Morrell v Department of Justice, Consumer Affairs Victoria* [2005] AIRC 41.

Awards, certified agreements and *Sex Discrimination Act*

In 1993, there were amendments to the *Sex Discrimination Act* and the passage of the *Industrial Relations Reform Act* 1993, broadening the scope of the principles of sex discrimination in the area of employment at a Federal level. Some further amendments were made when the former Federal industrial relations legislation was replaced with the *WR Act*. In 1999, the provisions in the *Sex Discrimination Act* were repealed and inserted as Part IIC in the *HR&EOC Act* when other similar changes were made.

There is a mechanism for the President of the Commission to refer a complaint alleging "a discriminatory act" under an award or a certified agreement to the Australian Industrial Relations Commission: *HR&EOC Act* s 46PW. A "discriminatory act under an award" is defined as meaning an act that was done in direct compliance with an award or a certified agreement and would have been unlawful under the *Sex Discrimination Act* except for the exemption for acts done under statutory authority.

Any complaint must be in writing and made to the President by a person who is "aggrieved by the act" on their own behalf or on behalf of themselves and others, or a trade union may lodge the complaint on behalf of its members. The President must then form a view about the complaint and whether there is a discriminatory act as described within the complaint. To reach this conclusion, she may need to undertake some investigatory steps and to obtain further information.

If the President forms the view that there is a discriminatory act, then she must refer the complaint to the Australian Industrial Relations Commission. If she considers the complaint to be frivolous, vexatious, misconceived or lacking in substance, she need not refer the complaint.

This provision has not been used and now has limited range due to the definition of "industrial instrument": *HR&EOC Act* s 46PW(7).

Certified agreements and AWAs

The *WR Act* established a system of Australian Workplace Agreements (AWAs) and certified agreements.

There is a range of provisions that impose limited requirements on AWAs and also mechanisms for enforcement through the Australian Fair Pay Commission and the Workplace Ombudsman. Laws proposed for 2008 by the Rudd Labor Government will remove the option of creating new AWAs and the statutory enforcement body will be renamed and redesigned.

Specialist texts and loose-leaf services should be consulted for a detailed discussion of these provisions as it is beyond the scope of this book to do so.

Appendix A

GROUNDS OF UNLAWFUL DISCRIMINATION

This table sets out the grounds of unlawful discrimination covered by the three Federal Acts and the Acts operating in New South Wales, Queensland, South Australia, Tasmania, Victoria, Western Australia, the Australian Capital Territory and the Northern Territory.

Key:

RDA:	*Racial Discrimination Act* 1975 (Cth)
SDA:	*Sex Discrimination Act* 1984 (Cth)
DDA:	*Disability Discrimination Act* 1992 (Cth)
AGDA:	*Age Discrimination Act* 2004 (Cth)
ADA (NSW):	*Anti-Discrimination Act* 1977 (NSW)
ADA (Qld):	*Anti-Discrimination Act* 1991 (Qld)
EOA (SA):	*Equal Opportunity Act* 1984 (SA)
RVA (SA)	*Racial Vilification Act* 1996 (SA)
ADA (Tas):	*Anti-Discrimination Act* 1998 (Tas)
EOA (Vic):	*Equal Opportunity Act* 1995 (Vic)
RRTA (Vic)	*Racial and Religious Tolerance Act* 2001 (Vic)
EOA (WA):	*Equal Opportunity Act* 1984 (WA)
CCC (WA)	*Criminal Code* Division XI – *Racist Harassment and Incitement to Racial Hatred* 1990 (WA)
DA (ACT):	*Discrimination Act* 1991 (ACT)
ADA (NT):	*Anti-Discrimination Act* 1992 (NT)

Grounds	RDA	SDA	DDA	AGDA	ADA (NSW)	ADA (Qld)	EOA (SA)	RVA (SA)	ADA (Tas)	EOA (Vic)	RRTA (Vic)	EOA (WA)	CCC (WA)	DA (ACT)	ADA (NT)
Sex		5			24	7(1)(a)	29(1)(a) 29(2), 35(1)		16(e)	6(k)		8		7(1)(a), 8(1)	19(1)(b)
Marital status		6			39	7(1)(b)	29(1)(c) 29(5), 35(1)		16(f)	6(e)		9		7(1)(d), 8(1)	19(1)(e)
Pregnancy or potential pregnancy		7			24(1B)	7(1)(c)	29(1)(d) 29(6), 35(1)		16(g)	6(h)		10		7(1)(f), 8(1)	19(1)(f)
Family responsibility		7A			49S, 49T	7(1)(o)			16(i)	6(ea)		35A		7(1)(e), 8(1)	19(1)(g)
Parental status					49S, 49T	7(1)(d)			16(i)	6(ea)		35A		7(1)(e), 8(1)	19(1)(g)
Sexual harassment		28A			22A-22J	118, 119	87		17(2),(3)	85-95		24-26		58-64	22(1), (2)
Race	9	7			7	7(1)(g)	51-63		16(a)	6(i)		36		7(1)(h), 8(1)	19(1)(a)
Racial hatred	18C											49A-49D	80A-80D		
Racial vilification					20C	124A, 131A		4	19, 22(2)		7, 24		77-80	65-67	
Disability			5-9		49A, 49B	7(1)(h)	66-78, 88		16(k)	6(b)		66A		7(1)(i), 9, 8(1)	19(1)(i), 21
Disability harassment			35-40												
Sexuality					49ZG	7(1)(n)	29(1)(b), 29(3), 29(4), 33(2), 35A		16(c)	6(l)		35O		7(1)(b), 8(1)	19(1)(c)
Transexuality					38B	7(1)(m)	5(1), 29(1)(a), 29(3), 29(4), 33(2), 35A		3, 16(c)	6(ac)		35AA		7(1)(c), 8(1)	4(1), 19(1)(c)

246

Age				14-15	49ZYA, 49ZV	7(1)(f)	85A-85E 85G-85L	16(b)	6(a)		66v	7(1)(b), 8(1)	19(1)(d)
Political belief or activity								16(m), (n)	6(g)		53	7(1)(i), 8(1)	19(1)(n)
Religious belief or activity						7(1)(j)		16(o), (p)	6(j)		53	7(1)(j), 8(1), 11	19(1)(m)
Trade union activity						7(1)(k)		16(l)	6(c)			7(1)(k), 8(1)	19(1)(k)
Breastfeeding						7(1)(e),		16(h)	6(ab)			7(1)(g), 8(1)	19(1)(h)
Associate	15-21				See definition (eg 7 for race)	7(1)(p)		16(s)	6(m)			7(1)(n), 8(1)	19(1)(r)
Transgender vilification					38s	124A, 131A						65-67	
HIVAIDS vilification					49ZXB							65-67	
Homosexuality vilification					49ZT	124A, 131A		19, 22(2)				65-67	
Religious vilification						124A, 131A	86	19, 22(2)		8, 25			
Victimisation		94	42	51	50	129-131		18	96, 97	13, 14	67	68	23
Incitement	17		43						9899	1516			27
Aiding and permitting	17	105	43, 122	56	52	122-123	90	21	98, 99	15, 16	160	73	27
Vicarious liability	18A, 18E	106			53	114-116, 132-3	91		102, 103	17	161, 162		105

Appendix B

AREAS OF UNLAWFUL DISCRIMINATION

This table sets out the areas of unlawful discrimination covered by the three Federal Acts and the Acts operating in New South Wales, Queensland, South Australia, Tasmania, Victoria, Western Australia, the Australian Capital Territory and the Northern Territory.

Key:

RDA:	*Racial Discrimination Act* 1975 (Cth)
SDA:	*Sex Discrimination Act* 1984 (Cth)
DDA:	*Disability Discrimination Act* 1992 (Cth)
AGDA:	*Age Discrimination Act* 2004 (Cth)
ADA (NSW):	*Anti-Discrimination Act* 1977 (NSW)
ADA (Qld):	*Anti-Discrimination Act* 1991 (Qld)
EOA (SA):	*Equal Opportunity Act* 1984 (SA)
ADA (Tas):	*Anti-Discrimination Act* 1998 (Tas)
EOA (Vic):	*Equal Opportunity Act* 1995 (Vic)
EOA (WA):	*Equal Opportunity Act* 1984 (WA)
DA (ACT):	*Discrimination Act* 1991 (ACT)
ADA (NT):	*Anti-Discrimination Act* 1992 (NT)

Areas	RDA	SDA	DDA	AGDA	ADA (NSW)*	ADA (Qld)	EOA (SA)*	EOA (Vic)	ADA (Tas)	EOA (WA)*	DA (ACT)	ADA (NT)
Applicants for employment	15(1)	14(1)	15(1)	18(1)	8(1) race 25(1) sex 49D(1) dis	14	30(1) sex 52(1) race 67(1) dis	13	22(1)(a)	11(1) sex 37(1) race 66B(1) dis	10(1)	31(1)
Employees	15	14(2)	15(2)	18(2)	8(2) race 25(2) sex 49D(2) dis	15, 15A	30(2) sex 52(2) race 67(2) dis	14	22(1)(a)	11(2) sex 37(2) race 66B(2) dis	10(2), 11	31(2), 31(3)
Commission agents		15	16	19	9 race 26 sex 49E dis		31 sex 53 race 68 dis		3, 22(1)(a)	12 sex 38 race 66c dis	12	
Contract workers	3, 15	16	17	20	10 race 27 sex 49F dis		32 sex 54 race 69 dis	15	3, 22(1)(a)	13 sex 39 race 66D dis	13	
Partnerships		17	18	21	10A race 27A sex 49G dis	16-18	33 sex 55 race 70 dis	30	3, 22(1)(a)	14 sex 40 race 66E dis	14	
Qualifying bodies		18	19	22	12 race 29 sex 49J dis	21, 22	36 sex 58 race 73 dis	35	3, 22(1)(a)	16sex 42 race 66G dis	16	33
Trade unions	14	19	20	23	11 race 28 sex 49I dis	19, 20	35 sex 57 race 72 dis	34	3, 22(1)(a)	15 sex 41 race 66F dis	15	32
Employment agencies	15(2)	20	21	24	13 race 30 sex 49K dis	23			3, 22(1)(a)	17 sex 43 race 66H dis	17	34
Access to premises	11		23	27						19 sex 45 race 66J dis	19	

Areas	RDA	SDA	DDA	AGDA	ADA (NSW)*	ADA (Qld)	EOA (SA)*	ADA (Tas)	EOA (Vic)	EOA (WA)*	DA (ACT)	ADA (NT)
Education		21	22	26	17 race 31A sex 49L dis	38, 39	37 sex 59 race 74 dis	22(1)(b)	37	18 sex 44 race 66I dis	18	29
Goods, services & facilities	11, 13	22	24	28	19 race 33 sex 49M dis	46	39 sex 61 race 76 dis	22(1)(c)	42	20 sex 46 race 66K dis	20	41
Accom-modation	12	23	25	29	20 race 34 sex 49N dis	82-85	40 sex 62 race 77 dis	22(1)(d)	49-52	21 sex 47 race 66L dis	21	38, 39
Land	12	24	26	30		77	38 sex 60 race 75 dis		47	21A sex 47A race		
Clubs		25	27		20A race 34A sex 49O dis	94, 95		22(1)(e)	59, 60	22 sex 48 race 66M dis	22	46
Govt laws & programs		26	29	31		101		22(1)(f)	67			
Requests for information		27	30	32		124			100	23 sex 49 race 66O dis	23	26
Sport			28						65	66N dis		
Super-annuation		14(4)				53-57	42-43 sex 63 race 78 dis			66P dis		48
Advertisements	16	86	44	50	51	127-128	103		195-197	68	69	25, 109

There are other grounds of unlawful discrimination in operation in New South Wales, South Australia and Western Australia and this table lists only the three main grounds, that is, sex, race and disability.

APPENDIX C

EXCEPTIONS TO COVERAGE

This table sets out the exceptions from discrimination laws covered by the three Federal Acts and the Acts operating in New South Wales, Queensland, South Australia, Tasmania, Victoria, Western Australia, the Australian Capital Territory and the Northern Territory.

Key:

RDA:	*Racial Discrimination Act* 1975 (Cth)
SDA:	*Sex Discrimination Act* 1984 (Cth)
DDA:	*Disability Discrimination Act* 1992 (Cth)
AGDA:	*Age Discrimination Act* 2004 (Cth)
ADA (NSW):	*Anti-Discrimination Act* 1977 (NSW)
ADA (Qld):	*Anti-Discrimination Act* 1991 (Qld)
EOA (SA):	*Equal Opportunity Act* 1984 (SA)
ADA (Tas):	*Anti-Discrimination Act* 1998 (Tas)
EOA (Vic):	*Equal Opportunity Act* 1995 (Vic)
EOA (WA):	*Equal Opportunity Act* 1984 (WA)
DA (ACT):	*Discrimination Act* 1991 (ACT)
ADA (NT):	*Anti-Discrimination Act* 1992 (NT)

Exceptions	RDA	SDA	DDA	AGDA	ADA (NSW)	ADA (Qld)	EOA (SA)	ADA (Tas)	EOA (Vic)	EOA (WA)	DA (ACT)	ADA (NT)
Special measures	8(1)	7D	45	33	21 race 126A general	105	47	24	22, 32, 39, 82	31	27	57
Genuine occupational qualification		30			14 race 31 sex	25	34(2) sex 56(2) race		17	27, 66s, 66zq, 50	34 sex 42 race 48 dis	35(1)(b)(i)
Pregnancy \ childbirth		31			35 sex		46 sex			28	37	54
Services for member of one sex		32				41		26(1)(b)		30	38, 40	42
Accommodation for employees \ students		34			20 race 34 sex 49N dis	88, 89	62 race 77 dis 40 sex		56	32, 35L	39	
Care of children		35				27, 28	85M	26(1)(c), 50	25(1)(a)	33	25	37(a)
Charities		36	49	34	55	110	45 sex 64 race 80 dis	23	74	70		52
Religious bodies		37		35	56	109	50 sex		75	72	32	51
Education institutions for religious purposes		38				41		53	76	73	33, 46	30
Age				youth wages - 25	49ZYA-49ZY	32, 43, 49, 106A	85M-85S	31-39	27A, 41, 62, 81	66ZM-66ZS	57A-57M	36, 44, 47(2)
Voluntary bodies		39		36	57				39(a)	71	31	
Capacity to work			15(4)		49D(4)	34	71(2)		32(1)(b)	66Q(1)	49	35(1)(a), 35(1)(b)(ii)

Exceptions	RDA	SDA	DDA	AGDA	ADA (NSW)	ADA (Qld)	EOA (SA)	ADA (Tas)	EOA (Vic)	EOA (WA)	DA (ACT)	ADA (NT)
Acts done under statutory authority		40	47	39	54	106		24	69	69, 35N, 66ZS	30	53
Insurance		41	46	37	37 sex 49Q dis	73-75	49 sex 85R dis	30	43	34, 66ZR, 66T	28	
Superannuation		41A 41B	46	37-38	36 sex 49Q dis	59-65	63	30	72, 73	34	29	49(2)
Sport		42			38 sex 22 race 49R dis	111	48 sex 81 dis	29	66	35	41 sex 57 dis 57M	56
Combat duties		43	53								56 dis	
Public health			48	42	49P	107			80		56	55
Migration			52	43								
Unjustifiable hardship			11		49C	5, 35, 44,51, 92, 100					47	58
Grant exemptions		44	55	44-47	126	113	92	57	83	135	109	59
Employment in a household	15(5)	14(3)	15(3)		8(3) race 25(3)(a), sex 49D(3)(a) dis	26, 27	34(1)		16		24	35(2)
Single sex accommodation		23(3)				30			28			
Workers married couples					31(2)(i), 46	31				29	35	

Appendix D

CONCILIATION AND INQUIRY POWERS

This table sets out the conciliation and inquiry powers covered by the three Federal Acts and the Acts operating in New South Wales, Queensland, South Australia, Tasmania, Victoria, Western Australia, the Australian Capital Territory and the Northern Territory.

Key:

RDA:	*Racial Discrimination Act* 1975 (Cth)
SDA:	*Sex Discrimination Act* 1984 (Cth)
DDA:	*Disability Discrimination Act* 1992 (Cth)
AGDA:	*Age Discrimination Act* 2004 (Cth)
HREOC	*Human Rights and Equal Opportunity Commission Act* 1986 (Cth)
ADA (NSW):	*Anti-Discrimination Act* 1977 (NSW)
ADA (Qld):	*Anti-Discrimination Act* 1991 (Qld)
EOA (SA):	*Equal Opportunity Act* 1984 (SA)
ADA (Tas):	*Anti-Discrimination Act* 1998 (Tas)
EOA (Vic):	*Equal Opportunity Act* 1995 (Vic)
RRTA (Vic)	*Racial and Religious Tolerance Act* 2001 (Vic)
EOA (WA):	*Equal Opportunity Act* 1984 (WA)
DA (ACT):	*Discrimination Act* 1991 (ACT)
ADA (NT):	*Anti-Discrimination Act* 1992 (NT)

Provision	RDA	SDA	DDA	AGDA	HREOC	ADA (NSW)	ADA (Qld)	EOA (SA)	ADA (Tas)	EOA (Vic)	RRTA (Vic)	EOA (WA)	DA (ACT)	ADA (NT)
Conciliation Procedures														
Written Complaint					46P(1)	88	136	93	62(1)	105	20(1)	83	72	64
Time limit					46PH(1)(b)	88(3),(4)	138, 168, 172	93(2)	63	110		83(4)	76, 81(2)(c)	65
Initial rejection				60	46PH(1)(c)	90	139, 140	95(1)	64	108(1)		89	81(2)(a)	66, 67
Confidentiality	27F	112	127	58	49					192		167	121	108
No civil action	45	111	126		48		266	101	69(2)	193		166	108J, 121	113(2)
Obtaining information					21, 46PI		156	94(2)	97(1)	114(2)(b)		86	108c	92(1)(c)
Compulsory conference attendance					46PJ, 46PK, 46PL	92(2)	159	95(4)	75	114(2)(a)		87	82	79
Interim Determination														
Application					46PO(6), 46PP	89A	144	96(2)	98(2)	131(1)		85	99(1)(b)	101
Making an interim order					46PP	112	144	96(2)	98	131(3),		126	99	101
Hearing and Decision														
Complainant reference					46PO, 46PW, 46PX, 46PY	91, 94, 95	155	95(8)	78					
Holding inquiry					46PO	96			86	159		107(3)	73	
Witnesses								24(1)(b)	79(3)			110	96	92

Hearing and Decision

Provision	RDA	SDA	DDA	AGDA	HREOC	ADA (NSW)	ADA (Qld)	EOA (SA)	ADA (Tas)	EOA (Vic)	RRTA (Vic)	EOA (WA)	DA (ACT)	ADA (NT)
Party joinder						98, 100	177	24(3)				109, 111	106	73
Representation					46PQ	101	187	24(4)	75(3)			112	95	95
Counsel assisting					46PQ	101A	185	95(9)						94
In camera							161	23(4)	75(5)			121	82(3)	86
Conciliation					Div 1	106	158	27	74	112		91	83	78
Evidence							201	25(1)	87			120	97	90
Offence	26	85	41	49			219	25(2)	106	201-206		157-159	108L-108O	110
Procedures, rules of evidence					46PR			23(2)	87(4)			120	92	90
Representative Complaints						102-105	146-152, 194-200		82			114, 115	78	
Dismissal						111, 113	210	96(2)	99	136(c)		125	88	102
Determination						113	209	96(1)	89	136(a)		127	102	76
Appeal						118	217	98	100			134	108D	106
Legal assistance					46PT, 46PU									

Appendix E

CONTACT POINTS

FEDERAL AGENCIES

*Human Rights & Equal Opportunity
    Commission*
Level 8, Piccadilly Tower
133 Castlereagh Street
Sydney NSW 2000
GPO Box 5218
Sydney 2001
Telephone: (02) 9284 9600
General Enquiries: 1300 369 711
Complaints Infoline: 1300 656 419
TTY: 1800 620 241
Fax: (02) 9284 9611
http://www.hreoc.gov.au

STATE AGENCIES

New South Wales

Anti-Discrimination Board
Stockland House
Level 4, 175-183 Castlereagh St
Sydney NSW 2000
General office number: (02) 9268
    5555
General Enquiry Service & Employers
    Advisory Service: (02) 9268
    5544
Fax: (02) 9268 5500
TTY: (02) 9268 5522
Toll free: 1800 670 812 (for rural and
    regional New South Wales only)
http://www.lawlink.nsw.gov.au/adb

*Newcastle Anti-Discrimination Board
    regional office*
Level 1, 414 Hunter Street, Newcastle
    West 2302
Telephone: (02) 4926 4300
Fax: (02) 4926 1376
TTY: (02) 4929 1489
Toll free: 1800 670 812 (only within
    New South Wales)

*Wollongong Anti-Discrimination
    Board regional office*
84 Crown Street, Wollongong 2500
Telephone: (02) 4224 9960
Fax: (02) 4224 9961
TTY: (02) 4224 9967
Toll free: 1800 670 812 (for rural and
    regional New South Wales only)

Administrative Decisions Tribunal
Level 15, St James Centre
111 Elizabeth St
Sydney NSW 2000
Telephone: (02) 9223 4677
Fax: (02) 9233 3283
TTY: (02) 9235 2674
Freecall: 1800 060 410
Email: ag_adt@agd.nsw.gov.au
http://www.lawlink.nsw.gov.au/adt

Queensland

Anti-Discrimination Commission
Level 1, RAMS House
189 Coronation Drive (cnr Cribb
    Street) Milton

PO Box 2122, Milton Qld 4064 or
 Brisbane DX 44037
Telephone statewide 1300 130 670 or
 TTY 1300 130 680
Fax: (07) 3247 0960
Email: info@adcq.qld.gov.au (all
 offices)
http://www.adcq.qld.gov.au

*Cairns Anti-Discrimination
 Commission regional office*
McLeod Chambers
78 Spence Street (cnr McLeod Street)
 Cairns
PO Box 4699, Cairns Qld 4870 or
 Cairns DX41346
Telephone: (07) 4039 8600
Fax: (07) 4039 8609

*Rockhampton Anti-Discrimination
 Commission regional office*
First Floor, State Government Centre
209 Bolsover Street, Rockhampton
PO Box 1390, Rockhampton Qld
 4700 or Rockhampton DX 41168
Telephone: (07) 4938 4466
Fax: (07) 4938 4459

*Townsville Anti-Discrimination
 Commission regional office*
Level 2, St James Place
155-157 Denham Street, Townsville
 Qld 4810 or Townsville DX
 41421
Telephone: (07) 4799 7020
Fax: (07) 4799 7021

Anti-Discrimination Tribunal
Level 1, 189 Coronation Drive, Milton
 Qld 4064GPO Box 487, Brisbane
 Qld 4001
Phone: (07) 3239 6408
Fax: (07) 3239 6397
TTY: (07) 3239 0718
http://www.adcq.qld.gov.au/tribunal

South Australia

Equal Opportunity Commission
Mercantile Mutual Building, Level 2
45 Pirie Street, Adelaide SA 5000
GPO Box 464, Adelaide SA 5001
Telephone: (08) 8207 1977
Toll free: 1800 188 163 (South
 Australia only)
TTY: (08) 8207 1911
Fax: (08) 8207 2090
http://www.eoc.sa.gov.au

Equal Opportunity Tribunal
Sir Samuel Way Building,
241-259 Victoria Square
Adelaide SA 5000
GPO Box 2465, Adelaide SA 5001
Telephone: (08) 8204 0285
Fax: (08) 8204 0544
http://www.courts.sa.gov.au/courts/
 district/equal_opportunity_
 tribunal.htm

Tasmania

Anti Discrimination Commissioner
Level 1, 54 Victoria Street
Hobart, Tas 7000
GPO Box 197, Hobart Tas 7001
Telephone: (03) 6233 4841
TTY (03) 6233 3122
Fax: (03) 6233 5333
Toll Free: 1300 305 062 (Tasmania
 only)
Email: antidiscrimination@justice.
 tas.gov.au
www.antidiscrimination.tas.gov.au

Anti-Discrimination Tribunal
23-25 Liverpool St
Hobart Tas 7000
Telephone: (03) 6233 8372
Fax: (03) 6233 5355
Email: adt@justice.tas.gov.au

http://www.magistratescourt.tas.gov.
au/divisions/anti-
discrimination_tribunal

Victoria

Equal Opportunity Commission
3rd Floor, 380 Lonsdale Street
Melbourne Vic 3000
Telephone: (03) 9281 7111
Toll Free: 1800 134 142 (Victoria
only)
TTY: (03) 9281 7110
Fax: (03) 9281 7171
Email:
information@veohrc.vic.gov.au
http://www.eoc.vic.gov.au

*Victorian Civil and Administrative
Tribunal*
55 King Street
Melbourne Vic 3000
GPO Box 5408 CC
Melbourne Vic 3001
DX 210576
Telephone: (03) 9628 9900 (Anti-
Discrimination list)
Fax: (03) 9628 9988 (Anti-
Discrimination list)
Email: vcat@vcat.vic.gov.au
http://www.vcat.vic.gov.au

Western Australia

Equal Opportunity Commission
Level 2, Westralia Square
141 St George's Terrace
Perth WA 6000
Telephone: (08) 9216 3900
Fax: (08) 9216 3960
TTY: (08) 9216 3936
Toll Free: 1800 198 149 (Western
Australia only)
http://www.equalopportunity.wa.
gov.au/

State Administrative Tribunal
Level 4, 12 St George's Terrace
Perth
Perth WA 6000
GPO Box U1991 Perth 6845
Telephone: (08) 9219 3111
1300 306 017
Fax: (08) 9325 5099

*Office of Equal Employment
Opportunity in Public
Employment*
Level 12, St Martin's Tower, 44 St
George's Terrace
Perth WA 6000
Telephone: (08) 9260 6600
Toll Free: 1800 676 607
Hearing impaired callers: 133 677
Fax: (08) 9260 6611
Email: deope@opssc.wa.gov.au
http://www.oeeo.wa.gov.au

Australian Capital Territory

Discrimination Commissioner
ACT Human Rights Commission
Level 2, 12 Moore St
Canberra ACT 2601
GPO Box 158
Canberra ACT 2601
Telephone: (02) 6205 2222
Fax: (02) 6207 0587
TTY: (02) 6207 0525
Email: human.rights@act.gov.au
http://www.hrc.act.gov.au/

Discrimination Tribunal
ACT Magistrates Court
4 Knowles Place, Canberra ACT 2601
GPO Box 370
Canberra City ACT 2601
Telephone: (02) 6217 4261
Fax: (02) 6217 4505
Email: tribunals@act.gov.au
http://www.courts.act.gov.au/magistra
tes/

Northern Territory

Anti-Discrimination Commission
7th Floor, National Mutual Building
9-11 Cavanagh Street
Darwin NT 0800
Post: LMB 22 GPO Darwin NT 0801
Telephone: (08) 8999 1444
Fax: (08) 8981 3812
Freecall: 1800 813 846
TTY: (08) 8991 1466
Email: administrationadc@nt.gov.au
http://www.nt.gov.au/justice/adc

INDEX